MEXICO MARCHES

MEXICO MARCHES

by

J. H. PLENN

▲

THE BOBBS-MERRILL COMPANY

PUBLISHERS

INDIANAPOLIS • NEW YORK

First Edition

PRINTED AND BOUND BY
BRAUNWORTH & CO., INC.
BUILDERS OF BOOKS
BRIDGEPORT, CONN.

9799

CONTENTS

CHAPTER   PAGE

   I   Mexico's March 11

  II   Blood and Oil 27

 III Mexico for the Mexicans 51

 IV A Mess of Kingfish 82

  V   Redeemers' Row 106

 VI That Man Cardenas 127

 VII Star Agitators 147

VIII The Little Red Schoolhouse 168

 IX New Gods for Old 191

  X   Land Lords and Liberty 212

 XI Rhapsody in Blue Denim 260

 XII Old Bricks in a New House 297

XIII The Forgotten Men 314

XIV Mobilizing the Muses 331

 XV In the Red 350

      Mexican Statistics 374

      Index 377

"And to me, the men in Mexico are like trees, forests that the white men felled in their coming. But the roots of the trees are deep and alive and forever sending up new shoots.

"And each new shoot that comes up overthrows a Spanish church or an American factory. . . . And soon the dark forest will rise again and shake the Spanish buildings from the face of America.

"All that matters to me are the roots that reach down beyond all destruction. The roots and the life are there. What else it needs is the word, for the forest to begin to rise again. And some man among men must speak the word."

Don Ramon in *The Plumed Serpent*
by D. H. Lawrence

I

MEXICO'S MARCH

1

By boldly seizing British and American oil properties, on March 18, 1938, in the name of his eighteen million people, President Lazaro Cardenas telescoped Mexican history into two significant epochs: Before Expropriation and After. This oversimplified, but tenable, approach to a revaluation of the country's past has instilled in many Mexicans the feeling that Mexico, as a nation, has just begun to live.

More than four centuries ago, another of Mexico's yester-days came to an end, and Tomorrow—Mañana—began. That swift bitter-sweet night of Conquest locked two civilizations in an enduring embrace: Cortez, Spanish, male; Malinche, Indian, female. The seeds of a new nation were planted.

Through the years the seedling nation strained for a bit of the sun that would bring it to flower. Each dawn brought new hope, and then another dreadful night. Tomorrow never came. Mañana was mockery, a down-dragging word, weighted with defeat.

Then, the explosion of 1910, and a whole people marching into the Mexican Revolution, with a new blood offering for another beautiful promise, the Constitution of 1917, pointing toward a better World of Tomorrow, a mañana of hope. And 1938—passion of expropriation. . . .

Today, Mexico still seems to be chasing a mirage, ever there, never reached. Or, at times, it may recall a theater magician and his trick hat: flags of many colors rise, as if from nowhere, float about the stage a moment, then disappear through the trap door of history.

What is to be found today in the Mexican sombrero? What will rise next? A hammer-and-sickle? A swastika? A fledgling American eagle? A road paved with question marks lies ahead of Mexico in the march toward her world of tomorrow, her mañana.

2

MARCH 18, 1938.

Dry season. Clear day. No rain. No clouds. Spring.

The sun, ready to plunge behind the mountains, was poised for a moment on the rim of Mexico City's bowl-like valley. In the *Zocalo*—Plaza of the Constitution—crowds moved like iridescent swirls of oil on a lazy, slow-flowing river: an airplane shot for a color movie, a strip of film cut from an endless serial story.

Four sides of the big square: one, the Cathedral, covered with stone statues and low-relief sculptures, high, richly-carved doors; directly opposite, the broad arcades of the municipal building; the third side, rows of store windows and, against all three curbs, chains of peddlers, their wares spread on the sidewalk.

Men, women, kids, crisscrossed through the geometrical park in the center of the square, pushed toward streetcars and busses that circled the park with a hum-buzz-roar-clang: office workers, laborers, housewives; barefoot Indian women with hampers of vegetables on their heads, babies slung across their backs; bootblacks, newsboys, policemen; camera-toting tourists dickering in front of a stack of multicolored sarapes.

All this on three sides and in the middle. The fourth was a broad silent lane of contrast. Few pedestrians, walking fast. No shop windows, no vendors. A solid wall of red and gray

stone, broken by big arched doorways and rows of grilled bal-
cony-windows: the National Palace, government headquarters
since colonial times. In front of one archway, uniformed
rifle-carrying sentries crossed back and forth in perfect tim-
ing: five paces, a swift turn to face each other, the left foot
swung down in a stiff Prussian step smack against the sidewalk, and the sentries crossed again.

3

Inside the Palace: a carpeted room tucked securely away
from the noisy patios where governors, congressmen, politicians, workmen, peasants, milled around all day long. In the
room, antechamber to the President's private office, twenty-
one men sat solemnly, on the afternoon of March 18, 1938,
around a long mahogany table.

At the head of the table a heavy-set man, in a gray business
suit. Straight black hair over a forehead that sloped sharply;
thick brows, shading sad eyes, greenish-brown in the light of a
French chandelier. Full mustache over a mouth in permanent
pout. His large ears quivered slightly as President Lazaro
Cardenas read to his cabinet from a stack of papers in front
of him. Twenty pairs of eyes watched him, twenty pairs of
ears listened to every syllable. The emergency cabinet meeting, provoked by the oil crisis, had begun.

4

Avenue November 20, named for the revolutionary move-
ment of 1910 which overthrew Porfirio Diaz, opens from
Constitution Plaza along one side of the municipal building.
In an old house, facing a side street that branches from the
Avenue, Madame Buleina was doing a crystal reading for a
newspaper reporter.

"Mercury and Saturn are in conjunction, a favorable sign for decisive action," the Madame said.

She read from a chart. It showed that the sun was approaching the sign of Aries. The sun would enter the sign at forty-three minutes after 12:00 P.M. on the twenty-first, beginning of the Spring Equinox when the day is as long as the night.

"The man you have in mind is dominated at the present time by the sign of Pisces," the Madame continued. "He can do big things. This is a sign of sympathy and understanding. He has excellent intuition, but lacks self-confidence. He must convince himself of his ability in order to act, he must learn to concentrate. He can overcome any obstacle if he wishes. There is a lack of egoism, there is sensitivity, good health, but he must abstain from alcoholic drinks and drugs. Some famous men born under this sign were William Jennings Bryan, Victor Hugo, Michelangelo, Enrico Caruso and George Washington. Two pesos please."

5

On the third floor of No. 12 Bucareli Avenue, news editors of DAPP, government press bureau, dictated bulletins for the morning papers:

Banco de Mexico suspends dealings in foreign exchange.

Oil companies in rebellion, refuse to accept Supreme Court decision.

Mexican Workers' Confederation calls demonstration to show labor's support for President.

Vicente Lombardo Toledano, head of Confederation, receives solidarity message from John L. Lewis, head of CIO.

Permanent commission of Congress called into special session.

6

Across the street, in *Excelsior's* editorial rooms, Assistant News Editor Jose F. Rojas Jr. sorted telegrams, hunting a good banner for Page One, Second Section. Among them were:

Puebla—Alejo Garcia and Francisco Ruiz, convicted slayers of Mrs. Rosalie Evans, British subject, in 1923, freed on appeal. This case, involving armed resistance by Mrs. Evans against land expropriation, had created an international sensation.

Monterrey—American Smelting and Refining Company stops smelter.

Tamazunchale, San Luis Potosi—Indian regional congress opens.

7

Around the Teatro Alameda, crowds pushed toward glaring searchlights for the world *première* of *La Zandunga,* first Mexican picture starring Lupe Velez, ex-chorus girl. Other movie houses offered: Bette Davis and Leslie Howard in *It's Love I'm After;* Tyrone Power and Loretta Young in *Second Honeymoon;* Greta Garbo and Charles Boyer in *Conquest;* Danielle Darrieux in *Abuse of Confidence;* John Boles and Jack Oakie in *Fight for Your Lady.* At the Folies Bergère, Mexico's all-the-rage musical comedy clown, Cantinflas, was wisecracking in *Time To Get Hot.*

8

Alexander Glyka, English-page editor of *El Universal,* reading copy on "Anglo-American Notes," learned that Mrs.

Dwight Morrow, widow of the late United States ambassador to Mexico, is resting at her home in Cuernavaca; that foursomes were drawn for the British and American golf tourney; that Union Church school will hear a talk by Miss Muriel Taylor on "Capturing Canadian Children for Christ"; that the Pan-American Round Table will have a program on Guatemala; that Sherwood Anderson is fishing at Acapulco.

9

In the same room at *El Universal,* Cable Editor Rafael Solana blocked in the headlines for his make-up dummy. Among his dispatches:

Barcelona—Debris cleaned up after sixteen air raids by Italian and German warplanes.

Vienna—Nazis take over; arrests and suicides continue; hundreds of Jews disappear daily; in Berlin, Hitler dissolves Reichstag.

Warsaw—General Rydz-Smigly delivers ultimatum to Lithuania.

London—Hoover says war not probable in Europe soon.

New York—Stock market nervous over European situation; many prices drop under 1932 quotations; May wheat closes at 88½ cents.

10

Throughout Mexico, farmers and peasants were on their way in from the fields for their evening meal. Some were beginning their spring sowing: tobacco in Oaxaca and Veracruz; alfalfa, chickpeas, wheat, on the vast plains of the highlands; sweet potatoes, sugar cane, rice, peanuts, in the lowlands. Others were harvesting fruits and vegetables which would soon be piled up on stands in the city markets: chile peppers, melons, squash, peas, beans of twenty different colors. Tons of cotton seed were being spread in the Laguna District of Coahuila and Durango, the government's subsidized-farm laboratory; along the fertile stretches of the Rio Grande valley, on the United States border, from Matamoros to Nuevo Laredo. Coffee and sugar cane and tobacco were ready for harvest in the hot lands. Everywhere, corn was being planted or harvested: corn, which has always been Mexico's staff of life.

Shifts were changing in many of the hundreds of mines which have been pouring billions in gold and silver to the treasuries of other nations for more than four hundred years: silver in Pachuca, in Guerrero; copper and lead in Sonora, Chihuahua; iron ores, lead, zinc, in Durango and Zacatecas; coal in Coahuila. In almost any mountain in Mexico you'll find rich ores: gold, silver, lead, zinc, graphite, iron, cadmium, arsenic, mercury, bismuth, vanadium, tungsten, manganese, generous heritage which has made the country a stamping ground for wealth-seekers through the centuries.

Factory whistles blew the close of the workday in the industrial centers in Mexico City, in Monterrey, Puebla, Guadalajara, Guanajuato, San Luis Potosi, in many smaller factory districts. In the oil fields of Tamaulipas and Veracruz, in the refinery at Mexico City, in the scores of filling stations that bore the emblems of the Mexican-dressed British and American eagles, eighteen thousand men awaited the approach of the zero hour for an industry-wide strike. In the groves of oil derricks, the blackish, viscous liquid—coveted by men for their machines, their locomotives, their airplanes and warships— pulsed from thousands of earth-holes in steady, valve-controlled rhythm.

The wires of the National Telegraphs buzzed a historic message from the offices of the National Oil Workers' Union to President Lazaro Cardenas in the National Palace:

"In spite of our good will, our earnest desire to comply with your wishes in the present case, we find it impossible any longer to maintain an attitude of patience, since the decorum of the nation demands putting an end to a situation which it is no longer possible to tolerate. . . ."

In the Hamburg Building, Juarez Avenue, Mexico City, on the top floor—rented entirely to the Employers' Union of the Oil Industry—translators, stenographers, office boys at duplicators, worked overtime. The copies they turned out went to the officials and principal stockholders of the seventeen oil companies involved in the oil dispute, most of them subsidiaries of the Mexican Eagle Oil Company (Royal Dutch Shell) or the Huasteca Petroleum Company (Standard Oil). At 8:00 P.M., an emergency meeting of the companies' legal staffs was scheduled to get under way in these offices, the Mexican headquarters of the Oil International.

11

The twenty-one men around the long table in the National Palace pondered that message from the union. For months the workers had been locked in a bitter struggle with the giant oil companies that boasted they were stronger than any government. There were other messages, too, piled high on the table: messages from peasants' organizations, "solidarity with our proletarian brothers of the oil fields." From teachers' unions, closing with the slogan, "For Education at the Service of the People." From the Bloc of Intellectual Workers, "the oil matter is but one incident in the social struggle of the nation—for the cause of mankind." From labor organizations in the United States. All urged the government not to let down the workmen, all closed with combinations of words in which hopes of the underdog have taken form:

Land and Liberty.
Liberty, Justice and Law.
Effective Suffrage and No Re-election.
Institutions and Social Reform.
Down with Imperialist Oppression.
For a Classless Society.
For the Social Revolution.
Toward a Democracy of Workers.

For nearly three hours the twenty-one men sat and argued. News of the momentous meeting had spread. Outside the room had gathered labor leaders, congressmen, senators, bankers, editors, lawyers, judges, newspaper reporters. The intangible vapor of their suspense penetrated the gathering of ministers. The twenty-one men had long ceased to be isolated in that meeting. They still heard the echoes of President Cardenas' husky voice as he told the American ambassador, Josephus Daniels, through a spokesman, how he felt about the pressure which Daniels had dutifully exerted, earlier in the day, on behalf of the oil companies:

> "Respectfully inform His Excellency, the Ambassador, that if the richest oil fields in the world stood in the way of maintaining our national dignity, became an insuperable obstacle to maintenance of that honor which we prize so highly, we would burn the oil fields to the ground rather than sacrifice our honor."

As they listened to his report of developments that brought the oil dispute to a climax, the ministers realized that they no longer heard the voice of just one man, a president, a stubborn leader of eighteen million people. From Cardenas' fleshy lips, with the insistent beat of a tom-tom, with the same ominous monotone, the words rumbled out of the depths; not from the depths of one man's entranced soul, but from the very belly of his people, a hungry, gnawing, unsatisfied belly that for centuries had been trying to eat promises and words, words, words, soft, smooth, caressing, musical, but indigestible, words that turned into lumps of hard clay, to bullets and gravestones.

At the head of the table, Cardenas was no longer speaking his own words. A host of unseen beings surrounded him, pressing him to act for them: ghosts of murdered Indians, peasants, workers, rising in the steam of oil-field swamps. Hilario Jacinto, Adolfo Merinos, Jeronimo Merinos, Manuel Gomez, Lino Cruz, were not just names. They and thousands of others had suffered the misfortune of living over pools of oil. Their bones now rotted in the slimy soil, along with those of Valentin Fernandez, who had no oil. But he had dared to drink water from a cup reserved for the foreign masters. He was shot down in cold blood.

Blood-memories of bitter centuries pounded through Lazaro Cardenas' heart, lashed against the hard walls of logic in his brain, walls of common sense, of convenience, erected by his many advisers, expert in the ways of practical politics. Iron in those memories: branding irons sent from Spain to mark Indian slaves after the Conquest; iron of British and French and American naval guns that had rained shells on Veracruz; iron and lead of Spanish and French muskets; of wheels and racks of the Holy, Roman, Catholic, Apostolic Inquisition; cannon balls from American fieldpieces trained on Chapultepec Castle in 1847; guns of Porfirio Diaz' "peaceful" days: overseers' guns in the tobacco hells of Valle Nacional, guns of White Guards in haciendas and oil camps, army rifles turned on mill workers in Rio Blanco, on copper miners in Cananea, blood and iron everywhere, to maintain the security of vast private empires, to keep up the market value of Mexican government bonds, stability as reflected in bankers' books, budgets balanced with the monstrous misery of a people, their birthright squandered for a mess of pottage.

These memories and more recent ones brought back to Lazaro Cardenas: his own experiences in the oil fields, the tankers slipping out through the night of Tampico harbor with the juices squeezed from Mexico's soil; the gambling dives and the whorehouses that infested the oil camps; the poverty, ignorance, and oppression which his people of the fields still endure, even twenty-eight years after the Revolution; and their loss of faith in the official "redeemers."

These things grew up with him, and he saw them over and over again on his trips of thousands of miles to every part of the country, sitting on the ground with Indian tribes, breaking bread in a peasant's hillside hut after a day of lone horseback riding, far from his official entourage.

Cardenas was living again through another moment as dramatic as the struggle in which he eliminated Calles, Big Boss of Mexico for many years, and the littler bosses, Tomas Garrido Canabal, Lord of Tabasco, and Saturnino Cedillo, Kingfish of San Luis Potosi. And through the speech of Minister of the Interior Ignacio Garcia Tellez, during the 1934 election campaign:

"Cardenas is the symbol of the revolutionary masses . . . his life is the history of our recent social convulsions. . . ."

And those two sentences which came from his own lips most often during his electoral campaign:

"I pledge my honor to the promise of fulfilling my obligations to the working class if I am placed in power. . . . My only hope is that some day you can say that Lazaro Cardenas fulfilled the promises he made as a soldier and citizen of the Revolution."

He must have thought, too, of the many betrayals his people had suffered. Of the talk now going around that trusted
political allies, even some of his close relatives, were merely
fronts to keep his name clear of graft, that the government
moves were just another phase of the old army game: putting
pressure on the capitalists in order to get bigger pay-offs. His
whole career ran contrary to any such accusations, but the
people didn't believe any more. The oil companies didn't believe, either. They had slid through court formalities and
figured on paying off at the right time for a favorable settlement. They had brought back-breaking pressure on the government, had withdrawn their deposits, broken the exchange
value of the peso, precipitated an artificial depression.

All these things Cardenas had slept with for months. He
felt he had already compromised more than was justified.
The welfare of the nation depended on solution of the oil
crisis. The situation had become intolerable. He was now
ready to call the oil companies' hand. He told his ministers
just that when the March 18th meeting began.

12

At three minutes to ten o'clock that night, the doors of the
cabinet meeting room opened and Lazaro Cardenas walked
into the corridor, followed by twenty men, weary but relieved
that the strain was over. The crowd in the corridor parted to
make a lane for Cardenas and his ministers. They walked—
Cardenas with his light cat-step—to the Ambassadors' Salon,
where microphones had been installed. As the President sat
down to read, the hundred or so important men, now just an
amorphous crowd, pressed around him.

At one minute to ten, radio listeners who were tuned in on
Mexican stations heard an announcement:

"Our regular program at this time is suspended in order to make place for a presidential message of vital national importance. When the President is finished, we shall resume our schedules."

More than 700,000 watts of electrical energy broadcast the message, via XEFO, the National Revolutionary Party station, on a nation-wide hook-up with all radio stations in Mexico, as well as with the government wireless at Chapultepec and the short wave broadcaster at the Ministry of Foreign Relations.

The President talked exactly eighteen minutes, beginning at ten o'clock. A bewildered nation heard Cardenas for about five minutes, unable to figure out quite what was coming next. But doubt vanished when he reached this part of his speech:

"We have here a clear and evident case that compels the government to apply the law of expropriation now in force, not only to reduce the oil companies to obedience and submission, but also because labor contracts between the companies and their workers have been rescinded pursuant to a decision of the labor authorities. Therefore, if the government did not take over the plants of the companies, immediate paralysis of the petroleum industry would follow, thereby working incalculable harm to all other industries and to the general economy of the nation . . .

". . . They hold that their economic strength and their pride shield them against the dignity and sovereignty of a nation that has with such liberality handed over to them its enormous natural resources and that cannot, by legal means, obtain satisfaction of even the most rudimentary obligations.

"It therefore becomes unavoidable, as a logical consequence, to take final measures, under our laws, to put an end to this never-ending state of affairs under which the country labors, its industrial progress checked by those

who hold in their own hands the power to throw all obstacles in its way, and the dynamic force of their activity,
employing the same, not for noble and lofty ends, but
for abuse of that economic strength, to such an extent as
to jeopardize the very life of the nation that seeks to
uplift its people by means of the enforcement of its own
laws, by turning to account its own resources, and by
freely managing its own destinies. . . ."

Nor was there any doubt about the expropriation decree,
signed at the cabinet meeting, and released the following day.
Its pertinent sections said:

"Article 1. The properties of the hereinafter named
companies are hereby declared expropriated to the nation, because of public utility; the properties including
machinery, installations, equipment, buildings, wharves
and other movable and immovable belongings . . . inso-
far as may be deemed necessary, in the judgment of the
Secretary of National Economy, for the exploration,
transport, storage, refining and distribution of the products of the petroleum industry.

"Article 2. The Secretary of National Economy, with
intervention of the Secretary of Finance as administrator
of the national wealth, shall proceed to the immediate
occupation of the property which is the subject of this
expropriation and to issue the necessary orders.

"Article 3. The Ministry of Finance shall pay the
corresponding indemnity to the expropriated companies,
in accordance with provisions of articles 27 of the Constitution and 10 and 20 of the Law of Expropriation, in
cash, and within a period not to exceed ten years. The
funds to make this payment shall be taken by the Ministry of Finance from a certain percentage, to be determined later, of the production of petroleum and derivatives, which come from the expropriated properties, and
the proceeds of which shall be deposited, while legal
proceedings are carried out, in the national treasury.

"Notify the companies and publish in the Official
Daily."

Since the expropriation law's passage in 1936, Cardenas had three times before ordered notification and publication of expropriation decrees. In May, 1937, he had ordered expropriation of the Alamos school lands in the State of Chiapas; in June, 1937, the National Lines of Mexico were expropriated; in December, 1937, the Agua Caliente resort properties.

An hour after 10:18 P.M., the President's office was swamped with messages of congratulations, and pledges of support.

13

At 1:00 A.M., Cardenas was still at the palace; among his visitors at that hour were cabinet members Suarez, Buenrostro, Villalobos, and Santillan, and labor leaders Lombardo Toledano and Juan Gray.

At 3:00 A.M., the lights burned in the Western Union cable office, and tired clerks were punching teletype machines loaded with stacks of messages from foreign correspondents. This was the first time in many years that the cable office had remained open after 1:00 A.M.

At 7:00 A.M., Doña Loreto was serving her last customer, before closing her portable lunch stand on Bucareli Avenue in Mexico City. While she fried an egg for his sandwich, the customer—a taxicab chauffeur—bought a paper from a passing newsboy: *El Nacional,* the National Revolutionary Party newspaper. Ordinarily he didn't read this paper, but he was eager to see the lottery list before turning in. It had been a bad night, and he hoped he had won something.

He glanced at the front page headlines: Expropriation! In his business, gasoline was important. Wonder if this is going to gum up the works like last year's strike. He turned the pages, hunting the lottery list. A bold-type editorial, set double-column, stopped him, and he skimmed through it:

"Independence . . . 1810—1938 . . . hour of national unity

has arrived. No Rights, no Lefts, no Moderates, no Radicals . . . solid front against capitalist tutelage, courage and stoicism to face the future . . . men who deserve statues as immortals . . . Cardenas . . . incarnation of the nation's genius at a critical instant . . . Latin-American liberty . . . our America south of the Rio Grande . . . awake . . . Mexican cry of alarm . . . demand from her expoliators return of what they have taken . . . guide of the continent . . . Revolutionary Mexico . . . takes the first step into what until yesterday was 'no man's land' because it was her own land."

To himself, the chauffeur mumbled: Nuts!

He found the lottery list on the next-to-the-last page. First prize, $100,000, number 23674, Mexico City. Second prize, $25,000, number 18268, Villahermosa, Tabasco. He scanned the list of smaller prizes. No luck. Two more pesos shot. He tore up the ticket, threw it away. Then he took a hard bite into his egg sandwich.

II

BLOOD AND OIL

1

MARCH 18th put the finishing touches on Lazaro Cardenas' niche in Mexican history. His expropriation speech was a 700,000-watt cry of vengeance broadcast to the world by an underdog nation. It crowned the career of a politically inconspicuous general, raised to the presidency by a well-oiled political machine, and engaged for more than three years in selling himself and his party's program to the Mexican people. Other generals had been carried into power on waves of popularity, products of military exploits in one or another of numerous Mexican revolutions. But when Cardenas was sworn in, people accepted him as just another stooge of the former dictator, Plutarco Elias Calles, and his all-powerful National Revolutionary Party. Cardenas came in like a lamb. When he goes out, he will go like a lion.

Popular reaction to the expropriation proved that Cardenas had done a good job of selling. If any doubts remained over his dramatic and victorious struggle against Calles—a struggle that marked a rebirth of the labor and agrarian movements in Mexico—these doubts were swept away in the tempest of expropriation. In taking over the oil properties, Cardenas struck the biggest gusher of nationalism in the country's long history of nationalist movements. A tidal wave of emotion, it swamped all else for a while, washed up class, caste and ideology like so many dislodged rocks and piled

27

them in a rugged and formless heap, monument to a dream: a united Mexico. The unprecedented support gave Mexico's President new courage for setting about to prove to the world that blood is thicker than oil.

The task of molding this outpouring of mass energy into a pliable instrument, a weapon against the foreign pressure sure to follow, became a supreme test of the government's Department of Press and Publicity. Cardenas had created this department on January 1, 1937, as part of his sales campaign on behalf of the Six-Year Plan, blueprint of his administration. The Department proved itself: booklets, leaflets, posters, newspaper articles, radio speeches, agitation in the schools, meetings, demonstrations, motion pictures, dramatic programs, shot from the DAPP (Department of Press and Publicity) offices in a steady barrage.

Labor unions, peasants' organizations, cultural groups, businessmen's clubs, all joined in support of the drive. Even the high Catholic clergy, enemy of the Revolutionary governments, enemy throughout Mexican history of all that stood for liberalism and democracy, did a surprising thing. In the past, the Church officially had given aid and succour to authoritarianism and monopoly interests—of which it at one time was the biggest—but now it made a public gesture in support of Cardenas' action. Paraders' astonished faces turned upward toward the towers as the clang of the Cathedral's bells mingled with the speeches, the shouted revolutionary slogans, the proletarian songs of the mammoth demonstration on March 23rd in Mexico City.

The DAPP campaign was a bombardment calculated to keep alive the morale of the people under the oil companies' terrific counter-offensive which had already begun to spread anxiety, to plant new doubts and fears. Every moment it became clearer that the battle had just begun. The surprise attack on the imperialist camp was successful so far, but the reserves of the oil companies are almost unlimited, and reinforcements were already being drawn up.

The heavy artillery of economic sanctions thundered across the border. The United States government announced it would stop buying silver from the Mexican government. Various foreign interests withdrew deposits from Mexican banks. In Washington and London, the foreign office aides assembled data for the official notes. First casualty was the Mexican peso, already undermined. The peso came crashing, from a pegged exchange rate of 3.60 to the United States dollar to five pesos for a dollar. This proved a boomerang measure. Unable to buy from the United States with a devalued peso, Mexico turned to other sources. The Mexican market was thrown wide open to the Germans, Italians, Japanese. Commodity prices skyrocketed, under the drive of speculators, the failure of crops, and the uncertain outcome of government-subsidized farming on newly distributed lands. The people were on the verge of panic, but when the Cardenas government called for a popular "National Redemption Loan," the citizens sent in—besides cash—personal jewelry, sacks of corn, chickens, gold and silver ornaments.

British and American newspapers were enlisted in the drive against expropriation. The whole business, they said, reflecting the companies' viewpoint, was a colossal steal, just plain highway robbery. It was all planned out ahead of time, years ago, so Mexican politicians could get control of the oil properties. The companies never had a chance. The courts were fixed. The labor board was stacked. The labor angle was all a blind. The companies were willing to meet the wage increases, but refused to let the unions run their business. Not only oil was at stake. All foreign business in Latin America might meet the same fate; American investments were menaced. Thousands of stockholders would be bilked.

Suspense mounted. Doubt, fear, unrest spread in the oil-fields. The companies had found a way out in the past. What would they do now? There had always been a general around to lead the way out of chaos. Who would be financed by the companies? Cardenas made a trouble-shooting trip to the oil regions, ordered more farm land expropriated and distributed. Things began happening, meanwhile, in San Luis Potosi, where General Saturnino Cedillo had been king-fish for many years.

Cedillo had quit his cabinet post as minister of Agriculture, and had refused a transfer of command to another State. Rumors spread: a revolt was brewing there, arms were being assembled, airplanes smuggled. The federal government moved in with a corps of engineers to trim haciendas which had remained immune from the agrarian program, and also carefully spread troops around the State, just in case. A manifesto appeared: the State government of San Luis Potosi withdrew recognition of the federal government. General Saturnino Cedillo had been named head of the "Army of Liberation."

Meanwhile, the British government had taken a stand identifying itself with the Compañia Mexicana de Petroleo El Aguila, known on the exchanges as the Mexican Eagle, subsidiary of the Royal Dutch-Shell combine, producing some sixty-two per cent of Mexican oil. There was no questioning Mexico's right to expropriate, but immediate payment must be made, adequately and in cash. And His Majesty's government did not see how Mexico could perform, since she was still in arrears on other debts, including a little British claims item of three hundred thousand dollars. Cardenas felt this was adding insult to injury. He told John Bull where to get off, wrote out a check for the three hundred thousand and ordered the Mexican minister in London to get out of the fog and come back to the Mexico City sunshine, thereby breaking off relations with the empire on which the sun never sets. David Cardenas had tweaked the nose of Goliath Chamberlain. So, on May 21st, the day after the Cedillo revolt broke, Owen St. Clair O'Malley, the British minister to Mexico, took the three hundred thousand and got jolly well off for home.

For a people who had always been stomped on, it was quite exhilarating to get up and kick John Bull in the broad seat of his pants. Cardenas couldn't have given the nation a better shot in the arm. The anxiety of the crisis was dispelled. There was no longer any hemming or hawing. You were either for Mexico or against her. And President Cardenas, whatever else you might think of him, was the voice and will of Mexico. For the folks on his side, he became more than ever the national liberator, a great statesman, a new Daniel come to judgment in a world badly in need of Daniels. His enemies, those opposed to his policies, saw him emerge Redder than their worst fears had painted him, branded him a raving Bolshevik, a Stalin of the west, puppet of Moscow. Some more moderately characterized him as a blundering, well-intentioned babe in the woods of *realpolitik* and the economics of imperialism. Still others saw him as an instrument whereby Standard Oil would outsmart Royal Dutch Shell, a tool of Washington against Downing Street. And there were those who saw him lining up with Hitler in the Nazi dictator's grab for Latin-American business.

All, however, even in their most violent attacks on his policies, admitted the man's courage, his frankness, his direct way of dealing, his respect for human life, which they were quick to recognize as new things in Mexican politics. Serious doubts remained as to the vaunted economic liberation brought about by expropriation and by Cardenas' firm stand against the defiant foreign powers. But nobody questioned the spiritual liberation that he had effected.

2

The blood that spouted from Mexican gushers, along with the black gold, never showed up on chemists' reports. The human tragedy, the sordid spectacle of murder, suicide, graft and greed that are a part of Mexican oil, does not appear in the industry's legal formalisms, in the constitutional articles, the decrees, enabling acts, diplomatic notes, plaintiffs' petitions and answers, experts' reports, labor board awards, appeals and injunctions.

The complete novel of Mexican oil still remains to be written: the epic imprint on two generations; the leveling of villages and towns rooted to the soil for centuries; the annihilation of entire families, the pitting of brother against brother, man against wife, father against son, in the frenzied rush for oil claims—the terrible impact of new rhythms that ripped ancient social patterns with the relentless power of drills plunging deep into the heart of the earth.

For the man who follows production charts and price tabulations, these things are undoubtedly the inevitable by-products of all great enterprise. In Mexico, they cut deeper and wider than the usual boom phenomena. The oil rush in Mexico came in the midst of a violent national upheaval, a period of war and revolution, when men left their work-benches and their farms and roamed the countryside with cartridge belts slung across their chests, rifles in hand. In this epoch there was little time for words or litigation. The only persuasive argument was the zing of a bullet, the gouging drive of lead into living flesh. The measure of a man's worth was how well he could shoot and how many more guns could shoot with him. The Revolution and the oil boom were welded into the same wild struggle; Revolutionary generals, waving the banners of anti-imperialism, became guards and protectors of the most rabid imperialists; the fate of presidents was decided at oil company councils. Legislators, judges, generals, were bought and sold like so many barrels of oil. Outside Mexico, the world was at war, clamoring for oil. The feverish race for profits on this bonanza market contributed to the cataclysm of the Mexican Revolution. Mexico today is still picking up the pieces, trying to build anew amid the debris left in the wake of this man-made hurricane.

A bare tabulation of men and women and children murdered to the greater glory of oil would fill a whole book. You could start with the nineteenth century exploits of Manuel Romero Rubio, father-in-law of Porfirio Diaz, such as the eviction of three thousand farmers near Papantla, Veracruz State. The farmers resisted. Federal soldiers opened fire. Three hundred farmers were killed. Strangely enough, it turned out later, after Romero Rubio's death, that there was oil under those farms.

You could go on down the line, through the blasting of the Merinos family for the rich Juan Casiano wells, to Hilario Jacinto and the Juan Felipe tract, Manuel Gomez, Daniel Gomez, Teofilo Cuervo, Lino Cruz, thousands, heaps of corpses in swamps, flatcars stacked with bodies, dumped to the sharks in the dirty Panuco, British against American, Mexican against Mexican, generals fighting for control of fields in order to collect tribute.

You can follow the career of General Manuel Pelaez, terror of the oil fields for years until General Guadalupe Sanchez was sent to clean him out. You would find federal soldiers becoming "white guards" to protect company property. You would find Pelaez organizing bands of white guards throughout the oil lands. You would find pirates who preyed on other pirates, boarding boats that brought merchandise into Tampico, that carried payrolls; boats smuggling oil out at night to evade export taxes.

You would find a swampy hell where men didn't just go to pieces. They melted like butter in a hot pan, their bodies and souls sucked into a miasma of booze, roulette chips, crap tables, whorehouses, syphilis, malaria. Men who worked in the oil fields wouldn't dream of having their families near them. The only women around were there on business. Is it any wonder that men ceased to be men after a few months, that their substance was drained from them as the oil was drained from the earth?

In Villa Cuauhtemoc, center of one of these fields, a young, lean army officer, schooled in the discipline of daily toil since he was a child, and in the field of battle soon after, saw all these things, and hated them. Fighting for a cause that promised to bring peace and self-respect to his countrymen, he saw corruption, booze, gambling and whoring destroying families, killing babies, spreading misery, perpetuating poverty. He saw fellow officers become partners in all this sordid business, and he, too, was offered bribes. This officer—Lazaro Cardenas—didn't need slogans, he didn't need elaborate ideologies, to tell him what was wrong, what had to be done. When, during his presidential campaign speeches, he promised to abolish booze and gambling, it was with the stench of the oil fields still in his nostrils. When he sat around the table with the oil company representatives, discussing the situation that had brought labor and capital to an impasse, these things—the human waste, and the waste of untold millions in oil and gas, lost through negligence in the wild abandon of the black-gold rush—all these things sat with him, and made him a very stubborn man.

3

The use of a foreign menace—real or imaginary—to whip up patriotic nationalism is not new in Mexican history.

"Death to the Spaniards" was part of the cry uttered by the parish priest, Miguel Hidalgo y Costilla, on September 16, 1810, when he launched the movement for independence from Spain. Demand for the death of some foreigner or other has figured in nearly all of Mexico's insurrections and riots since that time. This phenomenon became peculiarly acute during Mexican history of the last thirty years, much of which is inseparable from oil, an industry with a marked foreign stamp even in a semicolonial country where most industry and commerce is controlled by foreigners.

Madero, Huerta, Carranza, Villa, Obregon, Calles, each in turn tapped the reservoir of anti-foreignism, filled to the brim during the many years of partnership between the Mexican ruling classes and the non-Mexican interests. Mexico saw it all as a kind of hit-and-run procedure: men from other lands came, fought one another for pieces of land, sank pipe into the ground and carried away oil. They left only what they couldn't help leaving, some money in wages, some money in bribes, the rigs, tanks and processing equipment. Otherwise they were as alien to Mexico as if they had been operating in mid-ocean. Until 1912, they didn't even leave money in taxes. Porfirio Diaz' camarilla obligingly exempted the companies from this inconvenience, and in doing so they helped themselves, for the Mexican Eagle had thoughtfully bestowed shares of stock on important cabinet members.

The Yankee Edward L. Doheny, and the Britisher Weetman Pearson (Lord Cowdray) reveled in almost two decades of fantastic profits. By the time the new Mexican constitution was adopted in 1917, the scramble for Mexican oil had become a shambles. The new Constitution's Article 27 brought petroleum into the domain of nationalized subsoil, exploitation of which could be undertaken only by means of government concessions, the system followed successfully with mining properties for centuries.

Exploitation of subsoil wealth in Mexico first took a new legal turn with the Mining Code of 1884. Until then the Ordinance of Aranjuez, issued in 1783, had been in effect. Under the Ordinance, all minerals, including "bitumens," belonged to the Crown. Possession was granted to private individuals only on condition that they work the properties and pay taxes. Failure to meet these conditions made the properties subject to confiscation or cession to a new claimant. But under the mining code of 1884, reflecting the rise of the liberal bourgeois regime of Porfirio Diaz, although the nation retained the rights formerly held by the Crown, the surface proprietor was made owner of petroleum and coal deposits. All subsequent legislation during the Diaz epoch tended to unite surface and subsoil, definitely establishing private ownership. In the same way, the Diaz land laws wiped out the old community and township properties and made them the prey of private claimants. It was during this regime that a big part of their leases were acquired by British and American oil interests. Until 1925, when the Calles oil act was passed, legislation of the oil industry was on a basis of decrees.

The World War Armistice came on November 11, 1918, but the war over Mexican oil, still raging, was just really getting under way about that time. The companies had fought vainly to keep Article 27 from being adopted by the constitutional convention which met in Queretaro during December, 1916, and January, 1917. There was still hope that the provisions would not be put into effect, although Madero, during his presidency in 1912, had already instituted a system of oil taxes. On February 19, 1918, the Carranza government began to enforce the Constitution on oil, calling for registry of all lands where oil exploration would be carried on, and establishing a production tax. On August 8, 1918, the government decreed a system of concessions for oil exploitation, a radical departure from the system under which the surface proprietor was also owner of the subsoil. Besides her own legal tradition in these matters, Mexico had the precedent of United States Congressional action during Taft's administration, separating subsoil from the surface rights on public lands. There were also the British oil laws of 1917, in which the Crown is given exclusive rights to drill for oil in the United Kingdom. Mexican legislators pointed to the British government's direct participation in the capital of oil companies, and to the legal prohibition regarding transfer of oil company stock to other than British citizens.

The 1925 petroleum laws, which hurled President Calles into an open fight with the oil companies and brought him national support comparable to that developed by Cardenas in 1938, also unloaded an economic crisis on Calles' shoulders, due in part to economic pressure from the oil companies. In 1926 the Church-State dispute also reached an impasse and the Catholic clergy helped the oil interests by declaring an "economic boycott" of Mexico, suspending all church services, and bestowing blessings on Cristero rebels. Oil production, which had reached an all-time peak during 1921-1923, fell off sharply. Practically all exploration work stopped. The new laws established national oil reserves and protected rights acquired prior to 1917 by placing them under renewable fifty-year concessions, long enough for all practical purposes, but asserting the principle of government concessions rather than private ownership of the subsoil deposits.

That was the crux of the oil fight. The companies, especially the American companies, foreseeing increasing political control, balked at the concession principle. Independent oil interests rushed in, eager to get concessions which the major British and American companies spurned. Behind the united front of Standard Oil and Shell, these two competing interests were quietly engaging in cutting each other's throats, maneuvering for advantages, wangling privileges. Dwight

Morrow of the House of Morgan appeared on the scene as ambassador of the United States, poured diplomatic water on the troubled oil. An amended oil act was passed in 1928, granting "confirmatory concessions" for rights acquired prior to 1917. They were still "concessions," however, and inherent in a "concession" is the right to cancel, which becomes expropriation or confiscation, according to how you look at it. In the 1917 Constitution of the Carranza epoch, then, the seed of expropriation was planted, fertilized by the Calles oil laws, and brought to maturity under Lazaro Cardenas. The very nature of the Mexican political trends; the economic situation with relation to the United States; the growing world scramble for oil and war reserves; labor's steady pressure for protection against being made the goat of nationalist competition and economic depressions; all guided evolution of the oil problem inevitably into the path it took. Under another regime, with differences in the world situation, nationalization might have taken another form. It might have come a year sooner, or a year later, but nationalization has been in the cards for some time.

But in 1928 a *modus vivendi* was provided in Mexico. And the once-Red face of Calles bleached under the beneficent salve applied by the victorious Mr. Morrow. At this time, Mussolini doctrinaries, too, were already working on Calles' agile political brain. The oil crisis settlement, climaxed by the assassination of President-elect Alvaro Obregon, was followed by accession to the presidency on December 1, 1928, of Emilio Portes Gil, shrewd, squat, radical rightwinger. He built a smoothly-running political machine which continued to command attention of office-and-concession-seekers long after Portes Gil had been edged out of the official party control by the Cardenistas. Late in 1938, Portes Gil made two mysterious trips to Washington, after announcing he was going to the Mayo Brothers' clinic.

4

Above Wall Street, the Mexican Oil Workers' Union.

Wall Street is the name of a barber shop at the corner of Balderas and Juarez Avenue in Mexico City. The name is an anachronism from the days before March 18, when the Association of Petroleum Producers occupied the floor above. Now the oil workers have national headquarters in the upper story, and it is no longer rare to behold proletarians getting a trimming in Wall Street.

From isolated nuclei formed by nameless Wobbly apostles in the days when a discovered organizer was a dead organizer, has emerged this powerful labor organization. It is an industrial union with nearly twenty-five thousand members, today running the production end of the oil industry for the Mexican government, and with union leaders in fat jobs in the distribution end. Approximately eighteen thousand men are employed on the expropriated properties and the rest on federal oil reserves or with companies which were not involved in the dispute that led to expropriation.

The oil worker was referred to as the "spoiled child" of Mexican labor. His relatively high nominal salary, the social concessions in his contracts, were cited—among the latter, disability and death compensation, medical attention and recreational benefits. The worker replied that the oil zone climate is deadly, that work has to be carried on amid noxious gases and fumes, that as a result the length of life is greatly reduced. He said, further, that the real salary was actually not higher than that of other industrial workers, because of the high cost of provisions and rent. Housing had been neglected, and the oil fields had completely destroyed agriculture in those regions, so that all basic foods had to be brought in from other zones. The labor board, following an inspection of the oil fields during the litigation over the new two-year labor contract, prior to expropriation, made a report of what it described as terrible conditions. The board said most of the vaunted social benefits were mythical, existed only on paper, reported that the first-aid stations and hospitals lacked the most elementary supplies, that drinking water, drainage and toilet facilities were quite primitive. The labor board men were frankly astonished, because the visit of inspection had been announced at least a week ahead of time. Everybody had figured that the companies would at least make some show of having complied with these benefits called for in earlier contracts. This negligent attitude was reflected later in other acts of the companies, including their completely inadequate expert testimony, and led to the conjecture that the companies were reluctantly going through the legal procedure as a mere formality and counted on other means to win their case. Someday, perhaps, the little stockholders, who are used as instruments for spreading propaganda against the Mexican government actions, may investigate just how their officials acted in the case, and may demand a reckoning. At any rate, all this went into the record of the labor dispute, in some three thousand foolscap pages that provided one of the most detailed analyses ever made of any industry anywhere, a monument to Mexican scholarship.

The companies agreed to a forty-hour week instead of the prevailing fifty-six-hour week, to eight annual holidays and eight rest days with pay, and made other similar concessions. The companies at that time estimated that the new contracts would mean an outlay of some thirteen million pesos annually. The workers asked increases of about one hundred per cent over existing wages, stating that the cost of living had gone up ninety per cent since 1934, and that nominal salaries had risen only forty-five per cent. The companies offered increases of approximately twenty-five per cent. Then came the general strike of May 27th, called off by the workers under government pressure—after a tremendous publicity campaign by the companies, directed by imported press agents. The companies had apparently won, again, but their victory was Pyrrhic.

The union changed its tactic. Now, instead of raising a straight labor-capital wage dispute, which could lead only to another strike and another impasse, the union filed a plea "in a conflict of economic order," which is provided for in the federal labor law. That action, on June 10, 1937, was the beginning of the intense legal battle between the National Petroleum Workers' Union and the Employers' Union of the Petroleum Industry, a battle which reached a climax in the March 18th expropriation decree. The fight brought to a head not only the petroleum industry's capital-labor dispute, but also the beginning of a general showdown between the Cardenas government as the frank "protector" of labor on one side, and recalcitrant industry, champing at the bit of spreading unionization and consequent increase in strikes. That showdown is still under way, and its ramifications are many, affecting every aspect of Mexican life, spreading into the agrarian controversy, into politics, the army, the schools.

5

The expropriated oil companies claimed that Mexico owes them about $450,000,000.

The Mexican government, through its top-notch economic expert, Jesus Silva Herzog, said $10,000,000 would more than pay the companies in full.

And so the two sides squared off for another round in the knock-down-drag-out scrap that has been going on ever since the turn of the century, when the palefaces came poking into the asphalt seepages of the Mexican jungles.

Everything about the oil fight is like the estimates of expropriation indemnity: extreme, all black or all white, no middle ground. The companies said they couldn't pay the twenty-six-million-pesos annual increase that the proposed contract provided. The experts' commission said that the companies could pay twice that much, that the companies' profits have been ranging from fifty-one to sixty million pesos annually during recent years.

The companies said there was no need to expropriate, that the government had other legal means of enforcing the workers' demands. The government said the companies' intransigence, their defiance of the Mexican courts, not only flouted national dignity, but jeopardized the economic life of the country, threatened a political crisis, and hence forced the government to act as it did, without any other recourse in law.

The companies stated that the social benefits granted oil workers far exceed anything known in any other Mexican industry. The government said the mining, metal, railway, electrical, in fact, all big industries, give their workers far more in this respect than the oil industry, and, at that give only part of what the law calls for.

The companies held that the experts who studied the conditions of the oil industry and the companies' capacity to pay should have considered data of more than three years in order to form a complete economic cycle. The labor union answered that since the object of the study was a contract for the ensuing two years, a study of the three years immediately preceding was more than fair as a basis.

The companies claimed that oil prices used in calculations of profits were not real, that they were quoted market prices and not actual sales prices and that there were a lot of mysteries about the oil game that the experts didn't know. The latter answered that one mystery they had solved was the reason for the involved company structure of the Dutch

Shell interests. They said that the company hid real profits in order to evade taxes, that the Mexican Eagle had split into a production and distributing company in order to sell itself oil at a price that would show low profits, that it kept two sets of books on these matters.

The companies claimed that the proposed contract would represent an additional outlay of forty-one million pesos instead of the twenty-six million pesos called for on the face of the document. President Cardenas offered his personal guarantee that the companies would not have to exceed the lower figure.

And so on, into hundreds of points, on which the respective views were as night to day.

Basic, however, as precedent for future labor-capital-government relationships, was the neat use by the labor union of the "conflict of economic order." This legal device had been put into the labor law originally at the behest of the employers. It was designed for use in case an employer felt he could no longer live up to a union contract, so that, lacking any statutory reason, he might allege "economic incapacity." It was used by some mining companies in 1935, and by other employers since. It definitely placed the idea of "economic capacity" into Mexican labor law. But it remained for the oil fight to permit labor to use this same instrument for its own ends.

The companies set up a howl, denying that "economic capacity" could be considered in a labor dispute. Mexican labor procedure provides for two types of cases, those in "legal" conflicts and those in "economic" conflicts. An example of the first is a worker filing a claim for unpaid overtime, or for violation of a labor contract. This type of case goes to the conciliation and arbitration board as a complaint involving other laws might go to a justice of the peace: allegations, answers, presentation of evidence, argument, and a decision by the judge or jury. The second type of case arises when in a given industry or in a given region, circumstances of a general nature make it impossible to proceed under the existing conditions of labor-capital relationship. Then, the conciliation board is called on to intervene, as other arms of the government might in a case of public emergency that threatened paralysis of some phase of national life. The board seeks a solution, binding on both sides. Government experts are appointed to bring in findings. The findings are open to challenge by experts of the parties involved. The decision of the board can be appealed right on up to the Supreme Court, as was done in the oil case.

Thus the "economic capacity" theory became a boomerang. The labor lawyers argued: if companies could refuse to meet demands on the grounds of "economic capacity" then the same theory could be applied to prove that the companies were able to meet demands. The 1936 expropriation law, which permitted seizure of the oil properties, was a direct outgrowth of the original "economic capacity" argument. This law was definitely aimed at employers who were closing down their factories, alleging excessive labor demands on the grounds that they lacked "economic capacity" to continue operations. The expropriation law made it possible for the government to take over such properties, under the public utility clause.

6

Mexico said:

"Two billion barrels of oil, worth more than four billion pesos, taken from our soil, six thousand wells sunk, and what have we got to show for it?"

The new government oil set-up and the National Oil Workers' Union set about trying to prove that Mexico will have more to show under this type of operation than it ever could under the companies' regime. Some critics, both foreign and domestic, scoffed at the idea that the Mexicans could run the oil business. A booklet prepared by the companies said:

> "Expropriation transferred to the Mexican government physical properties unaccompanied by the intangible but essential factors of technical skill and executive ability. Expropriation also transferred to the Mexican government certain liabilities—reduced tax revenues,* curtailed economic benefits, disrupted commerce, strained relations with other nations, increased governmental expenses, and vastly augmented responsibilities—any or all of which might work to the extreme disadvantage of the entire nation."

Some of the boys waited around Tampico expecting the refineries to explode any minute, the wells to go boom, the pipe lines to burst. One reason for this—and this was part of the oil workers' complaint—was that the companies had carefully avoided teaching Mexicans the art of capping wells and other such intricacies of the oil game. The Mexicans were always just helpers, but a foreigner ran the job. The oil boys had forgotten, however, that as far back as 1913 Mexicans kept the Doheny properties running after all Americans had been evacuated. The same thing happened again in 1916. A similar situation had been taken care of on the railways. And in the meantime a new generation had grown up: geologists, engineers, electricians, and other Mexican technical experts, trained in Mexican and foreign schools, aching for a chance to put their training to use. Also available were foreign technicians in Germany and Italy, and independent American drillers. With the technicians had

---

* On December 23, 1938, the Mexican Congress passed a national budget based on estimated revenue of 445,000,000 pesos, largest in Mexican history.

grown up a corps of young men trained in business, in ac-
counting, in management. Besides, for nearly ten years the
Mexican government had been gradually getting into the oil
business itself. First through the Control de Petroleo, then
Petromex, and later the General Administration of National
Petroleum. These departments were created to direct production on public lands. Then there were the inspectors,
nearly all trained engineers.

The oil administration took down the neon sign over the
recently built volcanic-rock building of the Aguila company
and put up a new one that said "Petroleos Mexicanos,"
flanked by strips of light in the national colors, red, white
and green. Eduardo Perez Castañeda, twenty-eight-year-old
former confidential assistant of the Aguila field superintendent, became manager of the rich Poza Rica field. Perez had
been barred from the oil company grounds when it became
known that he was a member of the union. So it was with
special delight that young Perez, eight years before a newspaper advertising and subscription solicitor in Monterrey,
moved into the superintendent's house. Soon afterward, the
general whose troops had helped bar Perez from the fields,
was transferred. The new manager of the field, like so many
of the new bosses in the oil industry, had every incentive in
the world to make him try to show that the Mexicans can
manage as well as foreigners.

In June, Cardenas visited the Poza Rica field, made history again by ordering the first land parceling to farmers in
that region. Thousands of gas flares lighted up the field.
Workers and peasants trooped from the villages of Veracruz.
Schoolchildren brought him flowers. There was a big meeting. Speakers—Carlos Torres of Section 30 of the Oil
Workers' Union, Raul Rivera of Section 14, Señora Estela
Guerrero on behalf of the women—recalled that Cardenas
had personally financed a school when he was stationed in

Villa Cuauhtemoc. Hence, people of the oil region felt a special affection for him.

Cardenas learned that production had dropped off at first, and that the big problem was lack of storage capacity, made more acute by the international boycott against Mexican oil. He learned that fifteen wells had been drilled in Poza Rica, which is about thirty-five miles west of Tuxpan, and that two new wells had just been sunk; that twelve hundred men were at work on the pipe line from Tuxpan to the Atzcapotzalco refinery, which is just outside Mexico City; that five hundred thousand square feet of lumber was being cut for the first housing project, the "March 18 Colony," that the workers had acquired brick-making equipment, were installing water filters and sanitary services. Things didn't look so bad to him.

Soon afterward, the oil administration announced a general wage increase for workmen, averaging about forty per cent, as "the first step to putting into effect the labor board award," and ordered salary cuts ranging from fifteen to twenty-five per cent for the upper-salary-bracket employees, earning from one thousand to four thousand pesos a month. The administration also announced plans for ten new wells in Poza Rica, twelve in the Ebano field and twelve in the southern field of the Isthmus of Tehuantepec, in addition to budgeting six million pesos next year for workers' houses, other allotments for new pipe lines, a new refinery, new storage tanks, research to develop tetraethyl of lead, formerly imported from the United States, and withheld, after expropriation, by the American monopoly.

7

Criticism from the left and criticism from the right found common ground in pointing to dangers of political control

of the oil administration, and hence, indirectly, of the Oil
Workers' Union. The big If is: Will the oil industry be
administered on an honest, businesslike basis by bureaucrats?
Minor clashes occurred as a result of political appointments
to posts in the oil fields, and refusal of the union to recognize
these appointments. The government established a liaison
staff between the union and the oil administration to iron
out differences, and there were indications that there would
be more differences.

Critics on the extreme left charged that expropriation was
a device to keep the oil fields from passing fully into the
hands of the oil workers, as might have happened through
the process of embargo. They stated further:

That nationalization will benefit only the native bourgeoisie and labor leaders, who are getting good jobs in the
administration.

That no indemnity should be paid to the companies, because payment of indemnity means continued subservience
to foreign powers in one form or another.

That the workers were forced to renounce all the concessions they had won from the companies.

That the union leaders are trying to eliminate class consciousness among the workers and to substitute "social patriotism."

That, nevertheless, expropriation deserves support of the
workers of the world, for the sole reason that it "tends to
diminish the preponderance of imperialist capital in Mexico
and because it gives the proletariat the possibility of con-
quering better positions in the struggle for socialism."

From the right wing came this barrage:

That the only concrete gain from expropriation is additional prestige for Mexico in Latin America and the increase
of Cardenas' political stature.

That expropriation was a Standard Oil maneuver to oust

British interests and to keep the Mexican oil in the ground.

That payment of indemnity will force increased taxes on other industries.

That national economy will be impaired and permanent emergency measures will have to be taken to protect the national currency.

That Mexico's oil reserves will be exhausted at a faster pace than under private exploitation.

That the Six-Year Plan will have to be sacrificed entirely, with the exception of its section on petroleum, and the nation as a whole will have to postpone social and economic betterment for the exclusive benefit of oil workers and bureaucrats.

Between the extreme views is that of the government and supporters of its policies, a feeling of optimism that the problem can be worked out to the general benefit of the nation. And since the United States won't help, Mexico must turn to Germany and Italy and South America, for sale of its oil, for building of tankers. Great Britain stuck to her original demands that cash be paid or the properties be returned instanter.

The Democratic New York *Times* led the foreign press in pounding away at the Mexican government, a task undertaken with equal zest by the Republican Chicago *Tribune*. Mexican technicians were welcomed with open arms in Italy where they went to study plans for building a refinery which would take Mexican oil and pay in Italian automobiles. Other Mexican representatives went to Germany with similar assignments. More Italian and German agents arrived in Mexico to make hay under the glorious sun of antagonism against the Anglo-American world. The Japanese horned in on the deal, began to share in Mexican road contracts.

The boycott against Mexican oil continued. Mexican oil, at dirt-cheap prices, was smuggled into the United States. Mexico swung deals to sell oil to Central and South America.

The Ministry of Public Education awarded Mario Martinez a hundred-peso prize for the best oil publicity poster submitted in a school contest. Armando Sube and Francisco Dominguez composed the "Ballad of Petroleum," which goes something like this:

> On the eighteenth day of March,
> In the year of 'thirty-eight,
> Imperialism in Mexico
> Got the well-known gate.
>
> The companies for many years,
> Tied us up by foot and hand,
> Spread a reign of blood and tears,
> Ran amuck on conquered land.
>
> The workers in the fields of oil,
> Weary of the run-around,
> Demanded something for their toil,
> Besides a big hole in the ground.
>
> More power to our President,
> Brave leader of the nation;
> Knowing what our workers meant,
> He decreed expropriation.

But the Cardenas sun of a new Mañana is streaked with the shadows of ominous clouds: the hard facts of capitalist economics, the problem of feeding a nation, the political intrigue at home and abroad, the dreary record of past betrayals by Mexican leaders, all piled up to block the path of a nation courageously trying to get over the hump and onto the road of self-assertion.

III

MEXICO FOR THE MEXICANS

1

FOREIGN domination is the ball-and-chain that Mexico has been forced to drag along in its fighting march toward self development. One link on the shackling weight was made in Madrid, another in Paris, and still others in London, in Vatican City, and in Washington. The history of Mexico is a narrative in which one foreign flag after another has been raised over the Mexican flag during a moment of national crisis:

A. D. 1538—A Papal Bull, signed by Paul III, reaches New Spain, ending an ecclesiastical war that had raged since the first Catholic saint displaced an Indian idol in conquered Mexico. It rules that Indians are rational beings, even if they do not assume the Roman Catholic faith. As rational beings, they have souls.

MARCH, 1697—Riots in Mexico City provoked by high prices of grain, cornered by Spanish monopolists.

MARCH, 1808—Charles IV abdicates in Spanish crisis, marking beginning of Mexican independence movement. Spanish flag still flies over Mexico until 1821, when Iturbide finishes job started by Hidalgo on September 16, 1810.

MARCH, 1837—United States Senate recognizes Texan independence from Mexico.

MARCH, 1838—Mexican government says no answer to French claims will be given until French fleet leaves Mexican waters. Mexico feels her honor and decorum have been outraged. Later, the French shell Veracruz, land, raise the French flag on Mexican soil.

MARCH, 1847—United States fleet bombards Veracruz and captures the port, a decisive episode in U. S.–Mexican War. Stars and Stripes fly over Mexican buildings.

MARCH, 1867—Siege of Queretaro opens, beginning of the end of Maximilian's short and ill-fated reign as emperor of Mexico; Juarez and the Republic are triumphant.

The Hitler-led economic and ideological invasion of Mexico by the Berlin-Rome-Tokyo axis is another link being forged on the international ball-and-chain that binds Mexico.

2

The Ides of March, 1938, found Neighbor Uncle Sam rehearsing for a return engagement in his most famous role: the Mickey (Himself) Maguire of Latin America. The tough baby of the Western Hemisphere has been the pet nightmare of the twenty countries to the south for more than one hundred years: since the beginning of the struggles for national consolidation which followed the independence movements at the close of the eighteenth and the opening of the nineteenth centuries. But more than once the boys on the West Side of the Atlantic have thanked their stars, their saints and their idols for somebody in the neighborhood big enough to tell the guys from across the sea where to get off. The Monroe Doctrine, rejected by Latin America as a unilateral declaration of the United States, and as a pretext for American imperialist penetration, has undoubtedly served as a buffer against European ambitions in the New World. Today, in the face of an unprecedented Nazi drive in Latin America, United States foreign policy faces a crucial test.

In popularizing the Good Neighbor slogan, President F. D. Roosevelt made a smart and very necessary diplomatic move

to counteract the Bad Neighbor policy which other administrations had followed without calling it just that. The
other Roosevelt president, Teddy, represented the peak of
that policy. He kept the Latin-American neighbors awake,
turned his sharp-spurred gamecocks loose in their gardens,
spanked the neighbors' kids, and generally went about trying
to show the international neighborhood that if any of the
boys got to feeling their oats, they'd have to lick Uncle Sam
first. F. D. R.'s immediate Republican predecessors took
the Big Brother attitude, that of the fellow who knew what
was good for the Little Brown Brother, and who was going to
see that he got it, whether Little Brother wanted it or not.

The Good Neighbor idea didn't originate with the New
Deal. The treaty of Guadalupe Hidalgo, signed by Mexico
and the United States on February 2, 1848, said in its preamble:

"In the name of Almighty God: The United States of
America, and the United Mexican States, animated by a
sincere desire to put an end to the calamities of the war
which unhappily exists between the two Republics, and
to establish upon a solid basis relations of peace and
friendship which shall confer reciprocal benefits upon
the citizens of both, and assure the concord, harmony
and mutual confidence, wherein the two Peoples shall
live, as good Neighbours, have for that purpose appointed their respective plenipotentiaries . . ."

Only the peculiar irony of diplomatic documents can explain that harmony, concord and mutual confidence are
exactly the things which have always been lacking in the
relations between the two countries that meet at the Rio
Grande. From the infancy of the two Republics, Mexicans
have feared that the growth of the United States would be
achieved at the expense of Mexico. The annexation of Texas,
the United States-Mexican war, the shifting of the United

States boundaries to include all the territory north of the
Rio Grande and the Colorado, and roughly along the thirty-
first parallel, deprived Mexico of about half her former territory. This was a bitter pill, and not easily forgotten. It is
regurgitated with every new dose of foreign force applied to
Mexico, and it is not surprising that Mexican admirers of
Hitler applauded the taking of Austria and the Sudeten as
revindicatory measures, and expressed the fervent hope that
Mexico may someday be strong enough to recover her lost
territory. Others saw Hitler's aggression as a danger signal
to weaker countries which, like Mexico, live next door to a
big power.

Of course the feeling of animosity toward the United States
is not unanimous. There have always been counter-currents,
in which the influence of the United States is regarded as a
blessing to Mexico, in spite of Texas, in spite of the loss of
territory, in spite of United States battleships and marines at
Veracruz, the Pershing expedition, the economic sanctions
and ever-present threat of force on behalf of United States
big business interests operating below the Rio Grande. The
Mexicans who look with friendlier eyes on the United States
are those who find in the American political philosophy—
the doctrines of democracy and representative government—
a rallying post against absolutism, against government from
above, against the arbitrary rule of despots whether in the
name of a fictitious sword-carved peace or in the name of
exclusive appointment by divine providence.

The basic cleavage is essentially the same one which has
split the world into opposing camps, but it is sharpened in
Mexico to contrasts as dramatic as her mountain-valley land-
scapes, icy-tropical climate or her rainy-sunny days. The
European Holy Alliance drive early in the nineteenth century, aimed at "destroying the evil of representative government," hit a snag in the impassioned republicanism emanat-

ing from the United States, then fighting all over again to keep her independence from England.

In Mexico, the Church oligarchy and feudal nobility sought to stem the republican tide that swelled with the war of independence. Parish priests, hostile to the hierarchy, became leaders in the York Rite Masonic lodges, which rose against the Scottish Rite, stronghold of the old order. The first movement for independence—1810—was quelled with the aid of the ruling classes of Mexico. Hidalgo, the priest-leader, was excommunicated as "an enemy of the social order, and of property in land." He was captured and executed, and other insurgent priests, including Morelos, close to the misery of the people, met a like fate. Not until 1821, when the high clergy and their native allies, the landlords, merchants, and moneylenders, decided for independence from a Spanish regime moving toward liberalism, was the separation consummated. Efforts to retain the monarchial form were doomed to failure, however, and Iturbide as August I went to the grave, first and last emperor of the first Mexican empire. The Republic was definitely established—still to face many years of hostility—with adoption of the 1824 Constitution.

3

Today, two main currents of Mexican political tradition date back to this period. One hails Hidalgo as the father of Mexican independence. The other places the laurels on Iturbide's brow. In this civil conflict which was part of the independence war, the United States first appeared as a third party seriously concerned over the type of government to be instituted in Mexico, and the effects of such government on business with the United States. This country was represented by Joel Roberts Poinsett, first ambassador to Mexico, an ardent apostle of what the royalists called the "religion of republicanism," and an uncompromising enemy of everything British. Poinsett had even had the audacity to preach republicanism at the court of the Czar of Russia. The reply of Czar Alexander to Poinsett's arguments has become a classic of diplomatic annals:

"You are quite right, Mr. Poinsett, and you can be sure that if I were not emperor, I would be a republican."

This man Poinsett looms large as one of the originators and first standard-bearer of United States foreign policy, for better or for worse, in Latin America—a policy which combined political evangelism with the furtherance of economic advantage. To the Iturbidists, the traditional conservatives of Mexico, Poinsett is the incarnation of the very Devil, the evil genius of modern Mexican history, the man whose meddling in Mexican affairs did much to prevent the country from becoming an independent Catholic monarchy. Poinsett is blamed for the downfall of Iturbide, for the growth of the liberal Masonic order, for the introduction of Protestantism and the subsequent "undermining" of the Catholic Church's political hegemony. He is charged with having prepared the ground for imperialist penetration in order to keep Mexico from rising as a rival of the United States, which it might have become, according to the Iturbidists, if it hadn't been set against itself by foreign-fostered civil strife. Many Mexicans place another American ambassador in the same class of meddlers—Henry Lane Wilson. They hold this United States envoy responsible for the Huerta counter-revolution which resulted in Madero's assassination and subsequent years of bloody civil war.

Among the heirs of the Iturbidist tradition in Mexico today are to be found the most rabid anti-American Mexicans, railing against the presumption of an upstart country that called itself United States of America without consulting the other countries of the Americas. These traditional enemies of the United States stand ready to join forces with anybody who represents a threat to Uncle Sam's influence in Mexico. In their camp, British interests have found vigorous champions and have paid them well. Today's most aggressive rivals of the United States in Mexico—the Germans, Italians and Japanese—naturally turn to these same elements to further their political and economic ambitions. American interests, notably the oil and mining interests, have also utilized Mexican Iturbidists, opponents of Mexican popular movements, champions of Porfirio Diaz methods. Thence arises a paradox, one of many that make the Mexican picture a mosaic of paradoxes: the social democratic forces, represented by the dominant trend in the Cardenas administration—which are the most inclined toward friendship with the United States— are compelled to turn to the fascist countries. There Mexico seeks economic life belts in a threatened shipwreck, provoked by pressure from the democratic governments acting on behalf of their investors. The price for this fascist aid is paid not only in direct economic concessions, in purchase of commodities, but also in permitting fascist ideology to press its molds on Mexican political forms, still in a very plastic stage.

4

Summing up the Mexican grievances that tend to swing Mexican sympathy to the nazis or any anti-American force, we find the following as outstanding:

1. Loss of nearly one-half the Mexican territory as a result of the war with the United States.

2. Persistent meddling of United States officials in Mexican affairs.

3. The use of the United States Embassy as headquarters for the counter-revolutionary plotters who put Huerta in power and assassinated Madero.

4. Failure of the United States to give Mexico satisfaction on the question of the Chamizal district at El Paso, awarded to Mexico by an arbitration commission in 1911. The Chamizal question dates back to the boundary treaty of 1853. A few years after the international line had been determined, the Rio Grande shifted its course violently, leaving a four hundred-acre section of Mexican territory to the north of the river. This section later became part of urban El Paso. The arbitration commission ruled that according to U. S.- Mexico treaties, the Chamizal section belongs to Mexico.

5. The covetous eyes cast by some American interests upon the peninsula of Lower California. During the Porfirio Diaz epoch vast tracts were ceded to American companies with the understanding that they were to colonize the region. One of the tracts, the famous Flores-Hale concession, totaled more than five million acres. Most of this was recovered by Mexico in a purchase deal during the presidency of Abelardo Rodriguez. Accepted generally as a fact, although documentary evidence is lacking, is the story that on April 21, 1915, DuVal West, United States special agent, proposed to give Francisco Villa support and recognition of the United States government in return for cession of Lower California. At different times, American statesmen and legislators have declared Lower California to be a basic factor in well-rounded national defense plans for the United States.

6. Discriminatory treatment of Mexicans in the United States, especially in the Southwest. In some places, the Mexican children are segregated into separate schools. Elsewhere, Mexicans are not served in restaurants reserved "for whites only." Mexican consuls have protested numerous cases of alleged brutality by United States immigration and border patrol officers in handling Mexicans suspected of illegal residence.

7. Harshly-worded notes from our State Department,

considered an affront to Mexico's sovereignty. Some very hard-boiled messages were directed to Mexico City from Washington during the Coolidge administration on the question of Mexico's petroleum laws and their effect on American oil interests. The tenor of the communications was modified with inception of the Good Neighbor policy, but in the Hull messages on expropriated lands—following oil property expropriation—Mexicans thought they felt the familiar old big-stick, only slightly padded. Following an exchange of notes in which Mexico held firm, the two governments finally agreed to arbitration of the claims. The American representative arrived in Mexico City in November, 1938, for preliminary discussions. United States claimed Mexico owed ten million dollars for the land taken from American citizens. One of the points to be settled was how much of this land was actually property of Mexicans, registered under the names of Americans. The Mexican government later agreed to pay for the land at the rate of one million dollars a year.

8. United States press campaigns against Mexico, notably, in recent years, during the Church-State dispute and in 1937 and 1938 on the petroleum question.

9. The bolstering of Calles in his role as maker and un-maker of presidents, a policy which grew out of the Bucareli treaties which Mexico considered as onerous and which have been branded as a "sell-out" to the United States, with Obregon doing the selling in return for recognition of his government. The Bucareli treaties developed from conversations in 1923, when Charles Beecher Warren and John Barton Payne went to Mexico City to discuss with Mexico a general claims treaty to cover losses by American and Mexican citizens. Opponents of the Bucareli treaties held that they nullified Article Twenty-seven of the 1917 Constitution by granting special protection to oil and other foreign properties and by giving the United States interests a number of other special

concessions. Senator Field Jurado was slain for his opposition, and the treaties were pushed through the intimidated senate early in 1924 by Obregon, who got recognition from the United States. The Calles Petroleum law of 1925 brought the Bucareli treaties to public notice again. The United States charged that the new law violated the treaties. In the *modus vivendi* reached, Calles succeeded in abrogating a number of the special concessions granted to the United States. Many Mexican writers regard the treaties as illegal because they were ratified allegedly without a legal quorum and under conditions of terror following assassination of Field Jurado.

5

A pawn in the international chess game in which foreign interests jockey continually for advantages, Mexico turns first to one and then to another, seeking to utilize the battle of imperialisms as best she can. She aids Nicaragua against the U. S. marines, talks of secret deals with Japan during the Carranza epoch, grants British and French interests concessions in preference to American, flirts with Germany via the Zimmerman billet-doux in 1915, whereby Germany offered aid in recovering Texas and California: all this in an effort to counterbalance the insistent pressure of American capital.

Like the Indian in the market place, Mexico bargains with all comers, has developed a keen sense of horse-trading, a brilliant school of diplomacy, as part of the defense mechanism needed by a nation still trying to redeem her sovereignty from the hockshops of international big business, from the bondholders of Paris, New York, London, Berlin. In this struggle, Mexico finds common ground with her sister Latin-American nations. Blood ties are made faster by economic ties. The Monroe Doctrine exponents have been seeking a formula which would abolish Latin-American hostility toward it, perhaps even scrap the doctrine as such, and substitute an intercontinental treaty against European aggression. The Pan-American conference, meeting in Lima, Peru, in December, 1938, was considered a probable point of departure for this development. A certain note of optimism had developed in Latin America following inauguration of the Good Neighbor policy, made concrete in 1934 with the abrogation of the Platt Amendment which had given the United States the right to intervene in Cuba's internal affairs. Later events plus Nazi and Italian onslaughts on the idea of Pan-Americanism have tended to sour the note somewhat.

6

What happens in Mexico is of vital interest, then, to the one hundred million people who live to the south of Uncle Sam's next-door neighbor. They live on rich oil, mining, timber, and plantation lands, whose products are essential to the turning of the big machines in the highly industrialized nations. The majority of Latin-American countries have at least four points of heritage in common:

1. Blending of European—mostly Spanish—blood and culture with the Indian or Negro.
2. The Spanish language.
3. Imprint of centuries of Catholicism.
4. Colonial or semicolonial economy.

In this vast territory that stretches from California to the south and east, the United States has invested some 4,000 million dollars. More than 3,000 millions are in direct investments, and approximately 1,000 millions in loans. The biggest investments (direct and indirect): Cuba, $666,254,-000; Chile, $643,736,000; Mexico, $479,000,000; Argentine, $348,260,000; Brazil, $194,345,000; Venezuela, $186,286,000; Colombia, $107,548,000; Peru, $96,052,000.

The dollars working for the foreign capitalists are being

trimmed down by growing economic nationalism in Latin America. Nationalization of resources has become a general trend. In 1936, Bolivia expropriated Standard Oil properties. Chile has nationalized oil lands and the state controls refineries and regulates prices. State control has increased in Argentine. Brazil has laws which establish state control of petroleum. Costa Rica expropriated the Electric Bond and Share Company, and at the same time gave the United Fruit Company a monopoly of the banana industry. Ecuador has strict measures over foreign industry. Uruguay's government controls the refineries. Colombia and Venezuela in 1938 still remained the happiest hunting grounds for foreign capital.

The social reforms sketched into Mexico's radical constitution of 1917 have found varying echoes in legislation of several Latin-American countries, especially with reference to labor, formerly not considered in the basic political documents of nations. In 1924, Honduras included a labor clause in its constitution. Ecuador restricted property, giving it social modalities, and established legal protection for labor contracts. Peru's 1933 constitution recognized the "obligation of the State" to legislate on collective contracts, participation of workers in industry, security, workday, minimum salary, co-operatives, capital-labor relations in general. Article 15 of the Brazilian constitution orders the public authorities periodically to examine the standard of living, provides machinery for State monopoly of any industry or economic activity. Uruguay has moved closest to Mexico in giving labor special protective laws, recognizes the right to union organization and to strike, has opened the way to establishment of special labor board set-ups. The opposite extreme is found in Haiti where President Vincent said, "the lower the salaries, the more work for more men."

Social-Reform, however, is a big word and comprises the fascist modifications as well as the socialist. As a matter of fact, in some Latin-American countries the legislation on labor is modeled after the Italian corporative formula—suppression of class struggle, imposition of class collaboration. In most other countries, the so-called social reform laws are just so many scraps of paper. Peru offers one example of acute fascist penetration under the democratic form. The head of the state, Oscar Benavides, is president in name, dictator in fact. A personal friend of Mussolini, he has been an ardent admirer of fascist methods which he learned during service as Peruvian minister to Rome. Italians dominate the Peruvian financial scene and share economic domination with the Germans. Gino Salochi, head of the Italian Bank of Lima, sees to it that the bulk of Peru's war fleet of airplanes comes from the Caproni works. Italian instructors train Peruvian police in fascist methods. The Casa Grande trust, dominated by the German Gildemeister interests, controls sugar and cotton, has practically a monopoly on all South American sugar business. German technicians have established laboratories to develop methods of turning the excess sugar supply into explosives and war gas.

Brazil had a fascist movement developing as early as 1923, among Italian groups in Rio de Janeiro. The Integralista fascist group, formed in 1931, included among the sponsors Oswaldo Aranha, now minister of foreign affairs and formerly ambassador in Washington, and Francisco Campo, who became minister of justice. The Crespi and Matarazzo big business interests provided a steady stream of gold to build "a strong, integral, corporative, totalitarian Brazil." The political wing of the economically powerful Catholic Church, Catholic Action, persecuted liberal churchmen like the priest, Manuel Do Nascimento, and lined up with the Integralists. The United States State Department took a hand in the situation, and effected at least a surface change in the picture, where the main enemies of Brazil were painted as "Jewish capitalism in the United States" and "Jewish socialism from the Soviet Union." President Getulio Vargas, in 1938, rounded up Integralistas, but the leaders managed to escape. Integralista manifestoes had stated:

> "Integralism combats all parties, does not recognize classes, seeks a united nation, a national state, a strong state, a heroic state. The government must no longer be elected by parties which divide the nation, but by a totalitarian nation, by means of corporations . . . the liberalist evils of the French Revolution must be wiped out. . . ."

The Dominican Republic provided a tragically ludicrous caricature of all totalitarianism in the person of the dictator, Rafael Leonidas Trujillo Molina. This Caribbean Caesar rose, with the aid of United States marines, from his precarious existence as a cattle thief to become boss of the country, passing through the stages of guide and informer for the marines. His five-year-old son Rafael was made a colonel in the Dominican Army, and, unlike the honorary Kentucky colonels, drew colonel's pay. Trujillo's brother was appointed commander-in-chief of the army. The Dominican dictator crowned his career with the mass slaughter of Haitians, and the announcement that he was wiping out the Haitians so he could colonize the border region with fifty thousand Germans. The President of the Dominican Republic is, naturally, a Trujillo puppet.

In Central America, the fascist-dominated dictators have talked of reviving the Central American Unionist Party, in order to form the much-talked-of Confederation of Central America. Its aim would be to counteract the influence of Mexican Revolutionary politics and maintain the despotic status quo. Democratic Costa Rica, haven of Tomas Garrido Canabal, former Lord of Tabasco, Mexico, has become the propaganda base for the proposed Confederation's anti-Mexican program. When Antonio R. Osuna, representing the Mexican oil administration, made a trip through Central America, he was shunned by officials as if he had been some kind of reptile. The Central American dictators are frankly afraid of the admiration expressed among labor and liberal groups in their countries for that man Lazaro Cardenas.

All the Central-American countries have Nazi and fascist organizations, openly propagandizing, and with aid of the government, since each general in the presidential chair likes the idea of considering himself as another Hitler or Mussolini. German influence is particularly strong in Guatemala, where Berlin controls the coffee industry. Big shipments of arms and airplanes have reached El Salvador and Nicaragua from Italy.

It seemed quite likely that the Confederation would not be effected in the near future, however, because Jorge Ubico of Guatemala, Carias Andino of Honduras, Antonio Somoza of Nicaragua, Hernandez Martinez of Salvador, each wanted to be head man. But they did form a mutual assistance alliance, to help one another perpetuate themselves in power in their respective countries.

On February 5, 1937, Manolo Cuadra, Nicaraguan poet, and six Nicaraguan workmen, were arrested for attending a celebration of the twentieth anniversary of the 1917 Mexican constitution, sponsored by the Mexican chargé d'affaires. They were imprisoned, tortured, mutilated. In Mexico this was regarded as another assault of United States imperialism. It didn't help Good Neighbor sentiment a bit.

7

4-46-41.
6-09-62.
4-32-46.
These three numbers were among the busiest of all Mexico

City telephones on the night of March 18th. They correspond, respectively, to the German, Italian and Japanese legations, all terribly excited over the new commercial and political possibilities opened by the petroleum feud.

Mexico is the prize plum that the fascists from beyond the seas would like to grab out of the Latin-American trade pudding. For more than one reason; viz.:

Mexico is rich in raw materials.

Mexico has a growing industrial working class, still with a relatively low standard of living, a fine market for the cheap commodities produced in Germany, Italy and Japan.

Mexico has been in a state of political and social ferment for the last thirty years, has suffered many disillusionments, has mass organization psychology developed by dozens of demagogues; hence it is a fertile field for planting of fascist seeds.

Mexico is the perfect base for military and naval operations, for espionage, sabotage, and propaganda against the United States, as was shown in the World War.

The forms of fascist penetration are fourfold in Latin America: political pressure, economic drives, cultural infiltration, maneuvers for strategic war positions. Political pressure is applied for Latin-American recognition of the Hitler expansion program, of the Italian conquests, the Nazi-Italian inroads in Spain. In Mexico, the fascists encountered a regime which openly declared itself in favor of the Spanish government against Franco; and advocated economic sanctions against aggressor nations. *El Nacional,* the government party's organ, assailed Hitlerian racial and political doctrine, and championed the cause of Czechoslovakia.

The Spanish civil war gave Europe's fascists the key to the promotion of their interests in Latin America: Franco. The procedure became clear when it was revealed that arms, men and munitions were en route to Seville from Rome and Berlin. Throughout Latin America a well-prepared drive to enlist support for the Spanish uprising of July 18, 1936, bore fruit in the quickest possible recognition of Franco.

The Mexican government surprised many by taking her stand with the Loyalists, and eventually sending arms and ammunition. Many and varied reasons were advanced to explain this phenomenon. Two were most often repeated: Mexico owed Spain money for some coastguard cutters built in Spanish shipyards and was taking this opportunity to barter off some munitions at war rates; and the other, that the Cardenas administration, not yet consolidated after the head-on collison with the Calles steam roller, feared a fascist coup, in which case the Cardenas administration would be in the same boat as the Azaña government, standing full square on the legality of his side against the armed uprising of the other.

Despite the Mexican government attitude, however, the majority of the Mexican press vigorously espoused the Franco movement, and continued doing so with ever-greater weight as the Spanish fascists took more territory. The pressure on Cardenas became tremendous from inside and outside the government. Disputes raged about Mexican diplomatic precedents: whether it had been the policy to recognize de facto or de jure governments. But one factor outweighed them all—that Mexican governments in the past had always needed outside support to hold them steady against internal dissension or imperialist maneuvers. As she had condemned Italian invasion of Ethiopia, Mexico took her stand against any form of aggression, recalling her own defensive position in the network of international intrigue.

Mexico's many thousand Spanish residents split along lines similar to the cleavage in Spain, and the Franco side—because it could control a greater share of the press through advertising and business connections—automatically became the most articulate side. It was evident that Cardenas, although

he may have taken a popular stand, put himself in a dangerously bold position. The pressure on him varied from those
who advocated a "neutral" position such as that taken by the
United States, to the extremists who demanded recognition
of Franco. When he stuck to his guns, the opposition, including many industrialists with interests in Spain as well as
in Mexico, gradually began linking the fate of the Mexican
administration with the fate of the Spanish government.
Headlines such as this appeared: "Cardenas Defeated at
Teruel!" This phase of the pro-Franco drive was reflected in
hysterically jubilant news comments over the radio on occa-
sion of a Franco military victory. In the case of one radio
announcer, a Spaniard, the government stepped in and told
him to stick to the facts.

Among Spaniards are some of the wealthiest men in
Mexico. They own about sixty per cent of Mexico's acreage,
according to a study published in 1938 by the Instituto
Socialista de Mexico. Their interests in the mines and mining
concessions have stood up fairly well in spite of the inroads
of British, American, and, latterly, German operators. A large
percentage of real estate in Mexico City is owned by Spaniards. Their control of domestic commerce is well known:
clothing and food stores, theaters, movies, printshops, hotels,
saloons, restaurants, books, paper. The rise in commodity
prices, especially corn, beans, chickpeas, bread, lard and milk
was blamed on Spanish monopolists in control of the food-
stuffs industries. Two-thirds of the textile factories are Span-
ish-owned. The Spaniards' monopoly of the publishing business was declared responsible for the difficulty Mexican
writers encounter in getting their works published, and for
the high price of books.

Spanish capital figures in a big way in heavy industry.
Example: Adolfo Prieto, of Monterrey, one of the richest
men in Latin America. Spaniards or creoles (Spaniards born

in Mexico of families that have lived there more than one generation without marrying mixed-bloods or Indians) dominate the important industrial center of Monterrey. Spanish capitalists have an edge on the Anglo-Saxons in the matter of language, blood-relationships and cultural ties. Most of the Spaniards operating in Mexican business make their homes there, spend profits on residence and other construction, in new enterprises; whereas most of the American and British capital is strictly of the absentee type, for which Mexico is just an economic colony.

To be expected, then, was the discovery of a widespread pro-Franco fascist organization (Falange Español Tradicionalista) in the Spanish colony, with an associated youth organization, Juventud Obrera Nacional Sindicalista. In 1938, Mexican authorities investigating activities of the organizations found their headquarters on Prim Street, a stone's throw from the Ministry of the Interior, and in their receipt books discovered that many members of the Spanish colony had been contributing regularly for some time.

Meanwhile, the Mexican government made itself the guardian of some four hundred young Spanish children, refugees from the war zones. It established them in Morelia, capital of Michoacan State, providing quarters, food, schooling, recreation. Spanish widows, refugeed in Paris, cabled Cardenas, thanking him for helping Spain, wished him a long and happy life. Some of Mexico's best known leftists were assigned to diplomatic duty in Spain. In 1938 Mexico's ambassador in Barcelona was Adalberto Tejeda, one time governor of Veracruz, former cabinet minister, one time presidential candidate (and may be again), and known for his anti-clerical politics. As its representative in Spain, the Confederation of Mexican Workers named Narciso Bassols, former cabinet minister, later active in the Friends of the Soviet Union, noted scholar, translator of many Marxist works.

When Lauro Gonzalez Uzcanga, of a bakery workers' union, shot and killed Argimiro Lopez, owner of a chain of bakeshops, defenders of Uzcanga brought out, among other things, that Lopez had sent five thousand pesos to Franco. But, if somebody started shooting all the Spaniards in Mexico who have sent money to Franco—either voluntarily or under business and bank pressure—he'd be kept busy for quite a while. Not shooting, but wholesale deportation, was advocated in a broadside which appeared in October, 1938, signed by small merchants, peasants (who bring crops in for sale on the city markets) and a trade union in Mexico City. How the pro-Franco agitation is becoming identified with Nazi agitation in Mexico was indicated in the title of the broadside: "Spanish Kultur."

8

On November 22, 1937, while Mexican animosity toward the British and American interests was being roused to high pitch over the petroleum situation, Dr. Walter Hoffman, general manager of the Hamburg-Amerika line, arrived in Mexico. *Excelsior,* daily newspaper through which Nazism finds abundant expression, printed the following news story on Page One the next morning:

"Germany and Mexico Will Soon Do More Business and Will Enjoy More Tourist Trade. So stated Dr. Walter Hoffman, general manager of the Hamburg Amerika Linie, the biggest steamship company in the world.

" 'I have made the trip from Veracruz to the capital by automobile and I can state that this country has been a revelation to me, a country where so much is to be seen socially as well as scenically,' Dr. Hoffman said, continuing:

" 'The progress of Mexico is evident. As in the Third Reich of Germany, where the condition of the workers is being improved, this beautiful country has succeeded in realizing its great projects of the Six-Year Plan during the short time that President Cardenas has been in power. . . . I can assure you that the trade between Mexico and Germany during the last three years, and especially this one, has increased exceptionally and that exports to Germany have nearly doubled . . . this interchange will surely increase still further in the near future, for Germany is in a position to increase the imports of the many Mexican products in exchange for the products of German industry which I deem essential for the complete unfolding of the Six-Year Plan. . . . The project of the Mexican Confederation of Chambers of Commerce for an interchange of businessmen who understand each other's commerce and arts will do much to intensify the volume of business between the two countries.' "

Dr. Hoffman wasn't really telling any tales out of school because the Nazi campaign becomes more open every day, grows by leaps and bounds, has reached proportions comparable to the pre-War period when German influence was strong enough to make Carranza consider an alliance with the Kaiser and to refuse aid to the Allies. Highly colored newspaper stories, pro-Nazi editorials and articles appear in Mexican periodicals, and university students are organized into a National Socialist Party of Mexico. They greet one another with "Heil Hitler."

On September 16, 1938, anniversary of Mexico's declaration of independence, *Excelsior* published a special section devoted to the foreign colonies of Mexico. It was what the boys in the trade call a gyp section, with little advertising value as such. But its significance lay in the preponderance of German advertising and write-ups. German headache pills, German typewriters, German radios, German centrifugal pumps, German cameras, told their story in display ads amid lengthy articles extolling Nazi culture, Nazi economy, Hitler and his cabinet, beautiful relations between Mexico and Germany. Japan had the second biggest spread, Spain third. The British and American firms were conspicuously scarce. Several days before, Dr. Heinrich Northe, chargé d'affaires of the Nazi legation, had sent word around to all the German firms that they'd better take an ad for the greater glory of *der fuehrer* or else.

This type of pressure is the regular thing to German nationals in Mexico, watched constantly by the Gestapo. Several weeks before, Germans had been warned not to associate with, not even to speak to, any of the group of German exiles who had formed the anti-Nazi League for German Culture, and who were at that time arranging a series of lectures on National Socialism, discussing Nazi racialism, sociology, politics. Among the speakers in the series were Luis I. Rodriguez, president of the official Party of the Mexican Revolution; Alejandro Carrillo, director of the Workers' University of Mexico; Dr. Felix Gordon Ordaz, Spanish ambassador in Mexico; General Heriberto Jara, one of the Mexican army big shots; Dr. Matilde Rodriguez Cabo, wife of Minister of Communications Francisco Mugica; Supreme Court Justice Xavier Icaza, and Vicente Lombardo Toledano, head of the Confederation of Mexican Workers. What the speakers had to say about Hitler was not pleasing to Hitler's men in Mexico. Many anti-Nazi Germans were terrorized into staying away from the lectures.

They were taking no chances, for strange stories were going around about Germans who had been quietly liquidated by the Gestapo, about Austrian refugees warned to keep their mouths shut regarding Nazi atrocities in Vienna, about peculiar Nazi influences among minor officials in the immigration department. These officials could harass foreigners with passport technicalities, could delay and obstruct petitions of anti-Nazi refugees, and could—and did—expedite applications from Nazis who might desire to enter Mexico for one reason or another. The anti-Nazi Germans had heard, too, of a certain German army officer, ranked as lieutenant in the Mexican army, who lives sumptuously in a big mansion, on official wages of four pesos (eighty U. S. cents) a day, and who is one of the top-notch instructors in the National Military Academy, a job which is part of his chores in the line of Nazi military duty.

With the heightening of the oil dispute there suddenly appeared a violently anti-British pamphlet, published in 1917, and stored away these many years in a German bookstore that took over the stocks of the "German Information Service in Mexico," the anti-Allied, anti-American propaganda center during the War. The pamphlet is entitled *The Vampire of the Continent,* meaning Great Britain, and the author is Count Ernest Zu Reventlow. The pamphlet advertises other booklets, including *Wilson Unmasked* and *Uncle Sam Bared.* Reventlow is a veteran Hitler man and a persistent campaigner against the Monroe Doctrine. He is publisher of the weekly *Reichswart* in Germany.

These long-distance denudings are augmented by a steady stream of "news" releases from the official Nazi news agency Transocean; by teaching of Hitler worship in the German school; by German music and drama groups, forced to turn their talents to Nazi adorations; and, strongest and most insistent, by the short-wave radio programs which come directly from Berlin in Spanish, broadcasts financed in part by the tribute collected from the German colony in the name of the Winter Relief Fund. At one of the "cultural" programs in September, 1938, the principal speaker was Gerardo Murillo, a Mexican instructor, painter and champion of Nazism—a bizarre character who calls himself Dr. Atl (*atl* is the Aztec word for water), who for years has been preaching fascism to his many acquaintances in Mexican political circles. He told the group of specially invited guests—Mexican intellectuals, students, ex-army officers with political ambitions—what fine fellows the fascists really are, what great things race-consciousness could do, and that the time has come for militant Nazism in Mexico to stem the Red tide that is about to engulf the country.

The most direct form of building up Mexican sympathy for the Nazi program is undoubtedly the financing of Mexican writers and organizers of fascist groups, with a heavy play on anti-Semitism. In these activities, co-operation is forthcoming from Spanish, French, and other foreign commercial and industrial interests. A strong anti-United States vein runs through even the least virulent of the pro-Hitler articles in Mexico. Typical is the editorial in *Ultimas Noticias,* evening edition of *Excelsior,* on January 11, 1938, commenting on a speech by United States Senator Reynolds:

> "The senator's gall is intolerable. Because the Germans make an effort (quite a change from the saccharine Hollywood products in which all ends well, virtue à la American is rewarded, evil punished and fans go home pleased) to have the Latin-American public understand that the cinema, in UFA pictures, can be Art, it would be difficult to brand this a German conspiracy in America. . . .
>
> "Does the Nazi conspiracy perhaps consist in that the German automobiles now reach us in greater volume and show us that they give fourteen to twenty kilometers per liter of gasoline, that their price is low, and that they are not interested in seducing the buyer each year with new models that leave him broke, and that therefore we have stopped buying American automobiles?
>
> "Or is it part of that terrible propaganda that the possibility of establishing airlines with German planes would menace the monopoly of Pan-American Airways in our countries?
>
> "Of course European competition 'will affect the

United States.' And it will affect that country where its heart is—in the pocketbook, an unfillable heart-pocketbook, which swells with love for the Latin-American peoples in proportion with the privileges granted it by the people of Latin America. . . . But, in spite of the demagogic speeches of the Reynoldses, the people of Latin America know, and will not easily forget, that the Colossus of the North has a colossal stomach through which, like the ventriloquists, it speaks in accordance with its convenience."

The cheap automobile to which the editorial refers is the Fiat-size little Opel, made in General Motors' German plant. It undersells the lowest-priced automobile hitherto on the Mexican market in any quantity—the Ford—with which it does not compare in size, however. But it is much more economical to operate, its tires and other parts are cheaper to replace. During the last two years the Opels have swarmed into Mexico City traffic like an invasion of tourists from Lilliput, each auto not a messenger of "good will" from the United States—for the GM label does not appear—but a purring press agent for Nazism.

9

In 1938, the fourth Spanish edition of *The International Jew* appeared in Mexico—Spanish version by Bruno Wenzel.* Although neither this book nor the *Protocols of Zion* have a popular sale, according to the bookdealers, both have been used as standard textbooks by all the fascist and

---

* *The International Jew* is a collection of articles originally published in the Ford-owned *Dearborn Independent*. Franc Caser in a pamphlet entitled *The Jewish Menace* says this opus should be a "universal handbook."

In answer to criticism leveled against him for accepting a medal from the Hitler government, Henry Ford said on December 1, 1938, in an authorized interview:

"It is my opinion that the German people as a whole are not in sympathy with their rulers in their anti-Jewish policies, which is the work of a few warmakers at the top.

pro-Nazi mouthpieces of Mexico. Newspaper and magazine articles repeatedly make references to the two books, one writer with an argument as frank as this: "Even if we admit that the *Protocols* are faked, still they do give a picture of what is actually happening and thus reveal the Jewish plot to capture the world."

The International Jew, and the *Protocols,* however, are only part of a vast torrent of anti-Semitic writing that has been flooding Latin America, especially Mexico. The scope of the propaganda seems far out of proportion to the "Jewish problem" in a country where there are some fifteen thousand Jews in a total population of more than eighteen million Indians, mixed-bloods and Europeans. But the roots go deeper. The Semitic enemy is identified, by the pro-Nazi writers, with the Mason, the Protestant, the Liberal. And all of these, then, in one form or another, in pamphlets, leaflets, manifestoes, editorials, become identified with the United States, with American business, with American government: Roosevelt is a Jew, and so was Woodrow Wilson, Josephus Daniels is a Jew, Dwight Morrow was a Jew. And we have another Mexican paradox: articles originally appearing in a publication owned by that famous American, that great collector of Americana, Henry Ford, serving as a text for a campaign against the United States.

"My acceptance of a medal from the German people does not, as some people seem to think, involve any sympathy on my part with Nazism. Those who have known me for years realize that anything that breeds hate is repulsive to me."

The awarding of medals to Ford and to other American celebrities was carefully timed by the Hitler propagandists to precede the Lima conference. The most sensational of radio priest Coughlin's broadcasts in December 1938, also was delivered during the period just prior to the Lima meeting. In the *Nation* of December 17, 1938, The Reverend William C. Kernan traced some of the material of the Coughlin speeches to the Nazi sheet, *World Service.* If he had gone still further, he would have found that the material in the Nazi sheet and that in the Coughlin speech could both be traced to *The International Jew.*

The *Protocols* is an anonymous document long ago exposed as a fake. But it continues to flourish in Nazi-paid editions, and was reprinted by Coughlin in his house organ, *Social Justice.*

With continued agitation and increasing attacks, the Jewish question gave politicos, big and little, opportunities to develop a juicy racket. A campaign was begun to put over tighter restrictions on immigration, especially Jewish. One bill proposed to prohibit Jews from all commercial activities, to deny them civil rights and the privilege of naturalization. As a result of the new threat, professional "fixers," working hand-in-glove with certain officials, were able to raise the ante on passports for Jews. It was common talk during the summer of 1938 that a flat rate of a thousand dollars a head was being charged for any Jew who wanted to immigrate, and that one official had handled some five hundred cases, thus garnering a cool half million, thanks to the anti-Semitic propaganda.

In the welter of anti-Jewish agitation, an occasional moderating voice was heard, such as that of Antonio Luna Arroyo, well-known Mexican sociologist. Answering an obviously paid campaign, Luna Arroyo advised that the best way to solve the Jewish problem is not to create it. Let them alone, he urged, and don't treat them differently from other foreigners who obey the laws of the country; and if they disobey laws, punish them accordingly. "Whatever their faults," he added, "one thing is certain—they are hard workers, they produce, they live here, they do not carry away their profits, but re-invest them, build homes, and hence are useful to Mexico." Scrutinize carefully the petitions of new ones who wish to come in, he said, but the important thing is to give those who are here the same legal protection that other residents have. Most of the Jews quickly become naturalized. As their condition improves, he concluded, they themselves will be the ones who will least desire the arrival of further competition.

To link the Nazi racial doctrine with Mexican fascism, complex theories are evolved, designed to prove that the Germans and the Mexicans have certain racial affinities. Thus we find Dr. Krum Heller, the Gold Shirt representative in Berlin—in 1938 he was directing special Nazi broadcasts to Mexico—writing from Germany on May 28, 1935, to Nicolas Rodriguez, when the latter was "Supreme Chief" of the be-shirted racket:

> "Pursuing the investigations made by Wirth, I come to the conclusion that the Mexicans and Germans are the same race, Nordics all, not only because the Spaniards were Goths, but because the Toltecs were immigrants from the North, the same as the primitive Germans, and although the first Aztec Indians were blue-eyed and with blonde hair, as was the case with the Goths, the immigration of the Moors to Spain and the mixture with them brought about a dark skin. Serious studies by ethnologists of first rank prove the racial equality of the Mexicans and Nordics and this can be shown today even by blood tests."

Exposing the actual workings of the Nazi racial doctrine, the German Pro-Culture League created a sensation with its publication of copies of a Nazi Party official letter, ordering a German thrown out of the Party for marrying "a person of a second-class race, a Mexican." The League added that the man, employed by a Nazi firm, was fired from his job as a result.

The United States representative of the Gold Shirts—the fascist organization which was outlawed by the Mexican government has reorganized under other names—was a German, Walter Steinmann, whose New York offices were decorated with photographs of Hitler and with swastikas. The Gold Shirt organization, disbanded after a bloody clash with communist, popular front, and trade-union paraders in front of the National Palace on November 20, 1935, marked the peak of the first attempt to develop imitative, be-shirted, militarized fascism, with underworld elements hired at so much a head to start things off. The Gold Shirts, encouraged under the period of Calles domination, in order to combat militant trade unionism, had become a strikebreaking organization. Their principal activities, however, consisted of a shakedown racket, collecting under threat of strikes, prosecution, violence or boycott. These talents were directed against small foreign merchants, never against the big business interests. Violent manifestoes against Jews made the process work better, and a certain measure of support—based on the jingoist interpretation of the slogan "Mexico for the Mexicans"—was being obtained from Mexican merchants. But the main support of the fascist Gold Shirts, as well as of the Gold Shirt predecessors (Pro-Race Committee, Green Shirts) and the Gold Shirt successors (Nationalist Committee, National Union of Veterans of the Revolution, Nationalist Association, Mexican Nationalist Vanguard) came from the Nazi business houses, under pressure from the Nazi legation, or voluntarily in some cases; and from French, Spanish, Japanese and Mexican industrialists and big landowners, eager to quell the new competition, and to make use of armed mercenaries against striking workmen.

The Gold Shirts made the mistake of lining up on Calles' side in the dictator's split with Cardenas, then continued to play for aid, and got a certain amount, from the Calles oldguard elements which still remained in the government. They made a bid for Cedillo's support when that general was named Minister of Agriculture to succeed Tomas Garrido Canabal and his Red Shirts. Cedillo himself steered clear of any open association with the Gold Shirts, but they did get aid from subordinate officials in the agricultural ministry, including Ernest von Merck, ex-artillery officer in the Kaiser's army, who was Cedillo's military adviser, and who later fled to Texas.

Thoroughly discredited in Mexico, Nicolas Rodriguez, the "Supreme Chief" whose career ranged from California real estate promotions in which Mexicans lost their life savings, to filibustering expeditions which cost him a year in a U. S. federal prison, settled near the Texas border. He lived near the exiled Cedillo family, which had gone to Mission, Texas, while General Saturnino took to the Mexican hills. In February, 1938, the Gold Shirts, directed from Texas, invaded some ejidos (community farm tracts) near Matamoros, opposite Brownsville, Texas, and tried to capture some border cities, but were driven off by armed peasants and federal troops. Rodriguez and some American backers in South Texas continued their activities, trying to keep alive agitation in connection with the Cedillo revolt. They hoped to grab a ride on the gravy train of a Rightist uprising if it ever got up enough steam.

Cardenas' showdown with Cedillo, for many years kingfish of the rich State of San Luis Potosi, brought into the open the newer forms of Mexican fascism, subtler than the spectacular army of mercenary hoodlums "for saving the country from the invasion of Judaism and communism." The organizations revealed in the Cedillo affair also maintained that one of their aims was to "combat communism." Investigators found threads of this new fascist pattern leading to the confederations of chambers of commerce, employers' syndicates, middle-class confederations, into the National University and into the offices of public officials, congressmen, and former officials. They also found links with the Spanish fascist organizations, formed to aid the Franco cause, and to promote a similar movement in Mexico.

All these things, added to the close relations between the Cardenas and the Negrin governments, and the clever identification of the fate of both by anti-Cardenas writers, turned the Cedillo affair from a flash-in-the-pan family feud into a headline political crisis, from which Cardenas emerged stronger than ever. The slogan "Mexico for the Mexicans" has become a rallying cry among the Cardenistas as well as the anti-Cardenistas. Its interpretation has varied from Boxerism to regulated, but not exclusive, national economy. The widening cleavage of opposing economic, social and political interests led directly to another Mexican question mark: Mexico for which Mexicans?

IV

A MESS OF KINGFISH

1

THE news flashed to the world on May 20, 1938: Saturnino Cedillo rides again! One of the pillars of agrarianism turns against the Cardenas agrarian program! The last time Cedillo rode was in 1929, as a federal, one of three generals—each commanding a division—in the campaign, led by Minister of War Plutarco Elias Calles, to quell the Escobar rebellion. Another of the divisionary generals was Juan Andreu Almazan, for the last eight years zone commander in the important industrial State of Nuevo Leon. The third general was Lazaro Cardenas. Cedillo, former peon on an ixtle-fiber hacienda, had by that time become well intrenched as boss—kingfish—of the rich State of San Luis Potosi, rich in agriculture, rich in mining, important national railway center.

The kingfish system has been the political leprosy devouring Mexican national reform. Its roots go back to Mexico's authoritarian past: to the chief of the tribe, to the *comendador* system of paternalistic overlords among whom the King of Spain divided the conquered territory of the new world, and to the monopoly on souls held so long by the Catholic Church. It is a political reflection of the semi-feudal hacienda form of agriculture. The hacienda established economic absolutism; the land lord became the unquestioned ruler of the vast domain within his fences. His power extended beyond his fences, in a "sphere of influence" that ended where the sphere of the next hacienda began. In that radius, towns, villages and isolated clusters of huts were included. Their inhabitants were as much under control of the land lord as the peasants who worked the hacienda proper.

Under the kingfish system, the head man's word was law. Like the gods, he controlled the fate of human beings. They might plead with him, they might beg for his mercy, but none dared to question his right to pass judgment. There were big kingfish and little kingfish, and this system of ruling—developed to a fine point under Porfirio Diaz and his "cientificos"—was the antithesis of popular government, even when it took republican forms. Diaz was top kingfish. He appointed congressmen and senators and governors. Some of the legislators had never seen the districts they were supposed to represent. They, in turn, appointed the smaller kingfish, in the towns and the villages.

This bossdom, known in Mexico as the *cacique* (chieftain) system, has persisted right on through the twenty-eight years of the Mexican Revolution. It has been the most effective dike for holding Mexican social evolution within the old bounds. Against the *cacique* system, discharge after discharge of reform legislation spattered ineffectively, like birdshot against a stone wall. Labor laws, agrarian laws, had to have the blessing of the local kingfish before they could be put into effect. That was part of the price the big kingfish paid for support of the little kingfish. Enforcement of this law or that depended on the convenience of the local boss. And that convenience, as a rule, was on the auction block. Federal engineers who came to parcel lands were driven out or killed by gunmen of hacienda owners, in cahoots with the kingfish, sometimes with the aid of the kingfish's own police force. Labor laws were forgotten, unions wiped out. Probably the closest parallel in this country would be found in some of the "company towns," or cities dominated by corrupt political rings.

In trying to root out the old kingfish system, in which the local boss, more often than not, was in the service of the old order, the men of the Mexican Revolution found themselves substituting a new set of kingfish for the old. The new school sought a formula that would restore confidence of the masses for the reconstruction period after years of revolution and counter-revolution. The search blossomed finally into the National Revolutionary Party, by which Plutarco Elias Calles, schoolteacher, soldier, statesman, became the kingfish of them all. As war minister, finance minister, minister of industry, of communications, as president, and finally as Highest Chief of the Revolution, Calles put his stamp on a whole epoch. He brought into being about him a host of lesser kingfish who sought to perpetuate him in power so that they, satellites shining only by reflected light, could also perpetuate themselves.

Cedillo had risen to bossdom, via the military and civil governorships, after having cast his lot with Obregon and Calles against de la Huerta when the latter rebelled in 1923. Cedillo, with a following of armed peasants, was more important than Calles to Obregon at that time.

During that epoch the spark of antagonism between Calles and Cedillo was ignited. When the National Revolutionary Party nomination was made in 1933, Cedillo was more influential than any other one man in having the choice fall on Cardenas, much against Calles' wishes. Cardenas also had the backing of many other generals. The kingfish of San Luis Potosi supported the man who was later to destroy his feudal estate, not because he loved Cardenas more, but because he loved Calles much less. And the semiliterate, heavy-drinking, carousing provincial mogul hoped, through Cardenas, to move himself and his henchmen into the National Palace. Impatience—his own, and that of his political ringers who were no longer content with the pickings of just one state and were fearful of agrarian reforms heading toward

San Luis Potosi—swamped him. They got ready to move in
before the end of the presidential term. But Cardenas, no
slouch in military affairs, and learned in the ways of his
fellow generals, beat him to the draw.

So on a morning in May, Saturnino Cedillo, rebel, rode
back into the hills whence he and his brothers, Cleofas and
Magdaleno, had come twenty-six years ago, to capture the
town of Ciudad del Maiz, and to lay the foundations for turning the more than fifteen million acres and the more than
five hundred thousand inhabitants into a duchy for the special benefit of the Cedillo family and their friends. Instead
of toward Mexico City, then, Cedillo headed his wiry little
Mexican horse toward a cave in the Sierra del Meco. With
him went an entourage of some forty men and women, whom
he sent back, with exception of a half dozen trusted henchmen ready to die with him if necessary. They all rode Mexican ponies, those short, thin descendants of swift Arabian
steeds brought to the new world by the Spaniards. These
horses looked weak but they could ride on endlessly up and
down through devious mountain paths that men seek out
after holding up a town or blowing up a train.

With Cedillo on that dreary trek into the sierras rode memories of a young peon who in his day had become the Pancho
Villa of San Luis Potosi. For a while he had roamed alongside that more famous chieftain, champion of the frontier
farm folk: with Villa, scourge of the big shots whose days
were ending with the sinking sun of Porfirio Diaz; Villa,
terror of the American border towns, will-o'-the-wisp of the
Pershing punitive expedition. Villa rode into the presidential palace for a brief day of glory, till the Constitutionalists
sent Obregon to tame the recalcitrant leader. But Cedillo
bided his time, like a man of the fields who knows that he
must pass through the risings and settings of many suns before the seeds he put in the ground are ready for harvest.

2

The tragedy of Cedillo is a familiar one in Mexico: men with the stuff of leadership, but in the raw; unprepared, except in the hard school of empiricism, acquiring most of their knowledge through mistakes. Cedillo was sucked into the vortex of the Mexican Revolution as one of numerous focal points around which the resentment of a nation clustered for action. His inarticulate insurgency found the answer in Emiliano Zapata's clearly-expressed agrarianism. Cedillo fought on the side of Madero and against him, fought under the banners of Victoriano Huerta and his counter-revolutionary dictatorship, with Villa, and as a guerrilla.

Then the magnet of Zapata's "Land and Liberty" cry, striking deep into the heavy hearts of a peasantry bewildered by false leaders, drew him to the "Plan of Ayala" which, in its 1913 reformed version, denounced Pascual Orozco and Huerta as traitors. Emiliano Zapata, apostle of peasant liberation, was to be slain in ambush, but the wings of Zapatismo would carry uninspired, clod-hopping Saturnino Cedillo to the inner councils of national government, to the very edge of the presidential chair.

A new generation had grown up around the "old revolutionaries," however, a generation intolerant of efforts to hold the Mexican Revolution to the crude political formulas of 1910. This was a disillusioned generation that had seen promised reforms forgotten in a new orgy of corruption from which the people got little but the new bosses got much. Against this rising tide of demands for something more tangible than phrases, Cedillo fenced in the spoils to which he and other generals felt they were entitled. The methods of dictators everywhere were put into force to show the upstarts that Cedillo was number one man around those parts, that what he said was law. And for a dozen years or more, it was.

Cedillo's word was law to such an extent that the laws of the nation, being put into effect with varying efficacy in other states, were dead letters in his. It came to be said that "the Mexican Revolution stopped at the boundaries of San Luis Potosi." Cedillo ruthlessly built his political machine. He named all political officials, from aldermen to congressmen, placed his gunmen in strategic posts. He had a monopoly of the ixtle-fiber industry, farmed soldiers out for work on haciendas, established a system of forced labor on others. The Cedillo administration got a monthly "subsidy" from an American mining company, and the local labor board favored this company in labor disputes. He suspended parceling of land, except to take tracts from political enemies, to be added to the domain of Las Palomas hacienda, Cedillo's huge estate. A sister, Higinia Cedillo, had a monopoly of the public abattoir. Profitable deals followed one after the other, such as the sale of an irrigation system, which cost the state seven hundred thousand pesos, to a land company for two hundred thousand pesos.

The Escobar revolution of 1929 helped Cedillo increase his power and turn his attention to the possibilities of playing a bigger part in national politics. As a divisionary general his sway went beyond the limits of his state. The rebellion gave him a chance to further his ambitions in the manner he liked best: direct, quick, violent action. No big sweep of the imagination, but a thrust, a guerrilla jab toward higher posts, a blow here and then a blow there, like dynamiting a train, grabbing what could be grabbed, and heading for the hills.

3

Cedillo's stolid Indian face came smack into the national political picture in 1935 with his appointment as Minister of Agriculture. Cardenas had named him to succeed Tomas

Garrido Canabal, kingfish of Tabasco, who not only had sided with Calles in the Cardenas-Calles tiff, but who had created a serious problem for the Cardenas regime by the invasion of Mexico City with his Red Shirts, a semi-fascist priest-baiting organization that served him well in Tabasco. The armed Red Shirts clashed with Catholics leaving a church in Tacubaya, Mexico City suburb, one Sunday morning in the summer of 1935, killed five of the churchgoers. After that, Garrido Canabal's departure was a settled matter. Soon afterward, Garrido Canabal was back in Tabasco, and a little later left with his family and belongings for Costa Rica, on an "agricultural mission" for the Cardenas government.

Garrido went, leaving a bad taste of anti-Church agitation behind him, rousing Catholics to the highest pitch since the bitter Church-State fight in 1926. Cardenas needed somebody in the cabinet to counteract the impression that his term was to become a period of militant anti-clericalism. He couldn't have found a better choice at that political moment than Saturnino Cedillo. The kingfish of San Luis Potosi had been preparing his accession to the national scene. He had been playing ball with the industrial interests who did not feel any too sure about what Cardenas might do in labor matters. He had come out flat-footedly against the amendment of Article Three of the federal constitution. This amendment provided "socialist" education in all primary schools. He also let the National University students and instructors know that he favored "liberty of curricula." This was the slogan of the group opposed to "socialization" of the schools, especially the university, a government-subsidized but autonomously-operated institution.

Furthermore, Cedillo had sent word out quietly that in San Luis Potosi the Church would not be restricted, that all priests and nuns who had to leave other states were finding a haven in San Luis Potosi, and that convents and seminaries, prohibited by federal law, continued as of yore. His sister Elena was known as an organizer of Church societies, and among the General's advisers were two men actively engaged in re-organizing the Society of Jesus (Jesuits), theoretically abolished these many years in Mexico. To top it all, Cedillo was known as a bitter anti-Calles man. Cardenas had been carrying the onerous load of a cabinet hand-picked by Calles, with one or two exceptions. The cabinet included Rodolfo Elias Calles, eldest son and heir apparent of the old dictator, as well as rich Aaron Saenz, political and business partner of Calles *père* and rejected suitor for the presidency.

The appointment of Cedillo was one of Cardenas' smartest political actions, brilliant even in a surprising array of smart acts for a man who was supposed to be a dunderhead, a boob, a dumb yokel. The naming of Cedillo not only showed the people that Cardenas expected to move out of Calles' orbit, but also gave the impression that his administration was turning to the right and toward a policy of conciliation with the churchmen. Nor was it so dumb to foresee that Cedillo's ambitions and tie-ups would become more transparent, that a possible rival for national support would be weakened, although apparently strengthened; that with Cedillo in the cabinet opposing factions would soon be at each other's throats, and that Cardenas would thus wield the balance of power, would become what he wanted to be in fact as well as in name: the chief executive.

4

There are some people in Mexico who will buttonhole a newspaperman silly enough to bring up politics, and begin explaining that leftist Francisco Mugica, frequently mentioned as Cardenas' possible successor, is already president in fact. They will state that Mugica, reputedly Cardenas' mentor and closest adviser, runs things; that the whole set-up is just a Trilby act, with Cardenas in a state of ambulant levitation actually expressing Mugica's will, and that Mugica is acting for Stalin, and that Stalin is the Voice of Wall Street, and that Wall Street operates according to Protocols of Zion, so that the Six-Year Plan is really just another Jewish plot. You'd swear it was all a gag, but the fellow in front of you is dead serious, and you reach for a drink, or smelling salts, and long to relax with something simple, like a Moscow wreckers' plot. Then another fellow will buttonhole you and whisper that not Stalin, but Trotsky, is the man who runs the government, via a triple-play: Trotsky to Mugica to Cardenas. And a third will solemnly insist that Trotsky is really an instrument of Stalin.

It is true, however, that Mugica and Calles disliked each other. Calles exiled Mugica politically by making him head of the penal colony on the Tres Marias islands, off the Pacific coast of Mexico. Communists and other anti-Calles militants were rounded up and shipped off to the penal islands every now and then during the Portes Gil, Ortiz Rubio and Abelardo Rodriguez terms. That was the period between 1929 and 1934 when trade-union action was repressed and the Communist Party was driven underground after several years of legality. Former Tres Marias exiles recall that Mugica made things a little easier for political prisoners. It is true, also, that the cabinet feud developed as expected, a feud that eventually polarized the factions around Minister of Agriculture Cedillo on the right, and Minister of Communications Mugica on the left.

5

Cedillo's arrival in Mexico City in 1935 to take his cabinet post was the signal for a concentration of rightist forces. The

Gold Shirts lined up in military formation at the railway station to greet him. From that day the anti-Calles—and at that time anti-Cardenas—groups outside of the National Revolutionary Party began to weave the legend of the new "strong man," the new knight in shining armor who would redeem the nation from its redeemers. Before long it became noised about that the "real president" was now Saturnino Cedillo. The Ministry of Agriculture became a political club again. Now, however, instead of Red Shirts from Tabasco, the desk-chairs were being filled with bureaucrats transplanted from provincial sinecures to more fruitful and greener pastures for political grazing. The Cedillo influence had begun to spread like a galloping rash.

Cedillo had brought with him to the Agricultural Ministry, Ernest von Merck, an artillery officer in the Kaiser's armies during the World War, for years the San Luis kingfish's personal adviser, and Inspector General of Police in the city of San Luis Potosi, capital of the State. Through von Merck, among others, the influences of German and Italian fascism trickled into the private councils of the Cedillistas. The Gold Shirts were now getting more aid from officials, either in cash or jobs for their members. Some of them still have government jobs today, and continue to prepare for *der Tag*. The Gold Shirts took larger quarters just across the plaza from the National Palace. More than once Nicolas Rodriguez, Supreme Chief Gold Shirt, would lean his paunch against the balcony, work up a Hitlerian messianic mood and wistfully comment to a visitor:

"Someday, soon, we shall be looking out from the balconies on the opposite side of the plaza."

Rodriguez had already added to his laurels the raiding and burning of the new Communist Party headquarters. This occurred soon after Cardenas had legalized the Mexican section of the Third International, as well as the Fourth, and the

Fascist, and all other Internationals, granting them all, along with the Vatican International, freedom of the press which had been denied under Calles.

Cedillo's influence continued to grow, and with it the budding fascist forces that had picked him as a front. The Gold Shirt clash, on November 20, 1935, with the Mexican popular front, communist, and trade-union paraders, led eventually to the nominal disbanding of the fascist outfit in April, 1936, and its transformation into various other "nationalist" organizations. The campaign to "smear" Cardenas as a communist was intensified. A dozen or more groups such as the "Confederation of Middle Class," the various "nationalist" unions, associations, parties, vanguards, legions, began to move closer to the powerful Employers' Center, inner ring of the Confederation of Chambers of Commerce. Gustavo Saenz de Sicilia, of the Middle Class Confederation, who collected subsidies from a group of German business houses, distributed pamphlets praising Hitler, as well as anti-communist and anti-democratic literature. He made a bid for direct Nazi support in a series of communications to the German minister, congratulating him for having a man like Hitler as a fuehrer and for the creation of the Rome-Berlin-Tokyo axis.

And in the meantime, on Cedillo's Las Palomas ranch, preparations were getting under way for military action. Airplanes were bought, new types of bombs were being tried, arms and ammunitions smuggled in, secret radio stations built. Foreigners arrived on mysterious missions. Cardenas agents, watching all these moves closely, increased vigilance when Lombardo Toledano, head of the Confederation of Mexican Workers, exposed what he said was a plot to overthrow the government. He gave names and addresses, and police picked up a pile of dynamite bombs, arrested a lot of alleged conspirators. Cardenas ordered them all released, and continued his policy of watchfully giving everybody all the rope they wanted. Cedillo's supporters insisted that the revolt scare was all a myth, that what the Cardenistas really feared was the rise of Cedillo as the leading presidential candidate. He was already being groomed on a platform "which does not promise more than can be fulfilled."

Cardenas broke up the Cedillo party before it was in full swing. The hitch came in failure to float a $1,500,000 loan which Cedillo agents had tried to put over in New York. Cardenas' organization had grown faster than Cedillo's. The President had been engaged in a sweeping program of land parceling throughout the country, solidifying the peasant support he felt the regime needed. The first rip came over an appointment at the Chapingo agricultural school. Students and faculty protested against the Cedillo appointee, charging that he was not technically equipped for the post and besides was a reactionary. The students struck. Cedillo asked for Cardenas' intervention. Cardenas sided with the students. On August 16, 1937, Cedillo sent in his resignation, apparently intended as a bluff, for the kingfish's yes-men had been telling him that without his support Cardenas would fall tomorrow.

But Cardenas accepted the resignation so fast it made Cedillo's head swim. The kingfish went back to Las Palomas, and with him a host of brooding henchmen. The War Department then ordered Cedillo to Michoacan State as military commander. Cardenas was bringing all the threads together. He wanted to give Cedillo a way out. The kingfish, after all, had been his strongest backer, and besides he was an old friend and an "old revolutionary." But Cedillo's wisenheimers told him to refuse, that it was a scheme to liquidate him. Cedillo pleaded illness, and was permitted to remain in San Luis Potosi. Then he asked for appointment of a certain general into his jurisdiction. Blunder after blunder.

Backers he had counted on failed him. He denied the charge
that he had sought a loan from the oil companies. However,
an agent of his made a rush trip to New York about the time
of the expropriation.

When the State legislature of San Luis Potosi announced
on May 15, 1938, that it had withdrawn recognition of the
federal government, Cardenas decided on quick action. Federal troops were already in the field, when Cedillo got the
bad news: Cardenas himself was coming to San Luis Potosi.
Cedillo charged that he had not revolted, that the federal
government had rebelled against him, trying to destroy the
legitimate powers of the State. Several bridges were blown
up, a train was wrecked, and the tourist season was shot to
hell. The incident was soon over, Cedillo was in the hills, and
his family across the border. His exiled henchmen and others
close to him continued to have hopes that he would ride into
Mexico City on a white horse. Cardenas said: "Cedillo is a
sick man."

Cardenas ordered land parceling in San Luis Potosi on a
large scale. The new provisional government broke precedents of many years by ordering some public works. The
people of San Luis Potosi, twenty-eight years after the Revolution, would soon have drinking water coming out of real
faucets, and sidewalks would be built, the Administration
promised.

From his hideout in the hills, Cedillo issued a statement,
explaining his rebellion via the magazine *Hoy,* whose photographer had marvelously located him when the army
couldn't.

The July 23 issue of the magazine quoted Cedillo as follows:

"First—I have no connection with the oil companies.
"Second—I enthusiastically defend the sovereignty of
my state and the government of San Luis which with-

drew recognition from Cardenas because of unconstitutionality and for trampling on the Constitution and trying to implant a regime similar to that of the Soviet.

"Third—There is a decree dated May 16, promulgated by the legitimate government of my state, in which it reasserts its sovereignty and appoints me commander in chief of the Constitutionalist Army, an army which will undertake to establish order and a constitutional regime.

"Fourth—Cardenas betrayed agrarianism, making it fail by trying to implant collectivism, whereas our peasant is not prepared. I defend the system of land parcels for the peasant on the basis of private property."

Which was clear enough, despite a few misspelled words. A system of private property parcels was definitely out of harmony with the system of ejidos (community lands) that the Cardenas program stresses. Cardenas had modified his program to provide adequate protection for privately owned small tracts of land, but he did not essentially alter the ejido plan. Advocates of the latter see in it all the benefits of individual small-tract farming without any of the drawbacks or dangers—such as resales of the tract to the newly-arrived land-grabbers. But there is a lot of argument on this point, and General Gildardo Magaña, governor of Michoacan State, and one of Cedillo's old friends—incidentally a close friend of Zapata also—was preparing in 1938 to run for the presidency on an agrarian platform which would stress the small farm property as basis of the agricultural system. Magaña knew of Cedillo's plans to revolt, and was said to have advised him against it.

On August 16, 1938, three months after the San Luis Potosi rebellion, a court edict appeared in the official gazette, notifying one Saturnino Cedillo that this notice was being published in the official gazette because the citizen's whereabouts were unknown; that unless he paid 37.50 pesos into the public treasury, his property would be embargoed to cover the fine and court costs. The charge against him: speeding on a federal highway.*

6

Prior to the Cedillo showdown, Cardenas had already faced the problem of returning another provincial potentate's domain to federal jurisdiction. Just as later he tried to ease Cedillo, kingfish of the mountains, out of a flat showdown, so, earlier, Cardenas gave Tomas Garrido Canabal, kingfish of the jungles, a way out of the tight spot in which he had got himself and the Cardenas regime in the summer of 1935. The President offered Garrido "an agricultural mission" in Costa Rica. If he had refused, some fireworks might have resulted. But Garrido was smart, took his person, his family, his personal belongings, out of the country in three airplanes. He left his political machine behind. Not a few of the politicos, in a position to know, were willing to bet even money that the Tabasco kingfish would be back in home waters for the 1940 presidential campaign.

Many enemies of Cedillo quickly labeled him a fascist. It is undoubtedly true that his arbitrary methods of government, his authoritarianism, his absoluteness, are the methods of fascism. It is true, also, that among his most militant backers were groups that want to see a system of fascism implanted in Mexico. However, one of Cedillo's big drawbacks as a fuehrer-nominee was precisely that he was not fascist enough. If he had been more of a fascist, if he had learned more thoroughly the demagogic methodology of fascism, if his machine had penetrated the labor movement instead of hostilizing it, he might have been throwing parties in Chapultepec Castle today. No, Saturnino Cedillo was not the man

---

* On January 11, 1939, Cedillo was reported slain in a battle with federal troops near Matehuala, San Luis Potosi.

the big shots wanted. They thought for a while that he might do. However, Mexican capitalists are noted for their extreme conservatism in all matters. That's one reason, for instance, they didn't go in for oil: too much risk. Let the crazy foreigners sink their money in the ground if they wish. The Mexican capitalists have always liked a sure thing, and preferably with a return of fifty per cent or upward on their investment, guaranteed, gilt-edge. The Cardenas mass-base being what it was, Cedillo was too much of a long shot, a dry-track horse running in the mud.

Garrido Canabal is a horse of another color. Red, in fact, which is good, for the Mexican workmen have been brought up on Red slogans. If only Garrido wasn't such a fanatic against Church, he'd be perfect, the big shots figure. They'd like to have somebody with the organizational methods and the demagogy of Garrido Canabal and yet with the covert blessing of the churchmen. Somehow, they don't stop to figure that the drive on the Church was one of Garrido's best tricks, that it found a quick response among workmen seeking a little something here and now, willing to accept a hunk of bread and take their chances on pie in the sky. They might have recalled that many of Lombardo Toledano's speeches to the workers assailed the clergy as arch-enemies of the labor movement, and that only a couple of years back he had issued "an open letter to Jesus Christ" which created a sensation.

Garrido Canabal, utilizing the tradition of socialistic doctrine familiar to the residents of the Yucatan peninsula, purposefully chose red for his uniformed legions' shirts and blouses. He named his daughter Zoyla Libertad (I am Liberty) and his youngest son was dubbed Lenin. Garrido's father was a rich hacendado, Pio Garrido Lacroix, who was an active supporter of the Victoriano Huerta dictatorship (1913-1914). When Carranza triumphed, the Canabal family left for Yucatan. It was there, amid the Socialist Leagues of Resistance inspired by Felipe Carrillo Puerto, that Garrido got the organizing technique which helped him to become governor of Tabasco when Obregon became president of the Republic in 1920.

Garrido was way ahead of the rest of Mexico in forming the fascist type, strikeless, controlled unions. The Calles tactic of diverting worker and peasant resentment from falling on the heads of employers and landowners—both of the old school and the ex-revolutionary–neo-conservative—was well employed by the kingfish of Tabasco. He rose from an obscure country lawyer (with questionable degree) to absolute master of this rich seacoast State that provides bananas, precious timbers, chicle and other tropical products for export, not to mention oil.

Garrido's defenders regard him as the father of the labor movement in Tabasco. There is no doubting the fact that with Garrido's rise to power practically every branch of activity in the State was organized into labor unions. These were not called "syndicates" as in most other places in Mexico, but "Leagues of Resistance," as in Yucatan. Tomas Garrido Canabal was head of the Central League of Resistance, labor branch of the Radical Socialist Party, which included nearly twoscore leagues in the various trades: stevedores, graphic arts, butchers, chauffeurs, fruit sellers, carpenters, marine cooks, land cooks, barbers, practically every field of activity in the State. And the undisputed boss of the party, boss of the trade unions, was Tomas Garrido Canabal. Any attempt to form an independent labor organization, not controlled by Garrido, was an indirect way of committing suicide.

Garrido, his henchmen and his family, grew rich, immensely rich, in the process of "socializing" Tabasco State. As supreme arbiter of all economic and political relations,

Garrido developed a system of tribute from the foreign companies in return for exclusive exploitation rights. Thus, he collected a rake-off for every bunch of bananas that left the State. In order to "develop local industry," he instituted a system of import and export duties on articles entering and leaving the State. A trail of blood was left across Tabasco as brothers, uncles, cousins, in-laws, of the Kingfish moved into public offices, acquiring monopolies of one activity or another.

Although many opponents of Garrido have the smell of the old plantation slave-driver about them, his most violent opposition came ostensibly from the Catholic groups, who unhesitatingly classified him as a "monster, a homicidal maniac, an anti-Christ." His laws on the Church—regulated by the States according to the Mexican federal constitution—were the strictest in the country. He did not forbid religious services, although the State government took over one church building after another. These were converted into schools and libraries. The number of churches was drastically restricted, however. He built up a strong anticlerical organization among the young people. Holy days of meek adoration of an image became gay fiestas climaxed by the burning of the saints' images. Begun in the name of fighting clerical fanaticism, Garrido's radicalism led to a new fanaticism, which found one form of expression in ecstatic poetry and song, fruit of a tropical, passionate, life-loving people, denying the existence of gods which had long abandoned them. For instance:

> How we rejoice! There is no god!
> Only to our party do we render account
> Of how we have lived our lives,
> How we treated our fellow man.
> No prayer opens the day for us.
> We greet the day as a comrade

Who will help us toward liberation.
Soon the workers will pass by the churches.
They will say: There lived the oppressors' gods.
We went in to seek him, too,
But all we found was a dried-out pelt.
And they will go on, singing:
How we rejoice! There is no god!

Garrido's drive against the clergy revived an epigram which had wide currency during Calles' tiff with the Church. He, too, was called a "monster," but one of his daughters was married with Catholic rites, and his children were properly baptized, quietly, at home, by Catholic priests. The wise-crackers said that Calles offered up a daily prayer, and it was a simple one:

"Thank you, God, for making me an atheist."

Garrido's clerical laws made it impossible for a priest to practice his profession legally and still be a Catholic priest. Besides other qualifications, the law provided that only married men could be priests, and they must be over forty years of age. Garrido's reasons for this measure: that there are too many bastards in the world now; that the priests of Tabasco are notoriously concupiscent, had destroyed the sanctity and morality of many humble homes, so if priests want to have children, let them assume the responsibility that other men must, give them a name and a home. No need to describe the holy horror which was raised by Garrido's bio-sociological observations. Especially since he himself was known to have a half-dozen mistresses staked out here and there over the State.

Garrido's defenders are willing to admit that he was no self-sacrificing Lenin, and that in seeking to raise the general standard of living, he raised his own standards, too. They will tell you that the tradition of social reform antedates Garrido, but that it was Garrido who gave it form and made it function, and that his program answered a real need of the people. They point to schools, libraries, public works, sanitation and health measures, instituted by the Garrido Canabal regime. They point to the high wages of the Leagues of Resistance, to the "new spirit of the common people, their fervent adoration of the dictator," their development of self-respect as contrasted to the abject attitude of the Porfirio Diaz days when the Indian knelt and kissed his master's hand to give thanks for the whipping he had just got. They tell how he introduced diversified farming in the State, imported pedigreed cattle and hogs. And, they add, if the people's atheism and their passion for social betterment tend to fanaticism, it is because the priests for years had been leading them into a blind alley of fanaticism.

Above all, however, Garrido's defenders point with pride to his war on alcoholism. From the beginning of his rise in politics, Garrido said that the two worst enemies of the people are the Church and Demon Rum, since the first "keeps the people in meek ignorance" and the second "wastes their energies which could be used for improving their minds and their living conditions." Garrido dried up Tabasco as thoroughly as if he had covered the State with blotting paper. His zeal against booze knew no bounds. The way he went after alcohol would warm the gizzards of our own prohibitionists, would bring a glow of rejoicing to our most rabid bluenoses. And nobody will question the fact that the abolition of alcoholic beverages has done the State a lot of good. The Garrido program provided social entertainment, country fairs, and whatnot as substitutes for the surcease and consolation which the spirit of the people had sought in the incense of altars or through communion with kindred—distilled—spirits. Even after Garrido's departure, the State remained bone-dry, and the one crime for which punishment was absolutely sure was the sale or possession of intoxicating liquors. Homicide, larceny, and almost any other violent self-assertion prohibited by the penal code could have mitigating circumstances, could perhaps be fixed in one way or another. But the man who sold a drink, or the man discovered drunk, or with a bottle of booze, went to jail.

It is really a shame to spoil this picture of a teetotalitarian paradise by calling up the devil of bootlegging. But as one for the book, and so that the prospective tourist may not steer clear of Tabasco as he would an arid waste and thus keep some badly-needed dollars from going to that lusciously beautiful state, it can be whispered that as late as the fall of 1938 there was beer and stronger for folks who just couldn't get along without it; and that the stuff could be sold only in one of the joints owned by one of the Tabasco kingfish's many relatives. Just ask any dockworker who has to spend almost a day's wages—and high wages as such things go in Mexico—for a round or two of suds.

Garrido went to Costa Rica, but his political machine kept on running in Tabasco. Oppositionists charged that they were denied freedom of the press and assembly, in spite of Cardenas' promises, and elections continued to be bloody affairs. The Administration answered that the opposition of the hacendados and "fanatics" is more like rebellion than ballot-box action. Hence, strong medicine; hence, the slaying of three university students who went to Tabasco in 1936 on a "liberating expedition."

Money continues to flow from Tabasco to Mexico City to win electoral favors in the government party, to influence federal intervention in the right direction, to provide the right kind of publicity. Young men who worked closely with Garrido had jobs in the national government departments and in the government party organization. In 1938, the Tabasco influence was still strong in the Mexican capital. Cardenas, during a visit to Tabasco in 1934, was enthusiastic about the reforms he saw there. The President is too much of a realist not to know the seamy side of the picture. He figures, though, that there were graft and corruption before, and without social reform, so the social reforms are looked upon as a measure of progress. Regarded as especially important is the organization of the underdogs who, Cardenas maintains, will clean house when they get strong enough, and meanwhile are learning that they must depend on their own organized strength rather than on patronizing charity or on fuehrer-politicos. One thing that political opponents of Cardenas kept throwing up at him, and that he had a hard time living down in his efforts to conciliate the Red Shirt-hating churchmen, was the fact that in the 1934 elections, which made him president, Cardenas voted for Garrido Canabal.

Reports from Villahermosa in 1938 stated that Garrido was planning to run for president in 1940. They added that the Tabasco kingfish flies to Mexico City monthly from Costa Rica for political conferences, and that some of his men, in government posts, fly to Costa Rica. Some political prophets in Mexico see in the next elections a showdown between leftist collectivism and rightist collectivism, both of which have been gaining ground under Cardenas' policy of giving the class struggle full play. Either side may try to jell the Mexican Revolution into its particular mold. Another Mexican paradox is that Garrido Canabal could conceivably appear as a standard-bearer for one as well as for the other. Actually, both sides would probably reject him, and his bid for power would be independent, and would attract support from both wings, with a platform that would be a melting-pot of isms.

7

The nation began to grow weary of Calles when his earlier
radicalism underwent a strange sea-change in the magic of
the Morrow (1925-1928) influence. The masses cheered the
Calles who, on September 20, 1923, shouted:

"I am frankly a Laborite and an ardent defender of
the rights guaranteed to labor by Article 123 of the
Constitution of 1917. My enemies are in the camp of
reaction, my friends are in labor's camp."

But by April 1, 1932, the masses were holding their collective nose. They had long been smelling a rat. On that
date, the new Calles made himself clear, a quality for which
he was always noted:

"All the sectors of society need attention: the labor
sector, the peasant sector, the industrial, the commercial,
all need attention. The Revolution should guard the
interests of all. The Revolution cannot be discriminatory; before all else it should be concerned with the happiness of the underdogs; but it must also act legally and
with justice toward those above."

Which may sound like common administrative sense, and
might even be considered quite Red because of the emphasis
on the underdog. But in Mexico, accustomed to the hot
sauce of eloquent radicalism, that kind of talk fell flat. The
people have got used to finding that a man who talks very,
very radical may prove to be a moderate reformer. So when
they hear a man talking conservatively, they figure that that's
not the half of it, and what he's really driving at is violent
retrogression, reaction.

Anyhow, the Calles-men had reached the end of their political rope as long as Calles remained boss. He no longer

talked the language of the people. What happened when the anti-Calles forces clashed head-on with the old King of the Kingfish on a labor issue might be described by one of *Variety's* ingenious writers as the laying of a dictatorial egg by Calles. But history will record ironically that one of the most significant contributions of the Calles epoch was that it permitted and encouraged the evolution of men like That Man Cardenas.

V

REDEEMERS' ROW

1

Every morning General Julio telephones God. The apparatus he uses is quite simple. He cups his left hand over one ear and talks into his clenched right fist:

"Good morning, Lord. What would you like to have done on earth today?"

If General Julio, who is not a general and whose name is not Julio, were in a more favorable environment, he might go places. But there is not much future for him in the Mexico City insane asylum.

The General is an interesting case, the doctor in charge explained. Ordinarily harmless, he would be dangerous if he had power over others, if he could control an army or run loose on the radio waves, or even if he just had a gun. The doctor continued:

"He suffers from a panphobic phantasy and lives in a world of his own creation. He is dominated by fear, and a feeling of inferiority, which he attempts to overcome by assigning divine powers to himself. This type of mental derangement occurs frequently during periods of war or acute social unrest. He lived as an apparently peaceful business man. Several years ago he began referring to himself with a military title, although he has never been in the army. His general demeanor changed, and he developed a curt, sharp manner of talking. Soon he was wearing boots, and a short while ago appeared at his place of business in uniform."

General Julio was arrested on a train, enroute to Mexico City with his wife's jewelry and their life savings in a suit-case. These took up only a small part of the space in the bag. The rest of it was packed with leaflets and pamphlets, trans-lations of speeches by Goebbels, manifestoes of the Gold Shirts, newspaper clippings, Gold Shirt "bonds," handbills signed by the General as "Supreme Commander of the Tiger Knights," and some French postcards. He told officials that he had to leave town because political enemies were plotting to poison him. He said he knew he would be locked up; that was the way it always happened—people always crucified their saviors.

2

Most of Mexico's home-town-saviors-who-made-good have not been at all daffy. Or, if they were, there was an awful lot of method in their madness. For many of them managed to acquire a bit more than their share of the good things of life which they insisted—while they were on the make—every-body ought to have. Big automobiles, diamonds, stables of fine horses, cellars of fine wines, haciendas, juicy bank ac-counts in London or New York or Amsterdam, luscious mis-tresses, revolvers with inlaid gold handles—all the joys for-merly reserved for aristocratic epicures—were some of the things which the winds of the Revolution blew toward the lads who rode the right bandwagons. This phenomenon—profiting by riding the winner's bandwagon—is not new to politics, in Mexico, in the United States, or elsewhere. But there was one distinguishing feature in Mexico during the last fifteen years or so, one sure sign that a politico had ar-rived: a palatial mansion, in the city or in the country, or both. A half-dozen or so of these magnificent residences were built in the same section of Mexico City, not far from Chapultepec Forest. The man in the street, with his peculiar talent for nicknames and apt descriptions, soon was referring to this array of splendid architecture as "Redeemers' Row."

In a country where about seventy per cent of the dwellings are adobe, thatch or frame huts, these mansions of Redeemers' Row stuck out like the big diamonds on the puffy hands of Luis Morones when he was the big-shot labor leader of Mexico. Lean-bellied, flat-buttocked men, who came from dirt-floor shacks to march in Morones' demonstrations, did not look approvingly on the luxurious palace that the ex-plumber had acquired, nor on his apartment houses, and his Mancera Hotel. Morones' mansion became one of the most notorious party houses in his day, a gathering place for the new-rich and the old-rich on unforgettable week ends of revelry and abandon, surcease from the workaday class struggle. Here, plump proletarian prophets, gone slightly rancid through contact with the over-ripe plutocracy, rubbed elbows and shins with the well-heeled, the well-padded, the over-stuffed.

3

Villa—Zapata—Carranza—de la Huerta—Obregon—Calles: six men on a horse, anti-Huertismo; anti-Huerta, Victoriano Huerta, the counter-revolutionary dictator who killed Francisco Madero on February 22, 1913.

Huerta was forced out on July 15, 1914, leaving the six men on three horses: Zapata on his own, Villa on his own, and the Sonora trio (Calles, de la Huerta, Obregon) on the third with Carranza.

A federal senator during the Diaz regime, later governor of Coahuila, Venustiano Carranza attained national power as chief of the Constitutionalist Army that rose against the tyranny of Victoriano Huerta. His pronounced nationalistic policy, especially defiant of the United States, rallied many Mexican patriots around Carranza. The Kaiser in 1914 offered him Texas and California for Mexico's support against the Allies. Japan flirted with him, and there was talk of secret treaties against the United States. Carranza squeezed all he could out of the nationalistic fervor that had been raised by the Gringo occupation of Veracruz, by border incidents, and the Pershing punitive expedition. The scattered forces of the Revolution grouped around the First Chief, and in 1917 Carranza became president.

Villa and Zapata were eliminated during his presidency, leaving four men on a horse, Constitutionalism.

Carranza's Minister of War was the former merchant-farmer, Alvaro Obregon, outstanding military strategist of the Mexican Revolution, with a perfect batting average, 1000 per cent—not one defeat on the battlefield. As his Minister of Industry and Commerce, Carranza named Plutarco Elias Calles, ex-schoolteacher, reformer, provincial politico, who had become a general. Adolfo de la Huerta was elected governor of Sonora, rugged, proud State of the Northwest.

The Carranza regime was marked by the establishment of the 1917 Constitution, by widespread corruption and by the rise of the labor movement which was to carry the Redeemers into power. Carranza and the men around him acquired immense haciendas and huge stables of horses. Public posts and concessions were openly bought with haciendas and other gifts to the men in the inner governmental circles. Carranza repressed organized labor, whose Red Battalions had helped raise him to the presidency. And he suffered from that perennial ailment of nearly all politicos in Mexico's history: an itch to perpetuate himself in office.

Carranza's term was due to expire in November, 1920. Alvaro Obregon, military hero, announced his candidacy. Carranza picked a dark horse, Bonillas, whom he had brought from the embassy in Washington. It was a rash act, bringing a total stranger whom the populace called "Mister." Calles, de la Huerta, and others the Sonora clique, supported Obregon. Carranza persecuted Obregon's followers, including the members of the Mexican Laborist Party, and Obregon had to flee, disguised as a railroad worker, to a mountain village in the interior of the country. Simultaneously, Carranza tried to break the Sonora group's power by invading their State. The pretext was nationalization of the Sonora rivers, which would give Carrancistas the water rights taxes. Carranza sent federal troops to Sonora. Calles resigned from the cabinet.

On February 1, 1920, Calles wrote to Governor de la Huerta of Sonora:

> "My position in the cabinet was no longer tenable, both because of the constant persecution against the Obregonistas, and because I was not disposed to become an accomplice of all the errors of the most corrupt administration in the annals of government in Mexico. . . . The small group of men immediately about Carranza are the most corrupt in the country, and they are responsible for keeping the country off the paths of honesty."

To Felipe Carrillo Puerto, Yucatan socialist leader, Calles wrote:

> "I have always had faith in the dispossessed classes and it is comforting to find the working classes taking the side of a good cause. Justice, ideals and the popular will are on our side, and our triumph will be the greatest in all Mexican history . . . we cannot be defeated, our aims are sacred, we shall not be abandoned by the people because we have not deceived them, but have been with the people in the days of their suffering, sharing their misery and their sorrows."

On April 23, 1920, the Plan of Agua Prieta, drawn up by Calles, appeared, withdrawing recognition from the Carranza administration. Five State governors joined the revolt. In Guerrero State, Obregon rose against Carranza. The country was in turmoil again. Carranza, fleeing from Mexico City in May, 1920, was captured and slain. Other Carrancistas got the works. Some pulled out for the United States with bags of gold, others empty-handed.

Adolfo de la Huerta was made provisional president until Obregon could be duly elected. Obregon was sworn in on November 30, 1920. The Sonora clique had taken over. This clique constituted the original crew of Redeemers, and as they consolidated their control—by appeals to labor and to the peasants, by demagogy, intrigue, diplomacy, violence— they drew into their orbit Redeemers, generals and kingfish from other sections of the country.

With Carranza out of the way, three men remained as top rulers—Obregon, Calles, de la Huerta, three men on a horse: anti-Carrancismo.

4

Alvaro Obregon, the most experienced revolutionary, the hardest-living, hardest-fighting man of the lot, was boss of the Redeemers who took power in 1920. Calles and de la Huerta, both in Obregon's cabinet, jockeyed for second place. The oil boom was at its height and Uncle Sam was in the picture, and in a big way. Recognition from him was the big prize that Obregon sought, for it would bring prestige, arms, munitions, money. This was the period of the Bucareli treaties, pushed through by Obregon and denounced by his critics as a "sell out" to the United States.

In 1923, Obregon had to choose a stooge to be placed in the presidential chair. For months he debated between Calles and de la Huerta; both were pulling wires to become heir apparent. Obregon finally picked Calles. De la Huerta, with the bulk of the army generals, and with backing from big landowners and the clergy, rebelled. He was licked, fled to Los Angeles, and later opened a singing school there.

Two men on a horse, Calles and Obregon. Calles, cold, calculating, was the brain; Obregon, ebullient, red-faced, hard-drinker, was the heart. The clergy's support of the de la Huerta uprising gave Calles the ladder he needed. Obregon concurred in the need to break the economic power of the clergy, which had become the focus of the counter-revolution, the active center of opposition to the Constitution of 1917. The banner of anti-clericalism was hoisted alongside the pro-labor banner which Morones was putting to effective use.

Obregon continued as head man, not only during his presidency from 1920 to 1924, but during Calles' term, 1924-1928, although during the latter period Calles was able to bring his personal following to maturity. Perhaps Calles remembered that when he, then Lieutenant Colonel Calles, had fought his first battle in Sonora and had been defeated, Obregon, already a seasoned general, had called him "Colonel Turntail." At any rate, it was not personal affection that held the two together, but common need. To the opposition, they were two heads of the same serpent.

There is a great deal of discussion about just when the Mexican revolutions became The Revolution, when the first foundations were really laid for today's political structure. The Constitution of 1917 was there, but it remained to be put into effect. The general concensus is that the beginning of the so-called reconstruction period dates from the consolidation of power by Obregon on a basis of personal following, still the *caudillo*, the leader, and that the institutional foundations were laid by Calles.

Unlike some of the other leaders, Obregon was not a prohibitionist, not an ascetic; he was for the abundant life, and
nobody ever called him a utopian. He knew where the enemy
was, but had no illusions about bringing in the millennium
overnight. He constantly referred to a desire to return to his
farm in Sonora. In the meantime he assigned himself the
monopoly on handling the chickpeas, important Mexican
crop. He organized the growers, most of whom liked the idea
because they had been bilked before by more exacting monopolists. Obregon was noted for a prodigious memory and
for his endless repertory of anecdotes and wise-cracks. One
of his favorites:

"I am better for Mexico, for the simple reason that I can't
steal as much as the others. I have only one arm."

His other arm had been shot off in a decisive battle against
Villa. He was constantly eulogized by the Redeemers who
were rising like mushrooms about him. His enemies accused
him of some very bloody acts, wholesale executions of prisoners, assassinations. His friends answered that it was war,
and that the other side had been much more atrocious in its
slaughters. He was said to have become very ambitious. At
any rate, the laws were changed so he could run for the presidency again to succeed Calles, who had counseled him against
such action. Two generals were candidates against Obregon,
Francisco Serrano and Arnulfo Gomez, the latter reputedly
with backing of the usual combination of landowners and
clergy.

1927. The Cristero (Catholic) revolt was at its height.
Ammunition, arms, supplies from government sources leaked
out toward the Cristero encampments. Army units sent after
the Cristeros dillied and dallied around the hills, while the
Cristeros went merrily on, wrecking trains and raiding towns.
Obregon's decision to become a candidate threw Serrano and
Gomez, the Anti–Re-electionist Party candidate, together, and

with them a part of the army. The government found that the opposition was impatient, and had decided to revolt. Serrano and Gomez were bumped off along with a lot of others. A bomb was thrown at Obregon's automobile. A priest, Miguel Pro, his brother, Humberto, and two other Catholics were arrested, accused of the attempted assassination, and lined up in front of a firing squad. Obregon was elected in June, 1928, and a month after his election he was killed while at a banquet arranged in his honor by Guanajuato politicos.

A nun, a priest, a Catholic organization, were held responsible for the action of Jose de Leon Toral, the young caricaturist who pumped Obregon full of lead during the gaiety of the banquet. The trial of Toral and Mother Conchita, the accused nun, renewed the Church-State agitation. Toral was executed, Mother Conchita was sentenced to the Tres Marias penal islands.

Calles remained sole boss. During his rule as president-maker, the people were to recall a manifesto issued by Obregon in his election campaign:

". . . How many parties have existed in the country? Just two: the Conservative and the Liberal, with diametrically opposed tendencies.

"How were these parties defined? From the first liberating movement, the Mexican family has been divided into two parties, one made up of the oppressors, the other of the oppressed, the first known as the Conservative and the second as Liberal. The first was made up of the wealthy, the high clergy, the foreigners with special privileges; the second by all the working classes, laborers, farm workers, professional people, farmers, cattlemen, and small industrialists. The latter class was a real majority of the Mexican family. . . . In the movements since Independence, the Conservative Party has been strengthened by leaders of the Liberal Party who prostituted their prestige, blinded by ambition or in defense of illicit fortunes, and these leaders have always been used as vehicles by the Conservative Party to return to power. This type of Neo-Conservative has always proved, in every epoch, the most serious obstacle to the realization of liberal principles. . . .

"The bitter fruit . . . of all our previous revolutions has been that we could not liberate ourselves from our liberators."

And this, frequently repeated by Obregon, the jester:

"We can get rid of clericalism, and we can get rid of capitalism, but who is going to get rid of us?"

5

Plutarco Elias Calles, the "terrible Turk" of the Mexican Revolution, was the author of the Plan of Agua Prieta, around which the anti-Carranza movement had crystallized. It complained of violation of States' rights, nullification of individual rights, and proclaimed for "restoration of democracy." Calles, in power, violated States' rights, nullified individual rights, and kept democracy hidden in the Pandora box of the Revolution. Unlike many other "Plans" that have appeared during the last thirty years, the Plan of Agua Prieta did not offer any advanced social program or any class appeal. It was strictly an anti-Carranza document and its slogan was "effective suffrage, no re-election," which had been Madero's slogan. This was to become the "tag line" on every official communication in Mexico, even while Obregon was preparing to be re-elected on a technical change in the law. That slogan is one of the great ironies of Mexican history, most fought for, most abused.

Young Calles was a schoolteacher while still in his teens. The graft in the school system, the difficulty of getting funds from the Diaz officials who pocketed most of it, the monumental task of making parents send their children to school, influenced the young teacher to seek a change of government. When Madero appeared as the leader of the anti-Diaz movement, Calles rushed to the frontier to offer his services. Calles didn't do so well, soon afterward, in his attempts to enter politics. He was defeated in the race for the state legislature, and went into business. He ran a grain mill for a while, then a store.

The revolt of Carranza against the Huerta dictatorship brought Calles full tilt into the movement. He saw things opening up for him. He distributed his stock of goods among his employees and went off to join the revolution under Obregon's command. With the overthrow of Huerta, Calles became governor of Sonora. The taciturn, reflective, iron-willed, aggressive, tireless teacher-storekeeper-general was on his upward climb. Four years after the defeat of Carranza, Calles was president. Eight years later, with the death of Obregon, Calles remained the "strong man" and he went on building his machine, garnering ever more power and wealth. Through his organizational ability, and by establishing certain much-needed reforms, he became the indispensable man of Mexico. He pursued the Machievellian principle of "divide and rule," applying it to agrarian leaders, as well as to politicos and to labor organizations. Calles defended labor unions, when other politicos wanted to destroy them, and he got the labor support. But by 1927, third year of his term, when he was being called a Bolshevik, a communist, a Red, he made his position clear on labor unions:

"Nothing is further from my mind than to interrupt the peaceful economic development of Mexico nor to interfere with the present economic system. But I must emphasize the fact that I consider the trade unions to be absolutely indispensable to this capitalist system. For the trade unions serve a two-fold purpose: They keep the growing might of capitalism in check on the one hand. And in the event of an attack being launched on the capitalist ranks, the unions serve as a barricade. The trade unions stand or fall by capitalism. But they should never intervene in political matters. Their sphere is purely economic, and once they meddle in politics they lose their character and their significance."

And his attitude toward the middle class:

"My friendly feeling for the middle class can in part be ascribed to the fact that I am doing everything in my power to create a class of small peasant proprietors. It is my ambition to see the peasants own the land on which they work. For to make every peasant a proprietor is the best way of avoiding revolution and political unrest. Thus is created a substantial personal and perhaps in a measure selfish interest in supporting the existing order of things. Capital can play its part, too, in founding of land banks, insurance companies, and so forth. In this way the bonds between capital and labor are strengthened."

Calles' term as president was marked by three major fights: with the clergy, the land lords, and the oil companies. Mexican business interests, on the whole, supported him, although they disapproved of his Church policies and were afraid of his "radicalism." But when he proved himself a right guy, they gathered around him, feeling they had found the man who could protect their profits and at the same time keep labor "satisfied." He succeeded at it fairly well for a while. In the petroleum fight of 1925, Calles was up against a pretty tough hombre, the United States government, which, in the person of Mr. Calvin Coolidge, chose to defend the oil companies.

This was rather an involved situation for Calles. He and Obregon were indebted to the Washington administration for support against de la Huerta. He knew only too well that the support could be thrown to someone else, against him. Mr. Morrow, then the United States ambassador, told him that Uncle Sam didn't want to get hard-boiled about it, really, and they could all work in harmony. Calles and Mr. Morrow got to be quite chummy, and the competent partner of the House of Morgan even helped bring about a truce with the Church later.

Calles capitulated to the big land lords also, declaring that the peasants were not prepared to cultivate the land properly, and it was best that it remain in the hands of men with sufficient capital. Among these, of course, by that time, were not a few generals and some civilian redeemers. Calles continued to find opposition from the clergy, kept that issue alive and, through it, managed to hold the support of many men of the Revolution who were anti-clerical. They were also not very partial to Calles, but regarded the menace of a politically powerful Church much greater than the menace of Calles.

6

On September 1, 1928, Calles delivered an historic speech in Congress, flatly rejecting proposals that he continue in the presidency following the slaying of Obregon. He stated he would retire at the end of his term and would no longer figure in politics.

"The time has come for us to make a basic change in our political attitudes," he said. "For the first time in our history as a nation we find ourselves without any *caudillo*. Let us direct the nation along the path of real institutional life, so that we may pass, once and for all, from a historical condition of a 'one-man' country to a nation of institutions and laws. . . ."

The following year he was called in by the government to direct the campaign against the Escobar revolution. Two years later the government asked for his help in the financial crisis. An acute political crisis developed in 1932 during the Ortiz Rubio administration. Calles again took charge as Minister of War. The crisis which he was called in to solve was in a large measure due to the Calles hegemony over the administration, in which Ortiz Rubio was a mere figurehead. It was really Calles' first showdown with the strengthening anti-Calles sentiment that was later to rally around Cardenas.

Calles' administration shows a record of many roads built, irrigation works constructed, three thousand rural schools established in one year, reduction of the national budget by fifty million pesos during his first year, discharge of twenty thousand government employes and reduction in the size of the army.

Whatever his intentions at the beginning of his term, whatever measure of law and order he managed to institute, Calles was checkmated, willingly or unwillingly, by the big land lords and the big foreign interests. His regime became a brake on the Revolution of 1917. The Callistas could hold the basic laws over the heads of less powerful landowners and make them kick through for the private benefit of the Callistas rather than for peasants. Inevitably, the high-riding Calles clique sought a formula to perpetuate their man in power. They conceived the idea of making him "Big Chief of the Revolution" so he could continue as arbiter of the nation's destinies regardless of the temporary occupant of the presidential chair. In 1929, he formed a party designed as an effective instrument for keeping things in line. The new party's declaration of principles described it as "social democratic" and it was named the National Revolutionary Party. Through the machinery of that party, Calles continued to hold the reins from 1929 until 1935, a period of acute party dictatorship for the country at large, and of dictatorship by the Calles clique for the members of the party. Attempts to make it a mass organization failed. It remained essentially a party of government officeholders, employees and politicos. Most of its leaders, with exception, of course, of the die-hard Callistas, continued in government positions and became leaders of the Party of the Mexican Revolution, which Cardenas formed in 1938 to supplant the Calles organization.

7

Calles had not been strong enough to hold back the generals and politicians who for a long time had been champing at the bit because the small Sonora clique was hogging the public trough too long. The beginning of Calles' political decline came when he let his friends sell him on the idea of assuming the title of "Big Chief of the Revolution." It was the modern form of crowning Caesar. And there was more than one lean and hungry Cassius around ready to do his stuff. Calles' courtiers figured that the "old man" could be built up into another Porfirio Diaz, could rule perpetually on the pretext of maintaining "peace," rule in fact while the puppet-presidents ruled in name, sliding in and out of the executive mansion. Pascual Ortiz Rubio, practically an unknown whom Calles had put in the Palace on February 5, 1930, was too transparent a stooge, and the old dictator junked him on September 2, 1932, substituting Abelardo Rodriguez, the Minister of War.

The dual rule continued, and later precipitated a crisis which almost led to an open split between Rodriguez, "the Country Club President," and Calles, in spite of Rodriguez' great admiration for the "old man." Rodriguez, brought up on the border, had been a copper miner, storekeeper, professional baseball player. He became governor of Lower California in 1923, and rose rapidly in the army to the Ministry of War and the Presidency. He was popular among business men, because running a government was just plain business to him. Buy low, sell high. He talked their language. It had been mighty good business, too, in Lower California, during the time of prohibition in the United States. Booze and gambling joints in Tijuana and Mexicali brought tourists swarming, and with them a niagara of dollars that gave a lot of hard-fighting Mexican generals a start on the upgrade.

His California friends had a picnic when Rodriguez became president. To the big horse-racing and gambling resort in Agua Caliente was soon added the "biggest gambling casino outside of Monte Carlo," just at the edge of the Federal District in the State of Mexico, bailiwick of Calles' pal, Senator Riva Palacio. The casino, known subtly as the "Foreign Club," became a symbol of official corruption. Among partners in it were Calles and Juan Platt, Calles' millionaire friend, former treasurer of the National Railways, and some Hollywood movie big shots and professional gamblers. As a tourist magnet, as a hangout for politicos, and as a godsend for bored Mexican society, it was undoubtedly the stuff. The Rodriguez theory on the resorts was simple: people are going to gamble anyhow, and they're going to drink, and so on, and the country is poor, and can use a percentage of this money which people will throw away whether they can do it legally or not. Rodriguez' defenders will cite figures to show that even if he didn't distribute so much land and if he did clamp down on trade unions and unfriendly political parties, at least he balanced the budget, and left a surplus in the treasury. It all depends on how you look at it, on the system of bookkeeping. You can prove he left a surplus, or that a surplus was left to him, that the hand is quicker than the eye, or vice versa. One of Cardenas' first actions after he took office was to close up the Foreign Club, and later he forbade all gambling in the Federal District and territories, so that the National Lottery, run by the government, was left with a monopoly on gambling. But the lottery's proceeds go to maintain the Ministry of Social Welfare, so that's okay.

President Franklin D. Roosevelt and his ambassador, Josephus Daniels, were the innocent bystanders in a neat little plan that almost split Rodriguez-Calles as Cardenas-Calles split later and came near giving Rodriguez the historical medal for ditching the old dictator. But the time was not quite ripe. Being a shadow was not to the liking of Rodriguez, who had been governor, had been Minister of War, had been a big-shot general. He was getting fed up with the idea of having Calles-dressing every day on his official salad. Cabinet members ignored him, and they ran off whenever they had some problem to settle, ran off to Cuernavaca to get Calles' decision and deliver it to the President. Rodriguez, who had given promise of being different, of asserting his rights as president, was becoming the laughingstock of the country, as Ortiz Rubio had been. When he'd come in to the Nineteenth Hole at the Mexico City Country Club, his fellow clubbers, primed with a snootful of Scotch, would razz Abel about playing second fiddle. It began to get under his skin. Rodriguez sent out a famous circular telling all his cabinet members that government matters were to be taken up with him and not with Calles, adding that Calles was not running things, although Rodriguez was always glad to get advice from an old head. The ministers shrugged their shoulders and mumbled the Mexican equivalent of oh-yeah? and went right on making trips to Cuernavaca. Until the Case of the Roosevelt Letter.

The famous Roosevelt letter, dated March 22, 1934, was not an official document. It was a personal note given by the American President to a political friend in Texas who

was going to Mexico, and who thought it would be nice
to have FDR say a few sweet words about Calles. The note
referred to Calles as "the strong man" of Mexico and praised
him for maintaining peace and prosperity.* So far, so good.
And everything might have gone along as lovely as ever if
some of Calles' advisers—supposedly led by Dr. Jose Manuel
Puig Casauranc, ex-cabinet minister—hadn't got the idea of
converting that personal note into something really big. They
figured that it would be a marvelous bit of publicity, in view
of the rising sentiment against Calles, to have an official banquet and have Ambassador Daniels present the letter officially
to Calles. That would show the Mexicans that Washington
was still back of Calles.

When he found out about the proposed banquet at Calles'
estate in Cuernavaca, Rodriguez hit the ceiling. He got the
dictator on the 'phone and burned up the wires with some
good old profanity for which folks along the border are
noted: if that banquet went through, Rodriguez would not
only not attend, but would kick out every cabinet member
who showed his face there, and would issue a public statement all about it, a statement in which the frijoles would be
spilled good and proper. Calles told him to calm down, that
the idea wasn't his, but came from some of his clever friends,
and that he'd just as soon drop the matter right now if it was
going to get friend Abel all riled up. The banquet was called
off.

A short time later, about a month before Rodriguez was to
leave office, Ambassador Daniels was quoted in an interview
in *El Nacional* of November 3, 1934, as having delivered himself of great praise for Calles, which would have been a most

* A fuller account of the Roosevelt Letter incident can be found in *El
Presidente Rodriguez* (Pages 120-128) written by Francisco Javier Gaxiola,
Jr., private secretary of President Rodriguez. The book was published in
Mexico City, in 1938. A polemic over interpretation of the letter was carried
on in Mexico City newspapers in September and October of 1938.

impolitic thing at that time. Daniels told President Rodriguez privately that he had said no such untactful things, that a reporter had rushed up to him in Cuernavaca, and since Daniels didn't understand Spanish, had fired a few hot questions at him through an interpreter. Daniels said he didn't want to make a public denial because he knows, as a newspaperman, that young reporters frequently misquote people, but such mistakes should be forgiven, because the boys really mean well.

The Calles men, however, did not desist in their maneuvers to demonstrate to the people that Calles would continue to ride in the saddle during the next—the Cardenas—administration. The revolt against the Calles hegemony, meanwhile, had reached unprecedented proportions. The very thorough election campaign conducted by Cardenas in 1934, in which he began to emerge as an independent national personality, helped to jell the anti-Calles movement, and prepared the break which was to come before the end of Cardenas' first year as president.

8

Calles and Cardenas, the man that the National Revolutionary Party made president, split in June, 1935. Calles went to Los Angeles. He returned in December with Luis N. Morones, issued a call for formation of "conservative" labor unions against what he termed the radicals. This challenge was followed by an attack on Cardenas, whom he called a "communist," and an appeal for the middle class to join with the "conservative" labor unions. Congress asked him to leave the country because he was provoking disorders. Cardenas was asked to kick him out, and to expel Morones, but the President followed his policy of giving the boys all the rope they wanted. Calles remained silent for several months. On April 6, 1936, the Mexico City–Veracruz train was dynamited. Thirteen passengers were killed. The Calles agitators were blamed.

On the night of April 9, Calles was at his Santa Barbara ranch home near Mexico City. Dressed in black silk pajamas, he was studiously reading Hitler's *Mein Kampf*. In the Associated Press office in Mexico City, Luis Alvear got a tip over the 'phone that something would happen at the Calles home that night. Alvear telephoned Calles, and the old dictator answered, "I'm a prisoner." Early next morning Calles was on his way out of Mexico in an airplane, with a military escort. When he got off the plane at the Brownsville, Texas, airport, the squad of soldiers formed a lane for him to pass through, and stood at attention. Calles was still a general. He spoke harsh words to the soldiers, concluding:

"At least now I'm in a country where people respect me."

He still carried the Hitler book under his arm, and he told news correspondent H. G. Stilwell Jr.:

"I was exiled because I opposed the attempts to implant a dictatorship of the proletariat. The dynamiting of the train was a criminal act, due to the anarchy which prevails in the country."

Calles was bitter. The dregs of defeat had left a bad taste. During his fight with Cardenas, he had seen one after another supposed friend abandon him, many of them politicos who rode in on his prestige and basked in his glory. Calles, during his reign as chief Kingfish-Redeemer, had given the newspapers orders on what they could or could not print. But now, when he issued inflammatory statements (before, they would have been Page One Must), the newspapers did not use a line. All the medicine—except physical "liquidation"—which he had handed out before, was now given him, although in relatively mild doses.

Since 1936, Calles has been in Los Angeles. Some of the boys still nurse fond hopes that he might stage a comeback.

Most of the insiders say that he is too old, too discredited, too closely identified with the vested interests, to make any more splurges in Mexican politics, although you can never tell what might happen in a serious crisis. There are his sons, too, Plutarco Jr. and Rodolfo—whom he had been grooming for big things. The most general opinion is that if the Calles group attempts a comeback it will be under another front. Some regard Abelardo L. Rodriguez, ex-President, who recently published a series of articles highly critical of the Soviet Union, as a possibility.

Calles had taken the wheel of the good ship Revolution during a stormy period when somebody with plenty of guts was needed to keep the vessel afloat. Many question the value of the course he took. Others defend it as the only one left open at the time, that course or bust. At any rate, his procedure did not convince the masses that the Revolution was being kept intact. A government that merely maintained order did not seem sufficient. The country pined for a new fundamental readjustment. The idea was: if the people had been fighting all these years just to get new bosses, without protection of labor's rights, without land for the poor man to work, why they'd just as soon keep on at the merry game of war. A refrain from Zapata's campaign song, *La Valentina*, has become proverbial:

"If they're going to kill me tomorrow, they might as well do it now!"

Calles and his inner circle had repeated the same mistake of earlier rulers: they could no longer hold power, and they could not turn loose. In their panic, they tried to steer the Revolution into the cove of Reaction. But a new, confident, optimistic skipper had appeared. The first thing he did was to strike out boldly on another course, which was already charted, but which the old crew feared to travel. In taking over the controls, Lazaro Cardenas had his hands full.

VI

THAT MAN CARDENAS

1

PORFIRIO DIAZ was finishing his fourth term as president and getting ready for his fifth when, in the little town of Jiquilpan, State of Michoacan, another son was born to the Cardenas del Rio family. No earthquakes or floods announced the birth of little Lazaro, and his parents thanked God for another son, and also hoped that God would do something about helping to feed him and bring him up properly.

Lazaro's father died when the boy was thirteen years old, leaving the widow with eight children. Lazaro, although not the eldest, was the most "serious" of the children. No more school for him now. Young Lazaro got a job as printer's devil in a small shop. But the lad was apparently destined for public service, and by 1910 was an assistant to the town tax collector, and three years later was the town jailer. Madero had overthrown Diaz, Huerta had killed Madero, the nation was in turmoil. When Venustiano Carranza issued his call in 1913 for the nation to rise against the usurper Victoriano Huerta, Cardenas took his only prisoner from the jail, gave him a rifle, and the two went to join the nearest band of revolutionaries. In a couple of years Cardenas was leader of his own company. The news of organization of a major revolutionary army in Sonora reached him. He took his two hundred men and marched to Agua Prieta, where he placed himself under orders of Colonel Plutarco Elias Calles. Cardenas thus early in his career became associated with the

Sonora group that was to head the government into the reconstruction period.

From then on, the rise of Lazaro Cardenas in the army was swift. He had the qualities most in demand for the army in those days, much more important than preparation in the manual of arms or military tactics: loyalty, decision, energy. In October, 1915—he was twenty years old then—we find him as head of the 22nd Regiment. Two years later he is chief of the expeditionary column that went from Sonora to Chihuahua, and for three years after that, until June, 1920, he was general of the First Sonora Brigade.

Cardenas had just passed his twenty-fifth birthday when he was made governor of his home State of Michoacan, as well as chief of military operations. The following year he was transferred to the Isthmus of Tehuantepec, then to Guanajuato, wherever there was need of a trusted man. By 1923 he was firmly established in his military career. Offered a big command by the de la Huerta rebels, who had won over the biggest part of the army, Cardenas remained loyal to Obregon, fought against the de la Huerta forces and was badly wounded.

The three years from 1925 to 1928 marked the beginning of Cardenas' political formation and the development of the social ideas which were to be his beacon lights. During those three years he was chief of military operations in the Huasteca region, a Gulf coast region mostly jungle, but also center of the greatest oil boom on the continent. The Tampico boom was just past its peak then, and had begun to decline.

Thirty-year-old General Cardenas had now been a soldier for twelve years. He had seen much of his country, the confusion of fighting men desperately clinging to any straw, no matter how frail, which gave promise of not breaking the minute they grabbed hold. Oppression, misery, ignorance and hopelessness, the four horsemen loosed by the Diaz "scientific" regime, were already an old story to him. But what he saw and what he heard and what he learned during his stay in the oil fields left him no doubts about the path he must follow. To all the other injustices which he had seen his countrymen suffering, now was added the double shame of Mexicans being kicked around by foreigners. For him, as for most Mexicans, there is no difference between men because of the color of their skin or the language they happen to speak. He could not understand why one set of men had neat, comfortable screened houses up on the hills, while others were dumped on the edge of the jungle swamps in miserable shacks. Vice, gambling, boozing, graft, corruption, completed the picture which was branded into Lazaro Cardenas' retentive brain.

In the delirious dance of the oil fields, Cardenas lived the same disciplined life that he had before, and which he continued to live after attaining the highest command in the country. Some of his fellow generals think that he was a sap for not getting his while he was in the oil fields. Lesser officers made their pile during those days. Cardenas did not lack opportunities. A favorite story is of the oil company official who offered him a new Packard, just like that, no favors asked. Shiny automobiles have always been a weakness of Mexican generals. Cardenas then had in his service a battered old jaloppy on which you could barely make out the name "Hudson." The company man drove the Packard out in front of the offices and Cardenas' aides clustered at the window to oh-and-ah. Cardenas was polite in his refusal: "No, thank you. The one we have now serves its purpose well." Three days later the general's car stopped running altogether. The oil company offer was still good. His subordinates urged him to take it. Nothing doing. He sent a colonel around to the automobile agencies and finally arranged to buy a modest Dodge on installments of one hundred pesos a month.

His friends who knew of this incident and others like it were not surprised when he refused to live in Chapultepec; when he showed up in a dignified, dark business suit amid the swallowtails of a diplomatic gathering; or when he refused to have a special official license tag attached to his automobile, a tag which would give traffic privileges. Some of his political critics will swear it's all a pose and that Cardenas is smart, much smarter than people think, and that it's all a build-up. Whatever it is, the people seem to like it. Cardenas is the one recent president who walks among the people unafraid. No armored cars, no elaborate bodyguards. At times they'll almost crush him, the crowds will, trying to touch him, to walk a few steps by his side. Many foreigners cannot understand how much it means to the Mexican people to find a president who doesn't build a Chinese wall between governors and governed, who doesn't proclaim a divine mission for himself, who likes to lose himself in the crowd. If it's all a build-up, it's darn good, and that man is some actor.

Cardenas left the oil fields with his mind made up to go into politics. He already had a lot of ideas, including his belief that the soldiers and civilian workers should fraternize instead of being kept apart. He had founded a school—forerunner of what he was to do later as governor and as president—for the children of the private soldiers in his regiment. There was nothing in the army budget to cover such fantastic, non-military activities. So Cardenas clipped a bit off his salary, convinced some of his subordinates to sacrifice a few bottles of beer, and managed to scrape up enough to buy books and other materials and to pay a teacher. Every morning as regular as the sun, General Cardenas would show up at the school to see how things were going.

His campaign for the governorship of Michoacan took him not only to the towns, but to every village and hamlet and cluster of houses in the state. When election day came around, the people of his state knew that man, and he knew them. Cardenas' term as governor was a good indication of what might be expected of him as president. And precisely because he knew of Cardenas' devotion to the peasantry, his sympathies with the underdog generally, Calles opposed the nomination of Cardenas. It was Calles' contention that these things had been good in their time, when he had been on the make, but the country could not now stand the agitation which he knew would follow if such policies were put into effect. Cardenas now expressed the same general ideals that Calles had espoused in 1923, but Calles had gone a long way since, a long way from the days of the young Sonora governor whose first act as state executive was to forbid the sale and possession of intoxicating liquors. By 1933, Calles was a tycoon among tycoons, had his fingers in every political and business pie, was shareholder in every big industrial undertaking, sole owner of many.

2

Politicos who try to pull a fast one on Mexico's President have come to learn that they have to get up mighty early, as the saying goes, to get the better of Lazaro Cardenas. The reason is simple: Cardenas is out of bed at five o'clock in the morning, usually after about four hours of sleep, rarely more than five. The rest of his day is measured off with military precision. By five-thirty he has been in and out of the shower, if he is at home. If he is away on one of his frequent trips into the country which he has always loved more than the city, Cardenas will be splashing around in a river or lake, his smooth, muscular soldier's hands chopping into the water. His wind is fine, for he doesn't smoke, and his co-ordination and reflexes function like clockwork. No booze, no late parties, no carousing, no hangovers to cramp his style. He used to swim a little faster in the old days, before his bulging chest and beefy shoulders developed a neat cushion of fat. But he can still leave any of his party behind in the water, as he leaves them behind when he takes a long, brisk walk or is off on a horseback jaunt for hours at a time.

He likes his walks or his equitation during the first two hours after he's dressed. To ride out into the cool of dawn and to be on hand when the sun comes over the mountains is his idea of beginning a perfect day. Wherever he is, Cardenas goes about systematically exploring the countryside. He never tires of telling his less energetic aides that every soldier should be thoroughly acquainted with his environment for at least five miles in every direction. Some of his bureaucrats or congressional friends who happen to be along—and who like to take things a little easier, to get sozzled now and then—have come to refer privately to the President as "the boy scout." Like a boxer in his prime, Cardenas is always more or less in training.

By eight-thirty he will be wiping his abundant lips and neatly trimmed, thick mustache, after an ample breakfast of fruit, eggs, oatmeal, milk and rolls. He'll rest a bit after breakfast, glance at the morning papers on his way to the office, and at nine o'clock sharp—either at the National Palace or at the office in his suburban home—Mexico's President will be on the job. He'll stay on the job until two o'clock in the afternoon, meeting with cabinet members, congressmen, labor leaders, businessmen from all over the country, diplomats, visitors from all over the world. And rarely a day will pass during which he fails to receive one or more delegations of peasants or Indians. At times the anteroom to his office in the National Palace looks more like a peasants' convention than like the central salon of the federal bureaucracy.

Cardenas likes that, he likes to feel close to the men of the soil, to hear them tell their needs in a vocabulary too limited to admit hypocrisy. The peasant may be reminding him of the special seeds he promised to send on one of his trips, and which perhaps have been lost in a maze of red tape, or a committee of Indians may want to know what about that land they were supposed to get. Cardenas gave the orders, you can be sure, for he has a memory to which every little detail sticks like a grass-burr. He gives so many orders, as a matter of fact, on his trips, that his subordinates keep hoping for something that will make him stay in Mexico City a few months at a stretch. Every department has a spindle stacked high with orders: a fence for this man, a school here, a road there, an irrigation canal yonder. Sometimes the federal treasury has the money for the job, sometimes not. Don't get the idea that he grants everything proposed to him. Not by a long shot. But he'll listen to any reasonable request. He'll listen quietly, politely, absorbed, rarely ask a question. The petitioner always feels that his sales talk is a success. Then, quickly, as decisively as a line officer in battle, Cardenas will give the visitor the news: sometimes good, often bad.

The President is one Mexican who doesn't take a siesta, that age-old custom of the Latins which so delightfully makes two days out of one. Between two and three o'clock, Cardenas will have his dinner, and it's usually a much more modest affair than the multiple-coursed event to which most middle-class families sit down at midday. Since the Cardenas family nearly always has a visitor for dinner, and usually somebody interesting, there is no lack of diverting conversation to relax the presidential brain until he is ready to return to his office, where he arrives at four o'clock on the dot, remaining until about seven-thirty or later. A light supper, then perhaps a movie, or a little friendly gathering, usually a bit of horseplay with his five-year-old son, Cuauhtemoc, and with the young Spanish orphan, Fernando, who has been given a home in the presidential dwelling. And by ten o'clock Cardenas has ordinarily turned in, settled in an easy chair or propped up in bed, reading and studying, for two hours, sometimes three, sometimes longer. If he happens to have a pressing state problem on his mind, he may doze off only for an hour or so and get back to it. But he prefers to drop official business during the short period before he goes to sleep. He likes to read books on political and economic theory, or books suggesting practical methods adopted elsewhere, which might be applied in developing his country. He likes books on Mexican history, historical, biographical, or dealing with the life of the people. He is also up on the contemporary political literature of Spain. In his drawing room is an autographed portrait of Romain Rolland.

Cardenas, soon after he became president, decided against living in the gorgeous Chapultepec Castle, which had been the presidential residence for many years. He ordered the place turned into a museum where anybody could go. A lot of critics called it all a pose. Others saw in it a remarkable act of symbolism, in which Maximilian's gold-trimmed dinner service and Carlotta's bed, the luxurious furnishings and ample recreation quarters enjoyed by Mexico's official families, were exposed to public gaze as things belonging to a past epoch. Probably as influential as any other cause for the selection of a suburban villa, with a spacious garden, was that Cardenas really preferred not to live in the castle. The man is just that way. He doesn't like claptrap, he doesn't like stuffed shirts, and would rather roll up in a blanket under the moonlit sky of Michoacan than on the softest, smoothest inner-spring mattress in the world. The politicos who have been with him on the country trips will tell you that, in his direct, healthy, almost primitive way, he likes to have company under that blanket. But nobody in Mexico holds that against him. And as for the opening of Chapultepec Castle to the public, the thousands upon thousands who spend their Sundays in Chapultepec Forest, surrounding the castle, were frenzied with joy at being able to go through the place that only a chosen few could enter before.

Cardenas is noted for his discipline, his temperate habits, his sobriety, austerity, his frank loathing of gambling, his turning of thumbs-down on booze and booze-heads, his repugnance toward an atmosphere of liquor, tobacco smoke and fast ladies, so common to gatherings of politicos. As a result some critics call him an ascetic, a puritan, a wild-eyed reformer, a bluenose, almost anything implying that he wants people to deny themselves the good things of life. But quite the opposite is true. Health—physical, mental, moral—is the keystone of his character. His powerful physique has withstood serious bullet wounds, a siege of Malta fever that laid him low for a while, in addition to minor ailments that develop even in a healthy forty-three-year-old organism.

His tastes are essentially those of a man used to living simply, one who has spent most of his life in the barracks or in the field, and who had to keep in shape to keep alive. Because of this healthy approach, he has no need of artificial stimulants. He likes the spontaneous gaiety of a peasant festival, an Indian girl's musical laugh. He likes to tell stories and listen to them, the conviviality of a country gathering, unmarred by yes-men's rancid phrases. Cardenas is fond of dancing and of music—the fresh-air and not the wild-party kind—and suffers acutely in the stuffy atmosphere of diplomatic balls and the like to which duty sometimes takes him.

In 1923, Cardenas was about as near to death as a man can get without being a corpse. It was in Jalisco, near Ocotlan, during the de la Huerta rebellion. Obregon, who played the game of war for quick dramatic victories regardless of cost, sent General Cardenas and a small force to divert the enemy so the main force could attack from another flank. Cardenas and his men were routed, as Obregon calculated they would be, and Cardenas was wounded. As the rebels advanced, his staff was grouped around him. He told them to beat it, that they could do nothing for him. Cardenas was captured by General Enrique Estrada, who ordered that every effort be made to save Cardenas. In the hospital some days later, Estrada sought to win Cardenas over to the de la Huerta cause. Cardenas was adamant. He told Estrada: "You are fighting on the wrong side. You are making unnecessary war, and our country is dying for peace. Lay down your arms." The story still goes the rounds that Estrada personally paid the hospital bill.

And that may be the story behind a political event last August, when several congressmen—including the same General Estrada—announced formation of a new party, the Mexican Constitutional Democratic Front, to fight the "communism" of the government party, the Party of the Mexican Revolution (PRM). General Ramon Iturbe and Bolivar Sierra were the other two leaders, all members of the PRM. The PRM decided that since they were forming an opposition party, they should be expelled from the PRM, which means that they cannot appear in the party's primaries, in which nomination is tantamount to election, as in the solid Democratic states of the South. Sierra and Iturbe got the gate, after a trial, but Estrada stayed in the PRM.

Frequently this personal—rather than political—appeal will explain Cardenas' ability to keep the machine going when everybody expects it to explode any minute. Even men who disagree with him violently over policy are friendly toward him, different from the case of other political figures, like Calles for instance, toward whom bitter personal animosity was often the key to political opposition. The Calles method of dealing with men was that of the tough guy. Calles' friends say he had to be tough, that the period of his political rise was a dog-eat-dog period more than others. Almost anywhere in

Mexico you could find relatives or friends of men who had been killed or persecuted by Calles henchmen, carrying vengeance in their hearts against the old dictator.

There is nothing like that in the attitude toward Cardenas. He has no notches on his gun. His record on that score is unbelievably clean for the bloody years of revolution through which he moved. Cardenas could get tough—and he still can, and does, when he has to—but he'd rather settle things by the gentler route, and he usually has his way. This phenomenon, in Mexico's gun-toting politics, of a man who doesn't shoot first and ask questions later is so amazing that it seems like a myth. But nobody has yet produced an instance in which Cardenas killed off the field of battle, and there are numerous accounts of his sparing lives which could have been taken legitimately according to the laws of war. This respect for human life has done much toward establishing public confidence in his good faith. Folks will go along with a fellow like that even when he makes a mistake, because they feel he'll try to correct it when he can.

Cardenas is married to Amalia Solorzano, an unpretentious, attractive woman, typical of the middle-class *mestizo* families of Mexico. When she wears high heels, the top of her carefully coiffured head reaches well above Cardenas' shoulders. She is the mother of their five-year-old son, Cuauhtemoc, named after the last Aztec emperor. By a former wife, Cardenas has a sixteen-year-old daughter who appears occasionally at official functions. Señora Cardenas is interested in social welfare and her intimate circle of friends comprises the wives of several cabinet ministers with similar interests. Señora Cardenas began taking English lessons last year, likes the democratic manners of the Americans, admires the self-reliance, initiative and independence of American women. She refers to her husband as "the General." Other members of the President's immediate family, familiar in Mexican officialdom, are his brothers: Damaso, former federal senator, and later member of a firm specializing in government contracts; Jose Raimundo, studious, hard-working technical official in the ministry of finance; Alberto, and Francisco.

3

Soldier Cardenas was already known as a result of the various military campaigns and his term as Minister of War. Teacher Cardenas and Big Chief Cardenas were somewhat familiar to folks in Michoacan where he had built four hundred schools, was loved by the Tarascan Indians for whom he was *tata*—daddy. Citizen Cardenas had shown some notable qualities as president of the National Revolutionary Party, qualities of fairness and straight-dealing that made it inconvenient for the politicos to keep him there long. In the election campaign, a hitherto relatively unknown Cardenas, a Cardenas who was to be revealed more and more during his term as president, emerged: Comrade Cardenas, buddy of the workman and peasant.

Cardenas traveled nearly eighteen thousand miles over the country—seven thousand by airplane, five thousand by railway, five thousand by automobile, five hundred by motorboat, five hundred on horseback. The campaign was opened on December 8, 1933, and continued until election eve, June 30, 1934. The official election returns showed 2,268,567 votes for Cardenas; 24,690 for Antonio I. Villarreal of the Anti–Re-election Party; 15,765 for Adalberto Tejeda of the Leftist Socialist Party, and 1,188 for Hernan Laborde of the Communist Party.

Rightist politicians had already begun to develop concern, for on the very day he opened his campaign, Cardenas sent a telegram to the owner of the big Nueva Italia and Lombardia haciendas after "white guards" had killed three peasants and wounded twenty. In this telegram, Candidate Cardenas suggested that if the hacienda owners could not operate their estates and give their workers a livelihood, then the haciendas should be turned over to the workers for co-operative exploitation and arrangements could be made to pay the owner in installments. When Cardenas became president, a big part of these haciendas was distributed to peasants.

As this campaign unfolded, land lords got more and more worried and their only hope was that, like candidates before him, Cardenas had his fingers crossed, and that Calles could keep them crossed, when the candidate solemnly repeated:

"I pledge my honor to the fulfillment of my promises to the working classes if I am placed in power."

One of the big promises—which he had not been able to keep by the end of his fourth year in office—was that nation-wide prohibition would be instituted. A glance at some of Cardenas' campaign speeches is helpful in understanding the temper of the country at the time, as well as for an expression of the social and economic ideas which have guided him in his sensational term as president. Here are some excerpts from his speeches:

1. The Mexican people no longer fall for empty phrases like "liberty of conscience" and "liberty of teaching" and "economic liberty" because they know that the first represents the clerical dictatorship; the second, the dictatorship of reaction trying to impede the education of the people; and the third, the capitalist dictatorship opposed to salary increases and against state intervention in distribution of the public wealth for the benefit of the principal producers, who are the workers.

2. I have always desired that the organized workers and peasants have State power in their hands, so that they may be the most jealous guardians of the continuity of the revolutionary program, demanding the enforce-

ment of advanced legislation and combating, if necessary, the bad officials who fail in their duty . . . but to be deserving recipients of power, workers must first organize, must learn discipline, must develop broad social consciousness.

3. All political measures must have economic bases and economic significance.

4. The main road of the new phase of the Revolution is the March of Mexico toward socialism, a movement which departs equally from the anachronistic norms of classical liberalism and from those which are proper to communism that is undergoing an experiment in Soviet Russia. It departs from individualist liberalism, because this system cannot give rise to anything but the exploitation of man by man, to the unrestrained absorption of natural resources and to individual egoisms. It departs from state communism, because our people are not the kind to adopt a system which deprives them of the full enjoyment of their efforts, nor do they want to substitute the individual boss with the boss-state.

5. The function of the Mexican State is not limited to being a simple watchdog of public order . . . nor is the State recognized as a monopolist of the national economy, but our concept of the State is that of a regulator of the great economic phenomena which occur under our system of production and distribution of wealth.

6. Union organization is the best weapon of the workers, worth much more than protection of the laws and the public officials.

7. The definite adoption of the closed-shop system will not be effective unless the company-unions and minority unions, permanent cause of inter-union conflicts, are eliminated.

8. I believe that in the co-operatives—the consumers' and producers' co-operatives—rests the future of our country . . . but we do not speak here of the bourgeois pseudo–co-operativism, which has been with us since the time of the Dictatorship, but of genuine co-operatives, made up of workers, in which all can collaborate.

9. The formation of our own economy will free us

from the kind of capitalism interested only in raw materials and cheap labor, a capitalism which does not even reinvest its profits in Mexico, which arises as a danger to the nation, and which leaves us, in the end, dead earth, impoverished subsoil, starvation salaries and unrest that is a prelude to public disturbance.

10. Only by arming the agrarians, who have been, are, and will be the firmest bulwark of the Revolution, can they be prepared to fulfill their tasks. . . . I shall give the peasant a rifle so that he can defend his school and his land.

11. I regard it as antisocial for machinery to remain idle. . . . If I become president, all the idle factories will be leased and turned over to the workers, organized into co-operatives, which, under direction of the State, will operate them for the benefit of the workers themselves.

12. Our nationalist political economy does not represent a closed-door policy . . . foreigners are welcome, but they must respect our laws and our government. We desire that after coming here to make their livelihoods they build their homes, enjoy their possessions and pursue their enterprise, on a par with the sons of Mexico.

13. The Revolution cannot tolerate clerical interference in any form in public education, which is an exclusive faculty of the State . . . the Revolution cannot tolerate the efforts of the clergy when it tries to continue using our children and youth as instruments to divide the Mexican family, as backward elements in the nation's progress, and still less that it try to convert the young generation into an enemy of the working class. . . .

14. We must stimulate utilitarian and collectivist teaching, to prepare the students for productive activity, to teach them love of work as a social duty.

15. . . . that the teacher not stop at purely scholastic activities, but that he go to the shop, to the field, to defend the interests of the workers, especially to defend the worker's salary, because in so doing he defends the educational opportunities of his pupils.

16. The army should continue as the bulwark of our institutions . . . evolved in the revolutionary regime.

17. Women must organize, so that the home shall cease to be looked upon as a prison for them.

18. The Revolution is not content to sit back and wait for the children of today to grow up to put new ideas into effect . . . it wants the men of today to accept the responsibility of participating in the economic betterment which the entire republic seeks.

19. I call upon the workers to form a united front . . . independent . . . free of all official ties . . . so they can effectively co-operate with the beneficial acts of the government and to demand enforcement of the postulates of the Revolution.

20. I am the spokesman of the Six-Year Plan, placed in my hands by the convention which nominated me.

4

For years, a steel shell of what Porfirio Diaz intended as the framework for a magnificent new federal legislative palace stood in Mexico City, a gaunt architectural skeleton, reminder of a past epoch. During the period of Calles' domination, the framework was transformed into a huge arched structure, resembling the French Arc de Triomphe, and given the name of "Monument to the Revolution." Calles went out and the monument was still unfinished. The Cardenas regime proposed to put the finishing touches on it, and an elaborate park was laid out around the monument. By specific order of Calles, no portraits of actual persons appear on the sculptured groups at each corner. They are all symbolic.

Besides a number of half-finished edifices, the Revolution inherited a lot of unfinished social and economic business from the Porfirio Diaz regime, whose "cientificos" did their political building from the top down instead of the usual way of laying foundations first. During a breathing spell in the fighting, the Men of the Revolution took time out to remodel what was left of the 1857 Constitution after the Diaz regime had gone through it. Out of their deliberations came the political monument of the Revolution—the Constitution of 1917—in its day the most radical state charter in the world. The Obregon-Calles regimes worked on it for a while, and then reached an impasse in oil company opposition to enforcement of Article Twenty-Seven. Cardenas, then, inherited a Revolution-in-the-making, a wet clay figure, as it were, with the definiteness of a sculptural armature, but with a lot of modeling left to be done. The Mexican Revolution, under Cardenas, has begun to take a more definite shape, but it still is in a loose stage and its eventual form is conjectural.

Cardenas' blueprint for putting the finishing touches on the Revolution designed in the 1917 Constitution is the Six-Year Plan. This Plan is an Administration program produced in 1933 by the National Revolutionary Party, which also put Cardenas into the presidential chair.

The Six-Year Plan, written by Primo Villa Michel, then Minister of National Economy, and a group of politicos and economists who worked with him, was designed to provide the motive power for the 1917 Constitution, which had remained pretty much in abeyance during a hectic personal struggle for power. The Plan is to the Constitution what motor and fuel are to an automobile. And the automobile of the Mexican Revolution doesn't travel on tracks, so it can still be guided in the direction chosen by the man in the driver's seat.

Cardenas is not dictatorial, but he likes to get things done with as little friction as possible. Instead of throwing back-seat drivers out on their ears, as dictators are inclined to do, Cardenas will try to get them interested in co-operation. He'll hand one a road map to study, another will be assigned to keep an eye on the oil pressure gauge, and so on. Some critics call it buying off the opposition with jobs. And it is true that a number of men who carried the torch of anti-Callismo in the press and on the rostrum, but outside the pale of the official party, and who would naturally, then, be opposed to a program engendered by Calles, now have government jobs. Most of these returned prodigal sons—who consider themselves the real exponents of the Revolution—are veteran Carranza men of 1917, in favor of the Revolution, but according to their interpretation.

Cardenas went at running the federal government with the same discipline he followed as a soldier. He saw that things had to be done—definite objectives, if you please, to be achieved—and he had confidence enough in himself and the desirability of those objectives to make concessions that would help the main end. Some of his advisers told him he was being too lenient, that he was making too many personal concessions, and urged him to ditch the disturbers, just as later they wanted him to rattle the saber all over San Luis Potosi and take advantage of the Cedillo revolt to establish a nation-wide military dictatorship.

But Cardenas would rather conciliate, if the other fellow is willing to meet him halfway. An interesting anecdote is told of his period as governor of Michoacan. He was just taking over the reins and was trying to institute his program of schools and land distribution on a scale then unattempted. A young lawyer with an opposition paper kept riding the administration. That same situation in other States had led to wrecking of print shops, assassination of editors, harassing of their families. It was an old story under Diaz, under Calles, and other hard-boiled chiefs of the Revolution. Governor Cardenas called the young fellow in, asked him just what he was driving at, what he had to offer in place of the points he was attacking. Cardenas liked the young editor's ideas, invited him to collaborate. Cardenas got an alert young brain to help him, and the oppositionist paper became pro-

Cardenas. The same lawyer later coached him on making speeches in his campaign—a big help to Cardenas, then a timid orator. This policy, applied on a larger scale in his federal administration, has brought him good returns politically. At times it recalls a portion of the Obregon formula—for winning over rebellious generals: "I give them a shot—with a bullet if I can, or with a fifty-thousand peso wad of bank notes." Some wads have been going, indirectly, through government positions, to politicians who helped finance the Cardenas presidential campaign. These political obligations, which the Cardenas nature can't take lightly, are causing him a great deal of embarrassment, providing clear targets for the opposition pot-shots.

But Cardenas goes at the main tasks with hammer and tongs: building schools, unifying labor, distributing lands, unifying the peasantry, returning the army to civil roles, with the feeling that he is at least laying foundations that his successors, if they happen to be so inclined, will have a hard time blasting. In his attitude he seems almost to echo the prophetic words of Calles during the latter's campaign in 1923:

"I am armed with the conviction . . . blind faith in the triumph of our cause, and if by some fatality it should be defeated because the obstacles reared by the reaction prove too difficult for me to overcome, another will surely rise tomorrow, and triumph, for the redemption of the masses, liberty, human improvement, is, in the final analysis, the force of progress, and this can be halted by no one."

Some writers have called Cardenas the No. 1 agitator of Latin America, apostle of anti-imperialism, cheer-leader of nationalism, barker for Bolshevism. But there are a couple of agitators in Mexico that outshine Cardenas and all other human agitators. They are greater because they aim at abolition of personalist government, that curse of Mexican history, and would set up in its place government by institutions that will outlast the men who make them. These two star agitators of Mexico are the Constitution of 1917 and its streamlined vehicle, the Six-Year Plan.

VII

STAR AGITATORS

1

A BOTTLE of champagne—Vicomte F. Cantellane, Epernay—awaits the Last Man of 1917. For safekeeping, it is deposited in the vaults of the National Museum of Mexico. The bottle was put away on April 13, 1917, sent there after the banquet at which some two hundred delegates celebrated the final passage, on February 5, of the constitution designed to transform the social structure of Mexico. On a slightly faded label the words written by Venustiano Carranza, then president of the Republic, can still be read: "To be drunk by the last survivor of the constitutional convention."

At Tacabuya, a suburb of Mexico, in house number 33 of a street called the Dead End of the Revolution, an aged journalist breathed his last on August 13, 1938. His name was Ciro B. Ceballos. This man had been one of the delegates to the Constitutional Convention, had won his seat in that famous gathering at Queretaro for his unrelenting fight against the Diaz dictatorship. No champagne was drunk at Ceballos' funeral. In fact, his family had to borrow the money to bury him decently. Forgotten, in a state of bitter poverty, the man who had spent several terms in the Belem dungeon for writing anti-Diaz articles, the man who had written several novels—best-sellers in their day—achieved the posthumous glory of an editorial in the government party newspaper. The champagne has probably turned to vinegar by now, and the Constitution of 1917, inspiration of a new generation, has turned sour to the political palates of some men who signed the historic document.

2

The pedigree of the new constitution traces back to the Reform Constitution of 1857, which in turn is an outgrowth of the first Republic's constitution promulgated in 1824. The first constitution shows the influence of the French Revolution as well as of the United States' basic charter, and the defensive republican forms regarded as necessary to protect the young American nations from threats of renewed European intervention. This was the epoch of the Holy Alliance—Austria, Prussia, Russia—and its plan to aid Spain in regaining its American colonies and to help stem the tide of representative government. In this period the Monroe Doctrine was born, and Great Britain, hoping to stop a resurgence of Spanish power, hastened to recognize the independence of Mexico. Among Mexican leaders the big argument was whether to establish a centralist or federalist republic. The federalists finally won. Republican in form, the 1824 Constitution still carried over many of the social ideas of the preceding epoch, and the Catholic Church still had an official monopoly on religion by an article forbidding all other creeds. The social relationships underwent only minor modifications; the basic class relationships remained more or less the same. Instead of the big shots in Spain running the show, the resident big shots moved in after the independence movement. The rise of the native middle class continued in zigzag fashion as the arch-conservative elements, allied with the high clergy, tried to check the growth of the liberalism that was a part of the industrial revolution. The unceasing struggles between the conservatives and liberals reached a new climax in the Wars of the Reform, preceding the United States Civil War

by a decade, and coming ten years after Mexico's war with the
United States. The Reform Wars, from which Benito Juarez
emerged as the national hero, marked a definite triumph for
the liberalist forces, and brought to an end the all-pervasive
influence of the Church. This epoch produced the Constitution of 1857, which in turn led to the Reform Laws that gave
Mexican political evolution its new direction.

The Constitution of 1857 recognized natural and inalien-
able rights of man, as well as popular sovereignty, established
the federal form of government with executive, judicial and
legislative powers and paved the way for the Juarez law of
1859 which established freedom of religious worship. It
definitely sought to separate Church and State, provided for
nationalization of Church property, made marriage a civil
contract, prohibited convents and seminaries, and included
other familiar phenomena of the bourgeois antifeudal revolution. The Juarez constitution and laws also re-opened the
bitter fight over land, still going on, as a result of their provisions forbidding ownership of land by civil corporations.
Aimed originally at Church property, the scope of these
measures was such as to include community-owned lands
which formed the basis of many peasants' livelihood, and
prepared for the wide-scale land absorption by hacendados,
a fundamental cause of the anti-Diaz revolution.

Sixty years of hectic evolution marked the period between
the Juarez epoch and the Constitution of 1917, a period distinguished by the rise to power and the violent fall of one of
Mexico's outstanding political figures: Porfirio Diaz, through
whom the advancing bourgeoisie sought to perpetuate a
class dictatorship. The Diaz epoch, for which certain writers
like Owen P. White work up a nostalgic recollection of
"peace, gentle peace," was a period of blood-and-iron rule,
and the peace it proclaimed was enjoyed only by a favored
few. For the rest of the country, the Diaz epoch provided an-

other kind of peace—the peace of forced labor, contract labor, the peace of submission in the face of bayonets, the peace of no appeal from the insolence of office, the peace of slave-plantations, massacre of thousands, peace of starvation, dead souls, the grave. The fake peace of the Porfirio Diaz epoch—the violent suppression of inevitable economic and social conflicts seeking solution through legality—sired the real war that followed. Without a Diaz, perhaps there would have been no need for a Villa or a Zapata.

The Diaz epoch was also a period of national consolidation, of intensive development, building of railways, clearing of timber, spread of huge plantations, discovery of oil, influx of foreign capital seeking bigger returns than it could get at home. Diaz had distinguished himself as an officer in the liberal battalions that backed Benito Juarez. He turned against Juarez in 1871 on the issue of the latter's re-election, and went into exile. Meanwhile, Juarez died and was succeeded by Sebastian Lerdo de Tejada in 1872. The fight between expanding United States capitalism and British capitalism in the territory formerly held by Spain developed into a battle for government concessions in Mexico. The new president, Lerdo de Tejada, was partial to the British on the theory that Mexico's protection lay in encouraging European capital to counterbalance the growing threat of United States hegemony.

Lerdo de Tejada's announcement of plans for re-election, after having fought the re-election proposals of Juarez, stirred a new revolt in 1876, from which Porfirio Diaz arose as the central figure. In his Plan de La Noria of 1871, Diaz proclaimed against oligarchies and indefinite re-election. His manifesto concluded:

"Let no citizen impose himself nor perpetuate himself in the exercise of power, and this will be the last revolution."

During his term in office, Diaz amended the constitution

with a decree which prohibited re-election of the President
and State governors. Then, after repealing the no-re-election
laws, he went about consolidating a dictatorship marked by
six re-elections of Diaz, an oligarchy rule that lasted for
thirty-four years. The theory behind the repeal of the no–
re-election amendment: no–re-election prevents the free exercise of suffrage, hence it is much more democratic to permit
a nation to choose its rulers without such restrictions on suffrage. The fact is that the ruling clique, facing the tempting
offers of a big influx of capital, wanted a "strong man" and
they found him in Porfirio Diaz.

By 1900, the hogging of power by the Diaz oligarchy—
made effective through the terrorism of dictatorship, suppression of free speech and assembly, the guarantee of foreign
support by putting the nation's resources in hock through
budget-balancing loans—had become a heavy drag on the
people of Mexico. Getting rid of this new ball-and-chain
became the paramount political task of the Mexican people.
The turn of the century found the anti-Diaz sentiment seep-
ing through the caprock of suppression like the bubbling
flow of petroleum that was finding outlets after ages of imprisonment inside the earth. But any possible leader of the
people soon found himself in Belem dungeon or San Juan de
Ulua fortress, or in the hold of a slave ship bound for the
"Green Siberia" of Campeche.

The coming events which were to find formal expression
in the 1917 Constitution cast their first well-defined shadows
in the city of San Luis Potosi on February 5, 1901. Three
hundred men from all parts of the country gathered there in
the first Mexican Liberal Congress, and formed the Mexican
Liberal Party. The unifying force of this new movement
was the unanimous desire of labor, the peasantry and the
middle classes to get rid of the Diaz oligarchy. Prior to this
period there had been steady opposition developing, but

without any attempt at unification: Filomeno Mata, Daniel Cabrera and other courageous journalists; speakers in clandestine meetings of Liberal clubs honeycombed with Diaz spies; a few scattered labor organizers, many men filled with a yearning for liberty strong enough to make them stick their necks in a noose by assailing the dictatorship.

The binder that held these men together was hatred of the common enemy, Diaz, but the real power of the movement was the uninformed, inarticulate mass of the population: the peasant separated from the land, the factory worker made a cog of the machine, the trader and the small farmer harassed by arbitrary taxation and by commodity monopolies of official favorites. The stolid weight of the human mass could no longer be moved by vague formulas of justice and reform. In addition to these, it needed more concrete aims, and once set in motion it would obey the law of physics which applies to all matter; i.e., the greater the inertia the greater the momentum. The first Liberal Congress adopted a program which included land distribution to the peasants, the right to strike, the eight-hour day, social insurance. Camilo Arriaga, Juan Sarabia, Antonio Diaz Soto y Gama, Humberto Macias Valades, Ricardo Flores Magon, were names that figured prominently in this early movement.

The second congress of the Liberal Party was raided by Diaz police, the leaders imprisoned, repression intensified. Many fled into exile to save their lives. On July 1, 1906, the exiled leaders of the Liberal Party issued a manifesto from St. Louis, Missouri, signed by Ricardo Flores Magon, Juan Sarabia, Antonio I. Villarreal, Enrique Flores Magon, Librado Rivera, Manuel Sarabia and Rosalio Bustamante. This manifesto was rejected as "utopian" by hacienda owners and upper middle-class groups who saw no need of sweeping changes. They supported the Liberal Party because they wanted to get rid of the Diaz crowd. They felt that all the country needed was a change of faces, and some slight modifications in legislation to give new men a whack at public office, and to dissipate a few monopolies.

But Ricardo Flores Magon, and the little group of Mexican exiles who suffered persecution and imprisonment in the United States for their periodical, *Regeneracion,* had no patience with the minor reforms proposed. The brains of these men burned with a flame of liberty far too bright for the "practical" men of affairs who opposed Diaz. Yet the practical measures proposed by the "dreamers," such as minimum wages, eight-hour day, abolition of child labor, and many others, were the things that brought the men of Mexico out to fight. Diaz had closed the roads to gradual social reform. Mexico tried hard to get back on the road. It needed new vehicles, just as many Indians of Tabasco and Chiapas needed some new vehicle that would get them to the market centers during the time when the roads were impassable because of the steady tropical rains. The Indians finally found their vehicle in the airplane. It would seem ludicrous to tell these Indians that before riding in airplanes they must do as people had done in the past: first change to horse-and-buggy, then to horseless carriages, then to streamlined automobiles, and, when they had become accustomed to these, they would be "ripe" for riding in such new-fangled contraptions as airplanes.

One of Diaz' excuses for remaining in power was that the Mexican people were not yet "ripe" for self-government. To the advance guard of the Mexican Revolution the situation was simple and clear. Mexico needed a new vehicle to get out of the social-economic jungle of Diazism. And the tragedy of Francisco I. Madero, destined to lead the anti-Diaz revolt at the most intense moment, was that he thought he had climbed into a horseless carriage and found himself at the controls of an airplane that was moving faster, much faster, than he wanted to go. Madero, known as the "apostle of freedom," got planesick, was hacked down by Huerta in 1913. The blood of the Huerta counter-revolution, an orgy of slaughter, washed away the last illusions about the possibility of surface changes, mere changes of men, and stirred the nation to seek some fundamental readjustment. This new drive found expression in the Carranza movement, the formal beginning of the Mexican Revolution as it is known today. It matured in the Constitution of 1917, cornerstone of Mexico's reconstruction epoch, which still continues today.

3

The men who gathered in Queretaro City's Iturbide Theater for the seventy days of wrangling debate, birth pangs of the new constitution, brought to that convention the distilled essence that rose from decades of national ferment. The last few years were a steaming mess of armed revolution and counter-revolution. The men in Queretaro remodeled the 1857 Constitution into a new document which reflected the troubled past. From that day to this, the fight has raged over constitutional interpretation, and will probably be raging for many days to come. A number of the founding fathers are still around and active. Their paternal emotions vary. Some look upon their work with disappointment, see a noisy, snot-nosed, window-smashing brat instead of the well-behaved, polite and correct little man they had expected. Others behold a healthy, joyous, vivacious, growing kid who's glad to be alive, and shows it, and they are delighted that he has not turned out to be a sissy.

The debates over Article 130 were related to those on Article 3, and the aim of both was obviously to combat the renewed preponderance that the Church had acquired in educational and social matters during the Diaz period. Diaz, a

Mason, persistently refused to abolish the Juarez laws that
had nationalized Church property, and had restricted political activities of the clergy. But he had winked at violation of
these laws, and permitted the clergy to gain in power and
prestige, realizing, perhaps, that the Church could be of service in neutralizing discontent which might arise over the
hard Diaz rule. Article 3 definitely made public education a
government function, and took the Church out of the schools
by providing secular education. Article 130 set up a rigid
separation of Church and State.

Article 27 brought the Mexican government Don Quixotes
full tilt against the oil derricks of John Bull and Uncle Sam,
into the cold reality of foreign imperialism that wasn't going
to permit a little thing like a constitution to break up the
joyous picnic of profits. And its provisions for distribution of
land to the peasants found renewed opposition from the land
lords who had been willing to see a change of administration,
but not any alterations in their holdings. Article 27 established probably the most radical (its opponents called it
retrograde) principle possible under the capitalist economic
system: the social-democratic principle that property in land
corresponds originally to the State, and that private property
is a concession granted by the State. Inherent in this granting
of private property, of course, was the right to withdraw such
concession. It added, further, that "the Nation shall at all
times have the right to impose on private property the modalities deemed of public interest," as well as to regulate the use
of natural resources in order "to make an equitable distribution of public wealth and to guard its conservation." The
concept of landed property regarded as public domain was
extended to all subsoil deposits, specifically naming the hydro-
carbons, liquid, solid or gaseous, in order to cover the petroleum lands which had been left out of previous constitutions.
The Carranza government had, before this, paved the way for

breaking up the landed estates by the famous decree of January 6, 1915, that provided distribution of lands to the peasants. Attempts by the conservatives to limit the program to statutory legislation were overridden by the strong agrarian bloc in the convention, which insisted on establishing the constitutional basis for a permanent policy.

The article which provoked the longest hours of discussion was Article 123, regarded by Mexican labor as its Magna Charta. The original draft of the Carranza constitution submitted to the convention contained but a brief paragraph relating to industrial employer-employee problems, couched in vague terms that left the road wide open to future changes. When it was submitted to the gathering, a score of delegates rose to speak against it. For a moment, there was consternation among the Laborites, but they soon found that the opposition did not have its origin in an attempt to restrict protections for labor, but rather to enlarge upon the safeguards. This pressure of laborism led to the formulation of an entire new article in the constitution, one of the longest and most specific articles in that document, to take the place of the small paragraph that the original draft had timidly put forward.

Article 123—not to be made fully part of the nation's statutes until passage of the Federal Labor Law in 1931—opened the door to organization of labor, a factor which was to play a large part in the rise of Alvaro Obregon to the presidency in 1920 after the downfall of Carranza, who died ignominiously earlier the same year. While Carranza was slain in a trap that had been laid for him, the "brains" of his administration, a lawyer known variously as Luis Cabrera, Blas Urrea and Lucas Ribera, the latter two anagrams of his name, hid in a cave. On the condition that he put himself in a political cave, Cabrera's life was spared. His clash with the Obregon group came over his newly formulated slogan, "The

Revolution must be stopped," to take the place of the one he had used to justify earlier high-handed confiscations by the Carranza regime: "The Revolution is the Revolution."

By March, 1938, Cabrera had done pretty well by himself, having accumulated a goodly fortune as counsel for big corporations and through his prolific writings, in which he appears as spearhead for the permanent rightist opposition. During the Cardenas administration, and notably since the critical stages of the petroleum controversy, Cabrera came completely out of his political cave to take up the cudgels for the poor abused oil companies. This automatically made him a tart critic of Cardenas and Cardenas' policies and started talk again about making him a presidential candidate on an independent ticket in 1940. He turned down the nomination offered him in 1934.

Cabrera writes well, in a biting, ironic style that is perfect for his role of permanent oppositionist, and has a flair for coining phrases that stick like barbs in his opponents' flesh. He capped a polemic with Vicente Lombardo Toledano, head of the Mexican Workers' Confederation, by a play on Toledano's name, referring to him as "Atole Dando," a phrase from an old saw known to all Mexicans. Some of the very respectable friends of this very cultivated gentleman questioned the taste of such rhetorical coups but none questioned their psychological effectiveness. Another example of Cabrera wit: his reference to the government's Department of Press and Publicity—using the alphabetical designation by which it is familiar—as the Department of Presidential Praise. Fly in the Cabrera political ointment: a daughter of his married an American who edits *Mexican Labor News* for the Workers' University. Nasty things his opponents recall: Cabrera's forced loans, his issuance of worthless paper money, during his term as Minister of Finance in the Carranza cabinet. Cabrera is an editorial stand-by of the magazine, *Hoy* (Today) , a wide-awake, expertly handled, illustrated weekly, one of the favorite mediums for Hitlerites, Mussolinians and Francoists, and also the drainpipe for the totalitarian notions that flow from the faucets of Mexican fascism.

Cabrera and his school, a group of writers in *Los Ecos,* a political weekly which appeared during the fall of 1938, are the continuation of the tendency which they like to regard as the "orthodox" tendency in the Mexican movement, to which they refer as the "Revolution of Then" or the "democratic" as contrasted to the "Revolution of Now" or the "Bolshevik." These two trends were plainly visible in the Queretaro convention. At the time the opposing groups were known as the "Renovators" and the "Jacobins." Far and away the two most prominent orators, the two most decisively shaping influences in that historic meeting, were Jacobin Francisco Mugica, now Minister of Communications and Public Works, and Renovator Felix Fulgencio Palavicini.*

General Mugica, compactly built, stocky, short, baldish, ruddy, square-jawed, has an air of careless dynamism about him, like an idling motor. He is a leftist from way back, an ardent reformer who headed the constitutional convention committee that was given the Carranza project for definite formulation. At that time in his early thirties, Mugica was a popular figure in the convention, with his high-domed forehead, thick wavy hair and his imposing, upturning mustache which has been trimmed down proportionately to the thinning of the hair on his head. Some people call him the "Lenin of Mexico" and see a certain physical resemblance as well as a similarity in the social philosophies of the two men.

---

* On January 2, 1939, Palavicini was appointed Mexican ambassador to Argentina. On January 17, Mugica resigned his Cabinet post, presumably to run for president. The same day Minister of National Defense Avila Camacho also resigned to become a presidential candidate.

Inclusion of the social reforms in the body of the new constitution was regarded as a triumph for the young army officer from Michoacan, and when the final session was adjourned, fellow delegates lifted him to their shoulders and carried him to his residence. He suffered one defeat at the convention, however, the defeat of an article upon which he had set his heart: a proposal for establishing nation-wide prohibition of intoxicating liquors, prohibition of all games of chance, of cock-fighting, and—most audacious of all—abolition of bull-fighting! Some of the very sophisticated delegates at the gathering, nursing hangovers, beat down these proposals, suggesting that they were not basic, and should be left to local option. The anti-alcoholists charged that the liquor-makers, especially the *pulque* hacienda owners, had spent large sums of money to kill the plan.

Among the allies of Mugica in the Jacobins' efforts to make fundamental revisions in the 1857 Constitution was General Heriberto Jara, more interested in educational reforms than in fighting on the battlefield, although he has a good military record. Jara went into the Revolution from the Rio Blanco textile mills. He worked there at the time of the famous strike in which Porfirio Diaz' soldiers fired on the strikers after the hated company-store, where employees were forced to trade, had been set afire. Jara, now a white-haired dramatic figure who looks more like a composer than a general, is to-day Director of Military Education in the Mexican Army, and an important aid in Cardenas' program of "civilizing" the Army, abolishing the former policy in which the uniform was a bar to civic rights and duties.

In Tinguindin, a hamlet in the mountains of Michoacan, President Cardenas' home State, General Mugica was born on September 4, 1884. Son of a country schoolmaster, he traveled with his father throughout the State, learned at the roots the problems of the Indians and farm-folk. Like so

many other men who later became bitter enemies of the
clergy, young Mugica was educated in a Church school. He
joined the Madero forces from the beginning of that movement. When the Revolution was proclaimed on November
20, 1910, he was already a lieutenant in the anti-Diaz army,
military continuation of the anti-Diaz fight he had been
waging in the press. The 1913 Huerta counter-revolution
found Mugica a captain in Carranza's anti-Huerta army,
under General Lucio Blanco, for whom he was chief of staff.

Blanco and Mugica made agrarian history by performing
the first parceling of lands in the Mexican Revolution. This
action, taken on an hacienda near the border city of Matamoros, Tamaulipas, opposite Brownsville, Texas, provoked
the displeasure of Carranza, who had been a senator in the
Diaz congress, and who wanted everything done legal-like
even in the heat of a revolutionary surge. The distribution
of lands to the peasant-soldiers near Matamoros roused agrarian hopes, and caused skeptical European revolutionaries to
exclaim that now they believed that the Mexican revolution
was really a Revolution.

In 1916 Mugica went to the troubled State of Tabasco, later
to become the domain of Garrido Canabal, as military governor. This was after a year as customs chief in Tampico
where somebody had been needed to keep close watch on oil
exports. Prior to his arrival at the constitutional convention,
Mugica had assignments as military commander in various
states. By the time he got to Queretaro, then, he was prepared
to discuss many phases of Mexico's social and political puzzle,
not only prepared to discuss, however, but to insist that
something be done. It was this insistence that finally pushed
through the reforms which became known as Article 123.

During his term as governor of Michoacan, a post in which
he was Cardenas' predecessor, Mugica put the stamp of his
ideas on the legislation of the State. He pursued enforcement

of social reform laws and establishment of schools with the same vigor he showed in fighting for constitutional revisions at the convention. Mugica returned to active politics in 1933 as one of Cardenas' campaign managers. The new President appointed him Minister of National Economy and then, following the ousting of the Callistas, made him Minister of Communications and Public Works. In that post, Mugica is entrusted with carrying into effect the most tangible portions of the Six-Year Plan: highways, railroads, irrigation works, bridges, public buildings.

4

The conservatively inclined Renovators and lukewarm delegates were willing to insert a vague declaration to the effect that it was within the province of the State to regulate relations between employer and employee. But the Jacobins wanted more binding guarantees that the State would act, and concrete directions as how it would act. They got what they wanted, a revolutionary innovation in political constitutions, full and detailed groundwork for a new branch of jurisprudence, a new legal instrument for employer-employee matters, destined to guide Mexico's turn to the left, and to become a powerful political lever that eventually overturned Calles' steam roller.

Unlike most political charters, and different from what many delegates had expected, the 1917 Constitution did not merely state what was already an accomplished fact, merely give a name to a child already born. Rather, it opened the way for future reforms, that later converted the Constitution of 1917 into Mexico's prize agitator. The Mexican clergy a short time later issued a statement refusing to recognize the validity of that constitution. Article 123 stated explicitly that the Congress "shall pass laws . . . on the following bases," and then listed, among others: eight-hour day (seven hours for night work) ; special protection for women—no night work, no heavy work during the last three months of pregnancy, one month's leave with pay following childbirth, two daily rest-periods to nurse infants, same pay as men when the same work is performed, weekly day of rest; minimum wage; restrictions on child labor; employees' share in profits; double pay for overtime, and limitations on overtime; housing for workers and establishment of public markets in all work centers; compensation for occupational sickness and accidents; hygienic and safety measures in factories; right to organize for both employers and workers; right to strike or shut-down, according to regulations; establishment of arbitration and conciliation boards; legalization of labor contracts, collective and individual; social security measures.

Some of these provisions have been put into enabling legislation, principally through the Federal Labor Law of 1931, and the rest are still in the constitution, subject to statutory enactment, to amendment, or to continuing in abeyance.

It was the contention of the less intransigent conservatives at the Queretaro convention that the institutions would be stronger and more enduring if they were made as moderate as possible without sacrificing basic solutions. Champion of this point of view, the "democratic" as against the radical was Felix F. Palavicini, engineer by profession, political journalist by choice, campaign manager for Madero. A polished orator, he led the fight of the Renovators to guide the revolutionary current into the channels indicated by Carranza, to divert it from the radical agrarianism, laborism and the passionate anti-clericalism of the Jacobins.

Palavicini carried on his political fight in print for years after the constitutional convention had ended, and became one of the unquestioned daddies of modern journalism in Mexico, first maestro of several leading Mexican newspaper-

men of today. He founded *El Universal,* today Mexico's
biggest newspaper, among other journals, and kept up a constant fight with the anti-Carranza politicians who were push-
ing forward under the laborite banner. This put him behind
the eight ball as "an enemy of the labor movement" and gave
him tough sledding in his new journalistic enterprise.

5

The Mexican government's Six-Year Plan of action is
pretty explicit about what it wants, and how it is going to be
got. When this document was published by the National
Revolutionary Party in 1933 as a governmental program for
the next six years, few took it seriously. Mexico has been
used to flaming oratory, to utopian manifestoes, to word-
pictures of the new era done with all the plastic talent Mexicans show in their painting and handicrafts. And Mexico has
been used to seeing all these rosy promises go with the wind.
The Six-Year Plan was just another one of those things. To
a lot of people, but not to Lazaro Cardenas. He solemnly
swore to carry it into effect, read the Plan over and over until
it became a very part of him.

Early in 1933, Calles told newspapermen:

". . . and the time has come to formulate a detailed
program of action that will cover the six years of the
next presidential period; a program based on calculations, on statistics, on the lessons of experience. We
must study what we can accomplish, given the possibilities of our budgets and our reality. . . . I know that other,
more radical programs may be presented. To make
social experiments at the expense of the masses' hunger
is a crime. All persons who propose plans and projects
which cannot be carried into effect are insincere. They
know they lie. They think that later it will be easy to be-
tray their platforms and evade their promises. Of course,
they deceive themselves. They will not then know how to

escape from their own traps, and the masses will not pardon them, but will end by crushing them. . . ."

Candidate Cardenas, referring to the Six-Year Plan:

". . . The agrarian program will be completely solved, aid will be given for the organization of the United Front of Labor so that the raising of the standard of living may become a reality, the educational program needed by the masses will be carried out, and, in short, there will be realized in its totality, the doctrine for which General Calles has been fighting, to make of Mexico a strong and responsible country. . ."

The paternity of the Six-Year Plan is obscure. Its origins were really much humbler than the finished document would indicate. It started out as a campaign platform to be presented to the 1933 national convention of the National Revolutionary Party (PNR), Calles' organization. The fact that it was drawn up in the depth of the depression partially explains the sweeping formulation it took, in answer to mass unrest. The Plan was contemporary with the NRA and the growth of alphabetical agencies in the United States. The PNR committee to draw up the platform included the three leading presidential candidates, among them Cardenas.

Abelardo Rodriguez was president of the country at the time, named after Calles had ousted Ortiz Rubio. When the PNR announced its platform committee, Rodriguez immediately appointed a "technical advisory committee" that included Minister of Finance Alberto J. Pani, rich banker and property owner; Communications Minister Miguel M. Acosta, an army general; Education Minister Narciso Bassols; Labor Department Head Juan de Dios Bojorquez; and Minister of National Economy Primo Villa Michel. This advisory committee eventually became the actual PNR platform committee.

At this time Calles, and Rodriguez, who was one of the neo-conservative native industrialists closest to Calles, represented the right wing of the PNR. As president, Rodriguez proposed to the committee a four-point program covering education, labor, agrarian matters, and public works. In his labor plank, Rodriguez suggested that an effort be made to "harmonize the interests—apparently opposed—of labor and capital." He also stressed the idea of creating national mining reserves.

A bitter feud had been developing between Pani, ultra-conservative banker and career public official who had served under many administrations, and Bassols, crusading educator. Bassols quit the platform committee, and Rodriguez' private secretary, Francisco Gaxiola, Jr., was appointed in his place. Through the influence of Calles, Pani was forced to resign from the cabinet. The platform committee had reached an impasse. Calles was appointed Minister of Finance and as such, head of the platform committee. The group met in the Tehuacan health-resort, of which Rodriguez was a partner, and under the guidance of the "Big Chief of the Revolution," put through the platform, which was submitted to the PNR convention in December, 1933.

What finally emerged as the Six-Year Plan, the platform for the next presidential term, was something quite different from the Calles-Rodriguez proposal. Besides this official project, many others came from various labor organizations; from States such as Veracruz, where social legislation had taken a more radical turn; from peasant federations. One of the significant additions—bitterly opposed by Rodriguez—was the plank on "Socialist Education," offered by Manlio Fabio Altamirano, who was later assassinated. Instead of a four-point program, the Six-Year Plan became a complete restatement of the PNR's social, economic and political position, calling for sweeping reorganization. The emphasis of the completed document was definitely left-wing, and caused the Calles-Rodriguez faction so much concern that it insisted the Plan start at once in order to canalize legislation before the agrarian radicals and laborites moved in.

The original idea was to begin the Six-Year Plan on December 1, 1934, the date when Cardenas would receive the presidential band from the outgoing chief executive, Abelardo L. Rodriguez. But at the last minute a change was made and Rodriguez mapped out his last eleven months as president to fit in with the first year of the Plan, officially started on January 1, 1934. Among important portions of the Plan initiated during the Rodriguez term were Socialist Education and Minimum Wage legislation, and reform of the labor laws. The Plan, then, enters its final year on January 1, 1939.

State-directed economy is explicitly called for in the Plan. The Plan is described by its authors as marking the end of one epoch and the beginning of another, and as containing a "precise definition of our economic nationalism . . . a policy of legitimate self-defense."

In agrarian matters, the Plan holds that the limits to distribution of land and water will be reached only when all the agricultural needs of the rural population centers are satisfied.

The chapter on labor proposes to make unionization an obligatory point in all labor contracts, and affirms the individual's right to a job as a "consequence of the duty which society places on him of contributing his efforts to collective development." It definitely upholds the State's right to regulate labor relations, and: ". . . the State shall exercise vigilance so that the unions carry out their social functions as efficaciously as possible, without . . . becoming instruments of oppression within the classes they represent," which opens the way to political control over labor unions. This phrase was submitted by Rodriguez who, alarmed at the trend of the convention, sought to forestall what he described as "abuses of the labor leaders." Rodriguez was an ardent advocate of compulsory arbitration.

Attention, Standard Oil, Royal Dutch Shell, American Smelting and Refining Company, et al: ". . . the subsoil will be nationalized . . . measures will be taken to prevent foreign companies from continuing to monopolize mineral deposits . . . federal zones will be extended in order to protect permanently the nation's oil reserves."

Limitation of free competition, measures for fixing of prices, centralization and simplification of taxes, are called for in the Plan.

In addition to the measures which definitely mark out an era of controlled economy, the Plan provides a detailed constructive program, fitting for any progressive administration: public works, schools, highways, public health measures, social welfare matters, stimulating of commerce and industry. The sections on education state that the schools shall teach "the socialist doctrine sustained by the Mexican Revolution."

VIII

THE LITTLE RED SCHOOLHOUSE

1

TARGET practice has become part of the Mexican school-teachers' routine. To be quick on the draw and to fire fast and straight are as important as book-learning in the life of the public schoolteacher, especially in the rural areas. And again it is that Great Agitator—the Constitution of 1917, through its Article Three—which raised the steady pressure of land lord and clerical opposition to a new high pitch, led to violence on the teachers, ushered in the era of six-shooter-schoolma'ams. In self-defense, the poorly-paid teachers demanded that the government give them arms and ammunition. It was no mere academic request: Since March 8, 1935, when President Lazaro Cardenas signed the enabling act for the amended Article Three, establishing Mexican socialist education in the grade schools, nearly three hundred teachers, men and women, have been murdered, and many others tortured brutally, mutilated, raped and kidnaped.

2

Folks around the town of Acambaro, State of Guanajuato, had learned to like the new young schoolmaster who came from Mexico City early in 1938. Practically a kid himself—he was twenty-four—Juan Martinez de Escobar played with the school kids, visited their homes, became acquainted with the parents. Young Martinez de Escobar was typical of the new generation of federal teachers, drastically different from the old knuckle-busters who used to try to beat instruction into the children. And people in those days were glad to have even the old type of teacher, for they felt lucky to get any at all. Government schools were few and far between, in the Diaz days, the Church schools were even scarcer, and you had to be awfully "nice people" to get in.

The schoolmaster didn't act at all like the monster, the ogre, the very devil himself, that people had been told the Reds in Mexico City were going to send. All in all, he was quite a regular fellow, made no soapbox speeches, became part of the town's life. After school hours and on Sundays, he organized ball games, other athletic events, gatherings where there were singing and recitations. One thing that bothered him was the existence of feuds between various towns and villages, ancient grudges that traced back to fights for farming lands, to political intrigues, and in more recent days to the turmoil that followed the fall of Diaz. Trying to end these grudges, to transform them into a friendly rivalry which would help the people of different towns get acquainted with one another, the teacher arranged athletic contests in which teams from neighboring towns competed.

About seven o'clock on the evening of Sunday, June 12, 1938, Martinez de Escobar, two other teachers, and fifteen Acambaro school kids were returning in two automobiles from Hidalgo, about fifty miles away. They had gone there for a football game with the Hidalgo team. Professors and kids were talking about the game, some were singing, a few had dozed off.

A volley of shots from the side of the road, the clatter of stomping horses, commands to halt, brought the party to a stop at La Venta, a turn in the road, about a mile or so out of Acambaro. Armed men—twenty-five or thirty of them—surrounded the automobiles, ordered everybody out, searched the men, crowded the kids against the cars. The bandits saw there wasn't any money in the crowd, and fooled around, insulting the teachers, trying to provoke them, but apparently with intentions of just frightening them. The whole picture changed when a bandit found a pistol hidden under the front seat of one of the automobiles.

"Whose gun?" demanded the chief of the band.

"It belongs to the teacher—*el profesor,*" somebody answered, pointing to Martinez de Escobar.

"Oh, ho! So you're a teacher? Boys! Look, what fine game we've run into, and without hunting for it!"

The leader, called the "major," lined the children up in a semicircle, pushed the young teacher out in front, then said:

"I'm going to give you kids a lesson you'll never forget!"

He ordered two of his men to hold the teacher's arms pinned back, while two others beat him about the head, opening a big gash. They kept beating him until he dropped, limp. He wasn't quite knocked out and, still sprawled on the road, he raised his right arm to wipe the blood streaming down his face. The "major" pulled his gun, fired four times. Two bullets smashed the teacher's spinal column, one went through his lungs, another through his heart. The terrified kids scattered into the brush.

An unfinished scarf was among the objects placed in a cornerstone at the La Venta turn on August 18. The scarf was a wedding present for the teacher who was to have been married next September. The whole town turned out for the ceremony of laying the cornerstone for the monument to Martinez de Escobar. Even some of the mothers who were members of the Daughters of Mary, whose leaders told them not to have anything to do with these devils. A delegation from the teachers' union, the railway workers' union, students' society, Masonic lodge, marched to the site of the monument. The 18th Battalion band played a funeral march. School children sang the Athlete's Hymn, read short verses they had composed to the memory of the teacher. Colonel Roberto Calvo Ramirez delivered a eulogy: high mission of teachers, real fraternity of soldiers and teachers, both sons of the Revolution, the teacher fighting ignorance and the soldier fighting those who want to keep the people ignorant. A mound of flowers, covering the cornerstone, remained, as the kids, the women and the men, turned back to Acambaro.

3

Martinez de Escobar got off lightly compared to the treatment given some other teachers elsewhere. For instance, Maria Murillo, who taught in a rural school at Villa de Refugio, Zacatecas. She ran when a band of armed men rode toward the school. One of them lassoed her, tied the rope to his saddle and dragged her, feet first, over miles of rocks, literally tearing her to bits. Peasants gathered what they could find, buried the remains in three boxes.

On August 19, 1938, peasants in Tepames, Jalisco, sent word to Guadalajara, that they had found the body of a woman. She was identified as Maria de la Luz Avalos, a rural teacher, kidnaped the day before by the Medina gang.

In San Juan del Rio, State of Queretaro, Jose Luis Alfaro, nineteen, and Antonio Sanchez Rivas, twenty, rural schoolteachers who had only a few weeks back got their normal-school degrees, were murdered by a band of seven men. Rivas had eleven stab wounds, and mutilations reminiscent of lynch mobs. Alfaro was hacked with a machete in fourteen places, then shot in the head. Their bodies were being dragged to an irrigation dam when a group of farmers passed and spread the alarm. Five of the men were captured and said they killed to "give a Christmas present to the Virgin."

Their confession related that they were hired by the owner of a near-by hacienda, that they had killed forty men in all during the past year.

There were many others: Enriqueta Palacios, whose ears were cut off; Martin Sanchez, soles of his feet burned with live coals, then forced to walk over an ant-bed; Raul Maldonado, hanged; Pablo Jiminez, Juan Jiminez, David Moreno Ibarra, Apolonio Gonzalez, Alfonso Negrete, Flavio Gomez, Silvestre Gonzalez, Gilberto Mendez, Rosendo Martinez, Salustio Miranda, Enrique Rodriguez, Francisco Lopez. The list is long and bloody, a gruesome record of a systematic hunt for teachers by men shouting slogans so much alike and performing acts so much alike, in widely separated sections of the country, that the government felt it had reason to believe that they were acting under orders or encouragement from an identical source.

The Minister of Education ordered an inscription carved in stone letters placed across the width of the ministry patio. It said: "In homage to the rural teachers sacrificed for the ideal of socialist education." But the teachers wanted more than inscriptions. They asked that federal troops be assigned to guard the schools, that the government provide the teachers with arms and ammunition. The Ministry of National Defense finally authorized teachers to carry arms wherever they were believed to be in danger. Teachers were made members of the Rural Defense Corps into which peasants had been organized as auxiliaries of the federal army. That was in 1937. The attacks slowed down for a while when word got around that the teachers could shoot back. But the attacks did not stop. In July, 1938, the Union of Educational Workers complained to the President that twenty-five of their members had been murdered since the first of the year. The Union said that in most places no special measures were necessary, that armed teachers had definitely checked the attacks on them, but that in other places means were needed to repel the assaults, and that most of the teachers could not afford to buy guns. The Ministry of National Defense sent fifty rifles and pistols, five thousand rounds of ammunition, to each of thirty-three regional rural schools.

4

The slaying of schoolteachers did not begin with the Cardenas administration, nor with the Mexican socialist education amendment to the constitution. It has been going on ever since the federal government definitely took over education. The Ministry of Education had announced that it meant business in affirming that the task of providing schools and teachers is a function of the State. The big push to reestablish the school system got well under way with the Obregon administration in 1922. For two years during Obregon's term, the budget provided more money for the Ministry of Education than for the army, a sensational development in a country which had at that time been at war with itself for more than a decade. The school and the teacher not only represented inroads into revenue derived from private and Church schools. They also symbolized the government agrarian and labor program, anathema to the land lords.

Raids on schools and assassinations of teachers became part of the tactics of every guerrilla band that roamed the countryside. These developed on a large scale from 1926 to 1929, during the Cristero uprising, part of the State-Church fight that had flared anew with Calles' announced intentions of enforcing the constitutional provisions relating to the Church. The customary cry of school raiders—whether Cristeros or hacienda white guards or just plain bandits—became, "Long Live Christ the King! Death to the Communists!"

Back of the school fight, as of nearly every other major dispute in Mexico, is the fundamental antithesis of two opposed points of view: traditionalism and liberalism, the same opposition which divides men on issues of Catholicism and Protestantism, authoritarianism and republicanism, aristocracy and democracy. The Mexican paradox in this case is that the traditional authoritarians, the bitter opponents of liberalism and republicanism, are the ones who today clamor loudest for the very things—among them freedom of teaching—which their ideological predecessors, when they were in power, sought to suppress by blood and iron. And the inheritors of the liberalist trend find themselves adopting methods—they claim it is fighting fire with fire—that are branded by their opponents as authoritarian, dictatorial.

Just as big a paradox, if you wish to call it that, is the extraordinary tolerance of the Nazi religion and Hitler idolatry in a school system otherwise insulated against metaphysical intervention. There is the German school, for instance, in Mexico City, one of the oldest private schools in Mexico and with a reputation for solid teaching. Today the kids— and there are Mexican as well as foreign children enrolled— march in with a salute for Hitler's Swastika-draped photograph and the cabalistic "Heil Hitler." The children can't be taught, in public or private schools, that there is a God, a supernatural Being. But Hitler, in the Nazi school teachings, can be raised to Godhood. The Catholic catechism can't be taught because it involves "supernatural, metaphysical" instruction, but the pupils in the German school can be forced to memorize this mumbo jumbo: "I didn't think yesterday, I don't think today, I shall not think tomorrow, I don't want to think, I don't have to think, my Fuehrer thinks for me, what he commands I shall obey, and where he leads I shall follow!"

Whatever your attitude in these matters, however, whether you believe religious education should be part of the school system or that the priest should stick to his altar and confessional, there are certain glaring facts in the Mexican educational picture that nobody can deny. Undebatable is the strangle hold in which illiteracy and ignorance locked the development of the Mexican nation. The high percentage of illiteracy which still prevailed in Mexico at the turn of the century, nearly four hundred years after the Conquest had brought new gods, new masters and a new language, was a terrible indictment of the men who had held power over the centuries; an indictment, at least, in the eyes of an age in which people have learned to regard education as a right rather than a privilege. In 1900, after a quarter of a century of Diaz rule, seven out of every ten inhabitants over ten years of age in Mexico could neither read nor write Spanish. When the Obregon administration checked up in 1921, it found that there was improvement, but slight: the percentage of illiteracy was down to sixty-six. The population had grown, meanwhile, from 13,973,272 to 14,334,780, making it necessary to increase the number of schools at a greater rate.

Spreading the three r's in Mexico is more complex than it first appears. Besides a variety of races and dialects, the educator in Mexico runs into the problem of limited means of communication, lack of funds for buildings and materials, the extreme poverty of the people, which forces every child in the family to begin working at an early age (one breadwinner cannot support the family on the usual wages) ; and the ever-present crushing domination of the local political bosses; the land lords' hysterical fear of a peasantry that will read; the inclination to accept things as they are (God willed it thus), dregs of a preached meekness that did not inherit the earth.

In his "beautiful era of peace," Porfirio Diaz sometimes balanced the budget, by loans and concessions that helped put the country further in hock. Railroads were built. There were many years of good crops from soil that the hacendados left exhausted and unreplenished. One crop—the ultimate test of any nation—was neglected. That great mass of vitality, talent, courage—the common man of Mexico—was left uncultivated. In his gilded passage through the Mexican scene, Porfirio Diaz placed a lasting mark on many things. The legacy of illiteracy, which he left, far outweighs the positive achievements claimed for him. In tackling the mountainous problem of education, as in so many other problems, the men of the Mexican Revolution had to start from scratch. To move this mountain, they needed a new faith.

5

By seeking control of the public schools, the government in the Mexican Revolution from 1922 on entered the last stronghold of clerical influence, and perhaps in the long run the most important. The government moved full tilt now, no longer against the clergy itself, but in conflict with the prejudices of parents brought up in the Church. For the churchmen, the government educational program was more than an academic matter. It was not just a battle for the privilege of molding the plastic mind of young Mexico. For simultaneously with application of "lay" education provided in the 1917 Constitution, the Calles government in 1925 nationalized some twenty-one million pesos of Church property, which it planned to convert into schools and libraries that the limited federal budget could not provide. This blow in the pocketbook hurt, and more blows in the same direction were augured by the edict forbidding priests or religious organizations to establish primary schools, important for the seeds of doctrine to be planted there, and likewise important as significant sources of income. In the thick of the dispute, the Mexican clergy published a resolution passed some years before, disowning the 1917 Constitution.*

The opposition to the government school plans proved most effective outside of Mexico City, in the States where governors winked at violations of the Church laws, and where the lack of prepared schoolteachers led parents to seek private instructors. The benefits of this extra-legal tolerance were evident to some governors and other politicians with ambitions for bigger things. In some cases the public schools were completely neglected. In other cases, where the federal government opened schools, the State schools were immediately shut down. These and other obstacles continued to cross up the government school drive. Opening of new schools, either in transformed Church structures or in new buildings, continued. But the rub between the federal and State governments on these matters developed a movement in the left wing of the administration for federalization of education, a movement which still continued after the amendment of Article Three to provide Mexican socialist education.

That amendment, part of the Six-Year Plan, was regarded by the National Revolutionary Party left-wingers as an important instrument for federalizing education, and for definitely removing the influence of the clergy from the schools, both direct and through the parents. Passage of the amendment in 1933 provoked another acrimonious controversy between Church and State, eventually causing the resignation of Narciso Bassols, the Minister of Education. The furor arose from his announced intention of putting into effect the provisions of the amended article. President Rodriguez defended Bassols and in order to show where he stood, appointed

---

* The Church also refused to recognize earlier constitutions in which the "heresy" of Popular Sovereignty was set forth.

the resigned minister to the highest post in the cabinet, Secretary of the Interior. This was purely a gesture, however, and Bassols left the cabinet soon afterward. Before he left, however, he had brought a sex angle into pedagogy.

Bassols, reputedly author of the famous monetary law and regarded as one of the brain-trusters of the pre-Cardenas epoch, had a peculiar flair for getting a rise out of the churchmen. The Ministry of Education had prepared new curricula to substitute for the old ones, regarded as outmoded. Among the innovations was to be a course in physiology and hygiene that would begin in the lower grades and continue through the high-school grades. As announced in detail by the Ministry, the course contained more or less what is to be found in almost any elementary physiology text in our schools and a bit of "What Every Young Boy (or Girl) Ought to Know." It was a direct translation, in fact, of a standard physiology course in the United States. But Bassols dramatized it by calling it "Sexual Education." And he raised the roof. The opposition to government education seized this magnificent opportunity. For months a controversy raged, and the public at large got a wonderful sexual education.

Indignant parents, spurred on by a clergy jealous of its influence over children, clamored for the Minister's dismissal. "Sexual Education" gave them visions of shocking possibilities, and the enemy did what it could to make the visions more lurid. The original program of teaching the children about bees, trees, flowers, how a butterfly comes from a cocoon, chickens from eggs, plants from seeds and vice versa, pollenization and many other interesting facts of life, all faded from the public controversy. Meetings were held; pamphlets, manifestoes, booklets, editorials appeared, taking one side or the other. Bassols charged that the whole thing was clerical agitation aimed at nullifying Article Three of the Constitution, and that the meetings ostensibly protesting

"Sexual Education" always wound up with the cry of "Long Live Christ the King," and "Down with Article Three."

Freud, Havelock Ellis, Jung, psychiatrists and neurologists, foreign and Mexican, were invoked in newspaper articles discussing every phase of sex, normal, subnormal, abnormal and supernormal. The hypocrisy of sex attitudes and evils of the double-standard were attacked. Hands were raised in horror, the innocence of childhood was to be violated, it was charged, and whispered stories spread, about schools in which the classrooms were turned into infantile nudist camps and the most terrible things were going to happen. One side blamed the repression of sex matters by the Church teachings for the wrecking of many young lives. The other side said that the world had got along for thousands of years without Sexual Education and could go on as before. Occasionally a moderate voice arose, suggesting the argument be ended and that nature be permitted to take its course.

The furor had one effect that pleased the opponents of the reformed Article Three: it delayed passage of the enacting legislation. But the fight against the main enemy—Mexican socialist education—did not abate. Parents were warned not to place their children in public schools. A strike to keep children out of the schools was in effect. The government had to invoke legislation which made it compulsory to send children to school. The Church issued a long set of rules about socialist education, threatening ecclesiastical sanctions against parents who permitted children to attend the public schools. And teachers who taught socialist education were told that they were exposing themselves to excommunication. It was not until 1936, after Lazaro Cardenas had become president, that the enabling acts were passed and the government set about seriously reforming its whole system of education to conform to the program of Mexican socialist education.

6

Theoretical bases of this Mexican socialist school can be found in the "Plan of Action," published by the Ministry of Education in 1935. The "characteristics and aims" of the socialist primary school, as summarized from this Plan of Action, declared that the socialist school shall be:

1. Compulsory, so that all children of school age shall receive the benefits of education and so that non-attendance shall not develop because of misunderstandings, ignorance, negligence or for other reasons.

2. Free, so that nobody shall be deprived of the advantages of education because of economic reasons.

3. Of a welfare nature, where necessary, so that children suffering from malnutrition shall be provided with food, or with medical and other assistance.

4. Uniform, inspired by a social doctrine that will not vary from grade to grade.

5. Co-educational.

6. Integral, to cover physical, intellectual and social education.

7. Vitalist, to harmonize theory with practice, so children can learn by doing, and to help them understand social relationships to be faced as adults.

8. Scientific, to give a "real concept of the universe" based on the principles of causality and evolution.

9. Against fanaticism, to liberate the people from imposition of all forms of idolatry and superstition.

10. Orientating, to guide the student, to develop his special talents, to help him select a suitable vocation.

11. Favorable to manual training, which shall be compulsory in all grades.

12. Co-operativist, to develop in the pupil a sense of asso-

ciation and solidarity with the other pupils, to teach him to work in common and for the common good.

13. Liberating, to free the child from all prejudices and vices that arise in the social, economic, political or religious spheres, and to get rid of exploitation of human beings.

14. Mexican, to develop cultural, linguistic, ethnic unity, because the school is based on the historical experience and revolutionary traditions of the country. The school should "stress the peculiarities of our class struggles, and the great efforts of the masses to achieve emancipation, invoking the memories of the men who fought and lived in accordance with the ideals and interests of the proletariat."

The Plan of Action also contains a "Children's Bill of Rights" which lists a number of things that society owes the child and the duties which the child owes to society. Some of the rights are: to be born of healthy parents who are prepared in every way to bring up children properly; to receive proper nourishment; to develop talents and latent capacities, regardless of race, creed, economic or social position; to have sanitary, ventilated, well-equipped schoolrooms, fresh air, recreation. Duties include: to consider his fellow students as brothers; to work for the betterment of all and not selfishly; to guard his health; to love and respect his parents and teachers; to defend the rights of the workingmen; to fight idleness and vice; to organize school co-operatives; to serve family, the nation and humanity in the fight for social justice.

Minister of Education Gonzalo Vazquez Vela, in an address during October, 1938, stated that the philosophical basis of the Mexican public school system is "dialectical materialism," and that in practice this is translated to impart "functional" education which will best prepare the students to fulfill productive roles in society, and which does not confine itself to the schoolroom but which becomes a part of community life.

Against the State control of education, the principal opposition argues:

That education of the child is a natural right of the parent.

That Catholic taxpayers should have Catholic schools.

That the State has no right to become educational dictator.

That the "lay" and "socialist" schools are sectarian institutions.

That the "lay" school was established by the Masons, that it is un-Christian and atheistic.

That the Catholic religion should be taught in the schools of Catholic countries.

That Catholicism is not opposed to science.

That the socialist school teaches class hatred and not human brotherhood.

That the socialist school in Mexico has one main aim, and that is to combat drastically all religious ideas.

That teachers are merely political puppets of the higher officials and are not appointed on a basis of merit.

That the socialist school is just a mask, since it cannot be socialist unless it attacks property.

That co-education is immoral.

That the socialist school spreads communism.

7

One big defensive argument which its advocates bring forward on behalf of the Mexican socialist school is that it is meeting the educational needs of the people, and meeting them to an extent hitherto unknown in Mexican history. They admit that they made serious blunders; that there existed and still exists a shortage of well-prepared teachers; that there is a great deal of personal political influence which at times impedes the teacher's work; that many appointments are made for purely personal reasons.

But, they add:

That one of the first acts following establishment of social-ist education was the opening of new normal schools to train many more teachers and to permit the old ones to improve themselves.

That the teachers have organized into a powerful nation-wide union (STERM) which has already won civil-service rights for teachers, increases in pay, seniority rights, pensions, and the right to strike.

That the members of the Communist Party, a legal party, have the same rights as members of any other political parties in Mexico under the Cardenas regime; that among members of the Communist Party were found some of the best-equipped teachers and students of pedagogy; that it was the Communist Party members who accepted the government's education program, and not the government which accepted the Communists' program.

Figures are cited to show the tremendous spread of schools, the one big passion that all the presidents from Obregon to Cardenas have had in common. The statistics reveal an inter-esting phenomenon of the last years of Diaz' regime: an actual decline in the number of schools and a violent drop in scholas-tic registration. In 1907, the Diaz administration showed about 10,000 schools on its records, with registration of some 600,000 pupils. It was notorious even then that many of these schools did not exist at all except on the budget, like the 5,000 "extras" that appeared on the army payroll, just paper soldiers.

According to figures cited in a speech in 1936 by Francisco Castillo Najera, Mexican ambassador to the United States, a total of seven hundred schools was open in Mexico in 1910, and fewer than 100,000 pupils were enrolled. All of these were in cities and towns. The peasants' children had no schools. The budget for education was approximately seven per cent of the total budget. Illiteracy was rated at seventy per cent.

And here's what the official records showed in 1938:

Illiteracy—forty-five per cent.

Approximately twenty per cent of the national budget spent on education.

21,158 rural primary schools.

392 primary schools in the federal district.

375 urban, model and other types of rural schools.

1,541 schools known as "article 123" schools, maintained by industrial concerns, mining companies and haciendas in accordance with provisions of the Mexican Constitution.

33 regional agricultural schools.

33 schools for Indians.

29 high schools.

4 schools for soldiers' children.

21 pre-vocational, vocational, professional, industrial, commercial schools.

512 kindergartens.

17 night schools.

6 universities—Mexico City (2), Guadalajara, Morelia, Monterrey, Merida.

Total attendance—2,124,327, including adults (in night schools).

Approximately 50,000 teachers.

8

The most impressive achievement of recent Mexican administrations in the field of education has been, unquestionably, the development of the rural school. And it hasn't all been on paper, either, as Professor Graciano Sanchez can tell you with a grimace of displeasure. Husky, stout, with handlebar mustache that is far and away the most impressive thing of its kind in Cardenas' official family, Sanchez is the general-secretary of the National Peasants' Confederation and as such the spokesman for a couple of million peasants. Besides, he is head of the Department of Indian Affairs, entrusted with guiding, educating and protecting Mexico's more than two and a half million Indians who speak more than three dozen different dialects. Professor Sanchez, a former rural teacher, provoked the ire of the Union of Educational Workers by declaring in his annual report of the Mexican Peasants' Confederation, in August, 1938, that the teachers should confine themselves more to their school work and not spend so much time on extracurricular activities among the peasants.

The Union rebuked Sanchez for his harsh words, said they could serve no purpose other than to harm relations between the teachers and the farm workers. The teachers feel, added the Union, that their entire time belongs to the peasants and their families, and that they spend morning, noon, night, Sundays and holidays to carry on the good work, and to supplement schoolroom teaching, make it really effective, by relating it to the pupil's family and community life. There was a time when Sanchez heartily favored teacher participation in other activities. That was when he, as a teacher, rode with the agrarians. Now head man of the peasants' organization and of the government's Department of Indian Affairs, he guards his wards jealously against other influences, and especially against those of the city-slicker trade unionists. The teachers belong to the Confederation of Mexican Workers. Head of the Confederation is Vicente Lombardo Toledano. Sanchez and Lombardo don't hit it off so well together.

Sanchez' remarks caused quite a splash in the Mexican political pool, because it so happened that the very thing he squawked about was what President Cardenas and Minister of Education Vazquez Vela had stressed with pride: the rural schoolteachers are more than just instructors, they are guides and counselors, and one of their tasks is to help the peasants—most of whom can't write—draw up petitions for land. Which explains why the land lords do a little neat liquidating now and then at the expense of the well-meaning, hard-working, self-sacrificing teacher.

The rural teacher, in fact, under the Cardenas administration, has grown to be much more than a teacher, and the school has become the community center, the kids' gathering place in the daytime, and their papas' and mamas' at night. Besides transmitting the three r's, the teacher undertakes the duties of family counselor, of county farm agent, health and hygiene officer, scoutmaster, football coach, and all-round pal. In the school at night, the peasants can learn about such things as crop rotation, fertilization and seed selection, take their first lessons in ABC's so that they can continue their agricultural studies via the Ministry of Agriculture's publications. The peasants' wives learn how to make economical clothing for their children, how to vary diets on next-to-nothing per day, how to protect the kids' health by vaccinations and soap-and-water. Nearly always there's a school parcel of land on every ejido. This parcel is worked by the children and the peasants, voluntarily, and the proceeds are used for books, pencils, basketballs, and other equipment. Sometimes when the old school no longer serves, the villagers will put in their spare time to gather materials and build a new one. That sort of thing gives Cardenas a real thrill. These efforts and sacrifices, in the old days, went toward building churches.

This work of the teacher in the field is frequently augmented by an institution known as the Cultural Mission, a kind of traveling social-service bureau, formerly part of the Ministry of Education, later transferred to the Department of Indian Affairs. The mission's work is twofold: social service, and training of rural teachers. The missions, which carry portable equipment for presenting playlets, organize peasant leagues, health brigades, women's groups, sports teams, domestic-science classes, take the census, and establish schools where none existed before. An important part of the Cultural Mission's work is in the small, isolated settlements, especially Indian communities where Spanish can be used only through an interpreter.

9

A human arm and a leg dangle over the street from a balcony in Mexico City. Call the police! Murder? No, just another prank of students in the National University's School of Medicine.

Such macabre jests emanating from the government-supported but autonomously-organized University do not worry officials half so much, however, as the alleged conversion of that institution into a focus of political opposition. Leaders of the official party charged that the slogan of "Freedom of Teaching," under which the University remained relatively removed from Mexican socialist education, was merely a cloak for the clergy and the rightist groups agitating for sabotage of the Mexican Revolution. Whatever it was, government attempts to bring the University under the influence of its political doctrine met with much opposition.

The national administration said it had no intentions of trying to violate the school's autonomy, but that it was trying to bring the life of the University closer to the life of the people instead of permitting it to become "an incubator of enemies of the people." This echoed the regret voiced by President Cardenas a number of times to the effect that the great tragedy of "liberal" education consisted in turning out students who, instead of becoming champions of the underdog, serve "the enemies of their class." It was further charged that the students were being made dupes of clerical agitators and that the slogan, "Freedom of Teaching," really meant "Down with the Government" when translated into the political language of the day.

The Cardenas administration said it was mainly interested in having the University stress technical and scientific curricula more than the liberal professions. It argued that there are plenty of doctors and lawyers, and that the country's real need is for technicians, technicians and more technicians. To help bring about this shift of emphasis, Cardenas created the National Council of Higher Education and Scientific Investigation. A feud developed between the Council and the University administration. A concession was made to the government through creation of the "Department of Social Action" in the University, a department which was to serve as liaison between pundit and proletariat.

Cardenas hoped to see the National University take a turn toward the attitude for which the University of Morelia, formerly San Nicolas University, has been famous. That school, in the capital of Cardenas' home State of Michoacan, developed a reputation for liberalism in the days when the liberal was regarded as a dangerous radical by the dominant absolutism of the clergy. And in the Mexican Revolution, the Michoacan university became the only institution of higher learning where contemporary social ideas could get full discussion. There various philosophies influenced the curricula, an influence reserved, in the case of the National University, exclusively for the prevailing Bergsonian idealism and intuitionism of the top professors.

Among the men who shaped the Morelia University in recent years was Gustavo Corona, scholar, attorney, educator, an authority on Mexican labor jurisprudence. Corona was a student of the University and later became rector of that institution. In that capacity he sought to attract leading scholars and intellectuals from all over the world and from all parts of Mexico. He invited artists to paint murals in the University, and in the Morelia Museum, including several American artists. Corona had visions of making his campus an Athens of the New World. When Cardenas became president he invited the Morelia schoolman to collaborate in the Department of Labor. In the dispute between the petroleum workers and the oil companies, Corona was the government's representative on the arbitration board, serving with one representative of labor and one of capital. He was the author of that famous award which decided the dispute in favor of the workers. Lawyers regard the award as setting a precedent for all future disputes of this nature, because of its exhaustive analysis of practically every possible point that might arise in such controversies.

Unique among Mexico's universities is the Workers' University of Mexico, founded by Vicente Lombardo Toledano, head of the Confederation of Mexican Workers. Toledano, once a professor at the National University, directs this new institution. He is aided by Alejandro Carrillo, young laborite intellectual, educated in the United States and England, son of a former Mexican consul who later went into the curio business. An accomplished orator, tall, forceful, with a fluent command of English and French as well as Spanish, young Carrillo has taken a prominent part in meetings, conventions, demonstrations, and has traveled abroad as a representative of Mexican labor. His friends believe he'll go places in Mexican politics.

The Workers' University consists of six principal divisions, open to anybody with a registration fee of one peso. In addition there are five "study centers," night schools in industrial sections of Mexico City, taught by the staff of the University. The school provides courses in Marxist theory, co-operative organization and operation, languages, labor law, union organization, and special courses in a summer school for foreign students. In the Workers' University, Lombardo Toledano hopes to form leaders fully prepared to direct the Mexican labor movement—at the highest peak of organization in its history—to bigger and better things.

IX

NEW GODS FOR OLD

1

THE fine art of changing a nation's gods has become part of the equipment of all top-notch contemporary political leaders. Faith in human beings, fallible but subject to control, and their institutions, is preached in one place. Elsewhere, Blood-plasm, Corpuscle, Epidermis become a new trinity of racial religions. Wotan challenges Christ.

Competition for the soul of Mexico is fully as keen as the competition for her oil and her silver and her farmland. In Mexico, the technique of swapping old gods for new has the benefit of a rich storehouse of data on the subject. The clerical chroniclers of the Spanish Conquest were in many cases very explicit on the matter of knocking over heathen idols and setting up Christian saints in their place; on conversion of Indian seasonal festivals into adoration of Catholic images; on raising the cross atop an Aztec temple.

The Catholic Church is still inseparable from any solution of Mexico's problems. Mexican masters of nationalist technique frequently have come to grips with the delegates of the Vatican International. Along with breaking up the huge haciendas, the men of the Revolution undertook to break the soul-monopoly of the Catholic clergy. Various tactics were used. One extreme took a flat-footed stand of open warfare on belief in the supernatural. Another group sought to restore Quetzalcoatl, the Plumed Serpent god of the Aztecs who was banished by the Man on the Cross. Others tried the

Church's own technique, sponsored fairs, agricultural expositions, fiestas that coincided with the Church holidays, thus seeking to out-Jesuit the Jesuits in canalizing popular outpourings. Still another sector said it had no quarrel with religion at all but would fight tooth and nail against the Vatican's intervention in economic and political matters. This last-named group set up a church in competition to the Holy, Roman, Apostolic.

2

After you run into a half dozen or more strange-as-it-seems and believe-it-or-nots in Mexico, you will not be surprised to learn that the Pope is a Mason. And that his predecessor was a Mason, too. Meaning, of course, the Popes of the Redeemers.

The creation of a new church was part of Calles' tactics in his fight with the archbishops and the apostolic delegate. After all, he figured, if some fellow in Rome could call himself Pope, why couldn't another fellow in Mexico City also call himself Pope? Who was going to prove that the Mexican didn't have as much right as the Italian to be God's representative, if there is a God?

Today's Pope of the Mexican National Orthodox Apostolic Catholic Church is Jose Eduardo Davila, consecrated as Pope Eduardo I. The Mexican Pope, age twenty-nine, was the target of newspaper attacks on October 3, 1938, because of his streamlined methods of conversion. The press charged that Eduardo I and his followers were "shamelessly exploiting the Indians" in the mountain villages of Puebla, "taking advantage of their ignorance and superstition." Concretely, the charges were that the Pope had organized a band of boys to "borrow" images and religious ornaments from the Roman Catholic Churches in Mexico City and Puebla and then turned right around and sold these articles to the Indians. And not only to Indians, but to many nice people in the towns as well.

In answer to these charges, Eduardo I exclaimed:

"Calumnies of the Romans!"

Tall, thin, dark, the Pope lives in a small apartment on Belisario Dominguez Street, in the older section of the Mexican capital. He always wears a huge amethyst ring on his right hand. The schismatic Pope claims no fewer than a million members of his church. He "maintains diplomatic relations" with the Masonic lodges and Protestant churches and has organized a lodge of his own, the "Knights of Guadalupe," on the order of the "Knights of Columbus," but named after the Virgin of Guadalupe.

The first Pope had issued a decree permitting priests of the schismatic church to marry. But Eduardo I rescinded it and the priests are now required to be celibates. The same ritual as that of the Roman Catholic Church is followed, and the Mexican Pope has his "basilica" in the village of San Pedro. Eduardo I says he recognizes "the Roman Pope spiritually but not in matters of administration."

"I am infallible and my bishops are infallible," says the schismatic Pope. "I have recognized Pope Pius, but he cannot recognize me publicly because his church would go to pieces. But the time will come when we will work out a compromise."

Pope Eduardo and some of his high priests were mixed up with the fascist Gold Shirts, which confused everybody; for there were not a few Roman Catholics who thought the Mexican fascists were O.K. because they said they were against communism. The Mexican Pope carried a letter from the Gold Shirt commander "authorizing" him to make converts in "the eastern division of Puebla." The "bishop of Texas" for the schismatic group in 1938 was a German Nazi.

The fascist-schismatics did not miss any angles. As schismatics they took advantage of anti-clerical activity to win Catholics for their sect. As Gold Shirts, they sought help from Catholics, both American and Mexican, to fight the Mexican reds. Anti-Semitic in Mexico, the Gold Shirt exiles sought finances among Jews in Texas and California "to fight religious persecution in Mexico." The Mexican Pope petitioned the patriarchs of the Greek Orthodox Catholic Church to recognize him. Some of his followers in the United States said they were admirers of the radio priest Charles Coughlin. As Gold Shirts, they hoped they could get some help from him in fighting the Mexican government.

3

The European struggle for power between Church and State was brought to Mexico with the Spanish Conquest. The correspondence and the chronicles of the early colonial epoch are full of complaints by the conquistadores against the clergy, and by the clergy against the conquistadores: torture of Indians, accumulation of power, haciendas, industrial and commercial monopolies. In most cases, however, the clergy and the conquistadores worked together; souls and land were conquered simultaneously. Many members of the clergy even complained about their fellow brethren of the cloth. One of them became such an ardent champion of the Indians that Mexican anti-clericals later raised a monument to him. The monument—to Fra Bartolome de las Casas— stands today, crowning a fountain in one of the most prominent spots of Mexico City. It is at one side of the Plaza de la Constitucion, between the National Palace, seat of the temporal power, and the Mexico City Cathedral, seat of the spiritual.

Las Casas became known as "the Father of the Indians,"

and is one of the few clergymen who finds praise in the official textbooks. Las Casas spent years trying to obtain a decree from the King of Spain that would free the Indians, who had been handed out with the land to the conquistadores. The reformer-friar in 1539 published a work which condemned conversion by means of force, by war. This raised a storm among the clergy and the conquistadores. He obtained a special concession from the governor of Guatemala to try out his theories of peaceful conversions. The governor forbade armed men from entering that territory and within two years Las Casas reported that the territory had been Catholicized, and the Indians had vowed allegiance to the King of Spain. Las Casas was threatened with assassination, he was ostracized from the "best homes," and any aid he asked was denied. He continued his lone crusade, however, until the famous "Laws of the Indies" were passed, granting the natives special protection, but they remained dead letters on the statute books.

By the beginning of the nineteenth century, a movement for Mexican independence had developed, led by the native middle class, the professional people, and some of the lower clergy, all of whom were checked in their careers because, among other reasons, they were *criollos* (Spaniards born in Mexico, and hence of a lower caste than the Spaniards born in Spain). The members of the Mexico City board of governors proposed to the viceroy, Jose de Iturrigaray, that a constitutional congress be convoked and that the country be ruled independently.

The opposition of the high clergy and the Holy Inquisition helped squelch this early attempt at independence. The Holy Inquisition issued decrees condemning the theory of the sovereignty of the people, declaring it to be heretical and deserving anathema. The archbishop took part in a coup which overthrew the insurgent board of governors and the viceroy. Soon afterward, the archbishop himself became viceroy, and the persecution of all advocates of independence was carried on with increased fury. The secret dungeons of the Inquisition stank with the rotting bones of men who died in chains, proclaiming independence and freedom.

A parish priest, Father Miguel Hidalgo y Costilla, is regarded as the Father of Mexican independence. His call to arms against Spain, on September 16, 1810, is commemorated annually in Mexico's most important patriotic holiday. The alliance of the high clergy with the big shots who opposed independence led Hidalgo to exclaim in one of his manifestoes in 1811:

> "Open your eyes, Americans! Do not let yourselves be seduced by your enemies. They are Catholics only for political purposes. Their God is money. Do you think that he who is not a subject of the Spanish despot cannot be a true Catholic?"

Hidalgo and his followers were excommunicated and he was executed on July 27, 1811.

A declaration of independence, issued in Chilpancingo on November 6, 1813, stated that the insurgent Congress "does not profess nor recognize any religion other than the Catholic, and that it will not permit nor tolerate the public or secret observance of any other. . . ."

Lucas Alaman, noted Mexican historian and statesman, a Catholic, and defender of the clergy, estimated that at the time of consummation of Mexico's independence, in 1821, the Church owned about half the property and half the wealth of the nation. The Church had become the principal moneylender, and many hacienda owners were debtors. Vast stretches of land remained idle. Some Catholic writers contended that the wealth of the Church was only in proportion to the fabulous wealth of the leading families. At any rate, from the time of the conquest until independence, Indian labor, in most cases unpaid, went into the building of more than fifteen thousand Catholic churches. The gods were well housed and well nourished even if the people were not.

4

The triumph of the Juarez Reform Movement—marking the first triumph of the bourgeois Revolution in Mexico and its attendant liberal philosophy—hurt the power of the clergy. The preamble of the Reform Laws of 1859, in which church holdings were nationalized, listed a long bill of complaints charging the clergy with violence, bloodshed, treason, and other crimes in the attempt to retain control and to defeat the popular liberalist movement. The document placed the blame for Mexico's "backwardness, its shame before the other nations" on the maneuvers and intrigues of the powerful Catholic clergy that "had impeded the realization of Mexico's independence."

Mexico's Reform Movement, the anti-feudal wedge, opened the country to industrialization, to foreign capital, and theoretically, to freedom of worship. But Protestants, who had hopes of finding the last-named, discovered that the clerical power, although diminished by loss of property, still prevailed. American Protestant missionaries were slain, lynched in some cases by mobs instigated by priests. An interesting view of Mexico in 1875, just prior to the Diaz period was given by Gilbert Haven, one of these missionaries, who toured the country and wrote his impressions in *Mexico: Our Next-Door Neighbor*.

Haven concluded that it was impossible for "any single Church government again to possess exclusive jurisdiction" and "the Roman Catholic chiefs are recognizing this fact, and are said to be favorable to annexation, because they can get

yet larger liberties under our government than are allowed
them here." Haven tells of persecutions. At Toluca, a riot
broke up a Protestant church congregation and three persons
were killed. In Puebla, a preacher was mobbed "for daring
to speak in the name of Jesus." But, he hoped, "these outrages will last only a moment," for "like our Ku-Klux outrages, they are the dying blows of a dying evil." Speaking of
Mexico's great natural resources, Haven eloquently echoed
the fervent protests of the anti-clericals:

> "Mexico . . . poured forth hundreds and thousands of
> millions into the lap of earth . . . enriched thrones and
> subjects in all lands . . . yet the nation that produces
> them is poor and ignorant and blind and naked; a nation
> peeled and robbed by its own masters; a nation of blood
> and strife and desolation. How its splendid ceremonials
> of service, and magnificent altars and vestments, and
> golden shrines, and silver altar railings, and unbounded
> pomp and parade are rebuked by this poverty and peace-
> lessness of its people. . . ."

Haven blamed Pope Pius IX for the French invasion and
for the imposition of Maximilian. "Rome was mistress of
Mexico," he said. He gives a vivid picture of the ferment
that stirred in Mexico with the triumph of Juarez, of Catholic priests who rose in churches during mass and challenged
the archbishops to debate. He reports the lynching of the
"martyr, John Luther Stephens . . . born in Swansea, Wales,
murdered in Ahualulco, Mexico, March 2, 1874." He quotes
the *Missionary Herald's* description of the lynching, a scene
which seems to foreshadow similar happenings fifty years
later when the men of the Revolution sent schoolteachers
into the provinces.

The *Missionary Herald* reported on Stephens:

> "For three months he labored with success far beyond
> our most sanguine expectations, winning many souls to

the truth as it is in Jesus. He had gained, through his labor of love, the favors of the majority of people in Ahualulco. This grand success infuriated the priest, and the day before Mr. Stephens' death he preached a most exciting sermon to the numerous Indians who had gathered there, from the various ranchos and pueblos near by, in which he said, 'It is necessary to cut down, even to the roots, the tree that bears bad fruit. You may interpret these words as you please.' And on March 2, at one o'clock in the morning, a mob of over two hundred men, armed with muskets, axes, clubs and swords approached the house where Mr. Stephens lived, crying, 'Long Live the Religion! Long Live Señor Priest! Death to the Protestants!' "

Scores of Protestant missionaries and converts were stabbed and shot, their dwellings burned.

In *El Monitor Republicano,* issue dated September 27, 1873, the following advertisement appeared over a skull and crossbones:

"Death to the Protestants! To the people of Toluca: Either you are Catholic by name, or Catholic in fact. If you are Catholic in faith, give a terrible blow to these savages, intruders, and adventurers, who, to make themselves appear wise and important and to assure themselves a future without labor, attempt that which they do not understand—that band of filthy scoundrels, deluded sons of all the devils. Let us rise en masse to finish at once this accursed race, whose proper place is in hell, which is not complete without them. With one sure blow insure their death and the death of their families. Let a fiery death exterminate this sect of accursed wretches, who attempt to overthrow the Apostolic Roman Catholic religion, in which we will live and die. Unfurl proudly the standard of the Faith and shout, 'Long Live the Religion! Death to the Sons of Satan!' "

The ashen fruits of these seeds of intolerance were to be eaten by succeeding generations of Catholics.

5

Porfirio Diaz, although a Mason, did not make a major issue of the Church question. His main interest was in preventing any political opposition from developing. Diaz kept a close check on political activities of the Catholics, refused to permit formation of a Catholic party, or any other party. Many believed that Diaz himself appointed the archbishops and bishops. But he permitted the Reform Laws to slip into the background to a certain extent, so that the Church managed to acquire a lot of property, re-establish convents and seminaries and hold religious ceremonies in other public places besides churches—things that were prohibited by law.

An interesting picture of conditions in Mexico during the years of 1909-11, the final years of the Diaz regime, are given in some little-known letters written by Jesuit missionaries to their superiors. Most of the letters give statistics on the number of communions, marriages, confirmations and other ceremonies performed, and nearly all reveal a great preoccupation about the kind of lodgings provided, the meals, the reception. Occasionally one will contain a paragraph or two which helps explain the strong influence of anti-clericalism among the men of the Revolution. For instance, on November 23, 1909, Felix Aldasoro of the Company of Jesus wrote from Morelia, Michoacan, capital of President Cardenas' home State:

"... difficulties in arranging the ninety-eight marriages, because of the weight of the rites of matrimony against the pecuniary circumstances of those poor workers who hardly made enough to pay for their food, and I almost suspended the mission in order not to torture them uselessly. ... How could I threaten them with the punishments of hell fire if they were not properly married by the church, when this was impossible because

of the price of nine and twelve pesos per marriage for
people who earn thirty-seven centavos daily, and with
the price of corn so high, and there were many who
came from distant villages, waiting around eight to fifteen days for dispensation from the bishop. . . ."

Another missionary, Pedro M. Jimenez, was not so considerate. His letter of March 15, 1910, from Toluca, tells
how he and his companion went around to the people's
houses to pounce on the couples living in sin as man and wife
without having had the proper ceremonies performed. He
delivered sermons, and the civil authorities were very helpful, forcing the evil couples to come in and get a Church
wedding under the threat of jail sentences. They took, the
letter reports, a total of sixty-four pesos, two pesos a marriage.

From Durango, Luis Benitez y Cabañas wrote that the
sermons for the working people and the servants had to be
suspended, because no time was left after the sermons for the
"very select group of nice people from the best families."

On May 23, 1911, Father M. Jimenez wrote from Sayula
stating that he had found the authorities very co-operative,
permitting public ceremonies outside the Church. And the
Revolutionaries were even more considerate. They were all
ready to take the town, but waited outside the city limits until
the mission ceremonies were over and the priests had left.
Then they marched in and took the town.

Father Dionisio Cabezas in a letter dated Saltillo, Coahuila,
June 1, 1911, said that "there fell into the net of the Lord
some very fat fish, although few. . . ."

6

The Mexican clergy challenged legality of the 1917 Constitution and the laws deriving from it, declaring them to be

persecutory. The men of the Revolution charged that the clergy was using religion as a pretext for counter-revolutionary activity; that the Catholic Party had been in league with the dictator, Victoriano Huerta; that the clergy had spent huge sums in trying to smother the Revolution. The Church question became a vital political issue. The rising politicos raised the banner of anti-clericalism alongside the laborist banners.

On February 18, 1924, Calles and Morones established the Mexican National Orthodox Apostolic Catholic Church, and donated one of the centrally located Church buildings in Mexico City for this new sect. As Pope, they chose Patriarch Joaquin Perez, a Mason. With official support, the Church developed into a full-fledged schismatic institution, and before long numerous clashes were occurring between the schismatic church-goers and Roman Catholic church-goers, between laborists and Catholics.

By 1925, the blood-smeared hills of Mexico were again ringing with the cry: "Death to the Protestants!" And to this cry were added others: "Long Live Christ the King!" and "Death to the Communists!" The Cristeros—"Soldiers of Christ"—mobilized to fight the government's Church laws. Calles was president. Like his predecessor Obregon, he announced that he would enforce the statutes—recently amended—relating to the clergy. The National League for Defense of Religious Liberty threatened that it would bring about "paralysis of the economic and social life of Mexico." An "economic boycott" was declared in 1926, in retaliation for the government's seizure of churches (technically government property), the registry of priests, the banishing of nuns and priests from forbidden convents, prohibition of religious ceremonies or religious costumes anywhere except inside the churches.

In this maelstrom of hate, a great many excesses were committed by both sides. Property was stolen by generals from Catholics on various pretexts; in other cases, Catholics defiantly aided the rebels, and many of them even took up arms, spurred on by the reward of a "martyr's death" in some instances, and in others by immediate personal motives such as revenge for outrages committed by some of the generals under the pretext of crushing the rebellion. In Rome, the Pope ruled that the Mexican laws made it impossible for the Catholic religion to be practiced.

All the arguments advanced by the Church for guiding education on the basis of specific dogmas were brought into play to defend the government's position. The churchmen, past masters of absolutism, intolerance, monopoly, appeared as advocates of liberalism, tolerance, freedom of worship. But the two sets of values seemed irreconcilable, just as the association of the high clergy with the big landowners could not be reconciled with the peasants' demands for land.

In 1925, Archbishop Mora y del Rio denied that the Catholic Church in Mexico had failed to show proper concern for the social problems of the country. He made a public statement, answering the questions of a congressman, following appearance of a manifesto by the National Catholic Confederation of Labor. The prelate pointed out that as far back as 1903 the first national Catholic Congress had discussed labor problems. In 1912, he added, Catholic congressmen had introduced bills to recognize the legal personality of unions, to regulate the weekly rest day and to provide compensation for occupational accidents. The Archbishop recalled that Dr. Jose Refugio Galindo had traveled over the country as "an apostle of Catholic agrarianism" years before the Madero revolution. He also cited a program adopted in 1913 by the National Confederation of Catholic Workmen's Circles, which included compulsory arbitration.

But by 1926 the war of words had become a war of bullets

and had spread all over the country. Cristero uprisings broke out in a number of places. In 1927 a bomb was thrown at Obregon's automobile. Shortly afterward, a priest, Padre Pro, and three other Catholics were executed. Padre Pro became a martyr, his name a battle-cry and his photograph a battle-standard. In 1928, Obregon was assassinated and his slayer, Jose de Leon Toral, was executed. In 1929, following a secret conference in the San Juan de Ulua fortress in Vera-cruz, a truce was established between the government and the clergy. Anti-clerical Portes Gil was then president.

7

The dispute reached another peak during the presidency of Abelardo Rodriguez, 1932-1934, beginning with the publication in 1932 of the Papal Encyclical, *Acerba Animi,* and approval, in 1934, of the constitutional amendment establishing "socialist education." The clergy charged that the government had not lived up to the 1929 agreement, that new anti-clerical drives were being carried on in various States. The government said that the encyclical was a repudiation of the agreement, and that the document openly incited Catholics to rebellion against the Mexican constitution.

Archbishop Leopoldo Ruiz y Flores, the Apostolic Delegate, published a "message of protest" in which he warned of "tyranny" that would come as a result of President-elect Cardenas' "repudiation of freedom of teaching." The message said that no Catholic could be a member of the National Revolutionary Party, and also cast doubts on the legitimacy of the Revolution by stating that its triumph was due to the "frank and decided protection of the United States President Woodrow Wilson and its maintenance to the protection of the United States Government."

About the same time, Bishop Jose de Jesus Manrique y Zarate of Huejutla, issued his "Third Message to the Civilized World," in which he challenged Calles for the latter's statement to the effect that the children of the nation should belong to the Revolution. He described the new school program as a "Jewish-Masonic plan of which Calles is a worthy bearer."

Both prelates said a lot of things in their messages which Attorney General Emilio Portes Gil held were violations of Article 16 of the federal Constitution and of the penal code. Orders for their arrest were issued. But they had gone to the United States. All this happened in November, 1934, less than a month before Lazaro Cardenas was sworn in as president.

Cardenas became president on December 1, 1934. Along with a lot of other things, he inherited the Church problem. Garrido Canabal and his anti-clerical Red Shirts were at their height in Tabasco, and were moving into Mexico City. Garrido had been named Minister of Agriculture. One of the first crises that the new President faced grew out of the slaying of several persons by Red Shirts in front of a suburban Mexico City church. This was followed by a raid on the Red Shirt headquarters.

On September 8, 1935, all the archbishops and bishops of Mexico issued a joint pastoral letter on the "Civic Duties of the Catholics." The ecclesiastical authorities previously had threatened excommunication of parents who sent their children to "socialist education" schools and of teachers who taught there. The collective pastoral letter flatly defended the intervention of the Church in matters of "culture and progress" and rejected the theory that the Church should confine itself to "the narrow limits of the temples or the intimate sanctuaries of the conscience." The letter said that the Church should "organize and direct the integral life of man by means of its moral doctrines in all the spheres of human life . . . and action, within institutions and groups seeking . . . a better life, in the efforts of science toward investigation of truth and in the efforts of labor to obtain for the worker and peasant more abundant daily bread. . . ." The letter described the tasks "awaiting the Church" in civic, economic and political fields and called on the Catholics to use their rights as citizens to bring about repeal of the "laws of persecution." The document was regarded as a renewal of the clergy's challenge of the Mexican Constitution. Similar action had been taken each time a new president was sworn into office.

But this letter confronted Cardenas with serious questions for a man who had promised a democratic regime and whose acts indicated that he meant it. It asked, in effect: "Why is there no respect for the Mexican Catholics' rights of freedom of association, freedom of belief, exercise of their religion, and suffrage?" It continued with a rebuke for Catholics who think that their duty as Catholics ends with some acts of piety. They should, it added, "enter fully into the civic field . . . with the generosity and sacrifice demanded by the noble cause of Christian Social Restoration." Issued less than a year before the Spanish civil war broke out, the letter advised the Mexican Catholics to follow the example of the Catholics in Spain who had been quite active politically, and who, "with such laudable prudence, knew how to join in perfect union or confederation to face the unbridled persecution which followed the overthrowing of the throne."

Laymen of the Church were urged to form associations and other organizations, to conciliate other groups which seek the same ends, to publish and constantly disseminate booklets, periodicals, leaflets, "to clarify the facts, unify criterions, and co-ordinate the action of the various associations." The collective letter said, that on the whole, Mexico is no different from other countries in its social aspects, but "still it is true that not in all countries have the international secret societies been working so much and so insistently; that not all the countries have the grave difficulties occasioned by our geographical position; that the generation formed on the basis of atheistic laicism and absurd positivism seeks the remedy for our ills where they will never find it." The "geographical position" refers to the United States. The document recommended that the Catholics form a "united front" to work for "the efficacious removal of the children and youth from anti-religious teachings . . . and to organize 'Catholic Action' that will soon carry the nation to 'the conquest of its legitimate liberties.' "

In 1936, President Cardenas issued a statement in the State of Jalisco, hotbed of clerical opposition. He said:

"To break down the resistance of fanatics egged on by the enemies of the Revolution, the people in the communities must be organized. In those states where this has been done, the efforts of the reactionaries are null and void. . . .

"But this Government has no intentions of falling into the error of previous administrations. The duty of a revolutionary administration like the present consists in doing all that may be necessary to carry out the program of the Revolution, the fundamental aspects of which are social and economic in character. . . . It is no concern of the Government to undertake anti-religious campaigns, since all that is obtained thereby is a fruitless waste of the efforts of public servants, provocation of resistance and postponement, for an indefinite time, of economic and social principles basically essential to the well-being of the people. Action by organized masses in the fight against fanaticism and in support of the Socialist school is the best safeguard for the lives of their own members, for that of the teachers of their children, and for the social, economic and spiritual emancipation of the people."

On January 24, 1938, the new Archbishop of Mexico, Luis M. Martinez, stated:

"In truth, it is worth while to sacrifice our own ideas, excellent as we deem them, in order to maintain unity with our brethren around the ideas which seem inferior to ours, but which will make us all one; it is worth while to desist from our aims, holy though they may be, in order that we may join our hearts to those of our brothers, for, according to Saint Thomas, it is charity for man to want to realize the will of his fellow man as if it were his own, and it is a greater good to achieve concord and harmony among our brothers than to achieve realization of the highest ideas and the holiest aims."

Archbishop Martinez is from Michoacan, Cardenas' home State. It was probably just a coincidence that a Michoacan prelate should be called to the capital when a Michoacan man is president. At any rate, they seemed to have come to an understanding, and in 1938, the Catholic ceremonies and rituals were more publicized and more elaborate than they had been in a long time. For the first time in years, newspapers printed photographs of communions and other observances in which the crucified Christ—so long regarded as the Cristero's sign of rebellion against the government—appeared profusely.

In the State of Chihuahua, the parochial Eucharistic Congress was convened for the first time in twelve years.

Throughout the country in August there were elaborate three-day celebrations of the twenty-fifth anniversary of the founding of the ACJM, the Catholic Association of Mexican Youth, with attendant publicity and social functions.

Even Chiapas, which like Tabasco, had remained one of the two States of which the Catholics had complained most, permitted reopening of three churches.

In Puebla, a priest publicly joined in the debate over "freedom of curriculum" in the University of Puebla.

The month of October witnessed more Church festivals than had been seen in Mexico in many a day. The festivities, in which prelates from all over the country took part, marked the completion of the magnificent Basilica of Guadalupe, just outside of Mexico City; the twenty-fifth anniversary of the Catholic Youth Association; and besides, the year 1938 was a "holy year" in observance of the "four hundredth anniversary of the apparition of the Virgin of Guadalupe." The suburb of Guadalupe was thronged with visitors from all parts of Mexico. Pilgrims came also from other countries to win the "indulgence of the jubilee" granted for the first time to any country in the Western Hemisphere.

The railroads, government-owned and worker-operated, did a big business, conveying pilgrims. The sellers of wafers and candles and rosaries smiled again. Photographers were doing well, selling photographs of the new Archbishop, of the late Archbishop, and of Padre Miguel Pro. Two pseudo-pilgrims were arrested for placing counterfeit pesos in the collection plate and taking their change in legitimate coins. Every day free meals were served by the Basilica authorities to the first one hundred poor persons who applied for tickets. The *Official Gazette* published a notice to the effect that ten real-estate properties had been nationalized for infringement of the Church laws or because they were property of the clergy under the names of laymen. But this was offset by an amazing bit of news: a new church was being built in Mexico! A Catholic church, in the country where "religious freedom does not exist." Archbishop Martinez in August blessed the cornerstone for this new building, the Santa Rosa de Lima Church, patronized by the Belgian colony.

The many Church celebrations in 1938 seemed to indicate that the Cardenas policy of conciliation was working. Some were not particularly pleased about it. Among the displeased were the extreme anti-clericals who contended that leniency toward the clergy will strengthen reaction and bring on more revolutions. Others not too happy about it, either, included some good, loyal and devout citizens who had thrived on the restrictions. Some of these beneficiaries were politicos or lawyers. Others were the creators of a "persecution racket." These organized "private masses"—with all the mystery and intrigue of bootlegging speakeasies—a priest smuggled in to say mass, a collection taken up. Since these bootlegged masses were usually attended by well-to-do people, the organizers collected a good many pesos, paid the priest a day's wages and his meals, and pocketed the rest. The prohibition of religious education in the schools also brought with it considerable "bootlegging" of religious education in clandestine, un-licensed schools.

In November, 1938, a priest in the Santo Domingo Church, Mexico City, blessed a flag of the Spanish Fascist Falange, which was to be taken to Spain by a group of recruits for the Franco army.

The jubilee spirit ruled among the Catholics in Mexico in 1938. But the words of the Archbishop about secular organization were not forgotten. In January, the Archbishop reminded the faithful of the Apostolic Letter issued by Pope Pius XI on March 28, 1931, in which he urged that the secular organizations, through Catholic Action, co-operate with the hierarchy "in order to bring Catholicism back to Mexico." The Catholics of Mexico have been organized politically under the direction of Mexican Catholic Action, made up of four sections: Union of Mexican Catholics, Mexican Catholic Feminine Union, Mexican Catholic Feminine Youth, and Catholic Association of Mexican Youth (AJCM), the last named being the most active, especially among university students and in the preparatory school. All four organizations are ruled by a central committee which includes members of the clergy as ex-officio consultants since the law does not permit priests to take part in politics.

The membership of these organizations interlocks with the various "Nationalist" unions, vanguards, actions, federations, phalanxes, legions and what not. Some openly advocate fascism, others put on a democratic front. Their common point of departure is "anti-communism." Many are admirers of Mussolini, some "heil Hitler" and preach anti-Semitism, and then find themselves in a jackpot when Hitler attacks Catholics. In this muddy ideological delta, the streams of ecclesiastical authoritarianism find a common level with the streams of political and economic authoritarianism. And the politicos, the ever-fresh crop of redeemers, both within the Administration and in the camps of the Opposition, make the most of it.

X

LAND LORDS AND LIBERTY

1

MEXICAN history will picture Lazaro Cardenas with one hand on an oil derrick, the other on a tractor. Mexico's oil seizure may have been melodramatic, but the Cardenas farmland distribution is positively epic. It hit the country like an earthquake, jarring loose more fenced-in acreage in four years than had been revamped in the preceding twenty. Everybody was surprised, including Uncle Sam's Mr. Hull, when the Mexican government began handing out hunks of the good earth in a big way. Good Neighbor Uncle Sam got tough, reminded Cardenas that certain slices of that country had been sold—dirt cheap, it's true—to some of our boys, and that if Mexico wanted to be an Indian-giver with her own sons, that was her business. Americans, however, would have to be paid for expropriated lands, ten million dollars' worth, and pronto. But nobody was more surprised than the peasant himself when land actually began coming his way. For he had come to look on the whole agrarian program as another myth, something you talked about in speeches, you wrote about in editorials and articles, and then forgot.

If all the boloney written about the Mexican agrarian problem could be made edible, and distributed to the farmers in return for a reasonable amount of labor, under decent conditions, there would be no more agrarian problem. Mexico's most belabored public question, it has been attacked from every angle, hacked and battered by theorists of every color from infra-red to ultra-violet. Extremists of one shade have romanticized the peasant until the poor fellow seemed to be sprouting wings, no help at all in plowing. Extremists of another shade have pictured him as a hopeless clod, a sullen, sodden slug, a good-for-nothing who will work only when he's driven with a whip in the hands of his self-elected betters. Occasionally a critic came out of his rhetorical and ideological trance long enough to remember that the guy is human, after all, and that when the two-bit words are trimmed away, the agrarian problem is just another everyday bread-and-butter problem.

That's the way Cardenas has been looking at it for about twenty-five years, and for the last eight or ten he's been doing some serious thinking about it. A number of other Mexicans, politicos and technicians and economists, had also been wrestling with this eternal headache. When the Six-Year Plan was being drawn up, in 1933, they decided that the country had been dosed with political aspirin long enough, and that it was time to get to the root of the trouble instead of just attacking the symptoms. So they wrote into the Plan the resolution that the parceling of land must move along at a healthy clip. One of the major objectives listed in that famous document is the conclusion of land distribution, satisfaction of all land needs by the end of 1939. To soldier Cardenas, become nominee Cardenas, that was an order. He's been obeying that order, with emphasis on the ejido (community tract) system of land allotments. That approach provoked new argument and opposition, had the country in ferment again: many land lords, who had grinned with the thought that they had stopped the Revolution, now looked glum. Peasants beamed with new hope. The rest of the country anxiously awaited the outcome, for the land question, directly involving about thirteen million of Mexico's eighteen million population, has been the cause of social battle for centuries.

The fight for the soil has been waged back and forth for more than four hundred years. Since the time of the Conquistadores the man or men who owned the land ruled Mexico. In the struggle for power, the peasant was gradually squeezed out. The Church, the Spaniards, other foreigners, and native big-shots got more and more land. During the Colonial times, some tracts were restored to the Indian communities, when the grantees of the Spanish crown found that their land was worthless unless somebody worked it, and the terrified natives had fled to the hills.

From 1857 to 1868, laws were passed—known as the Reform Laws—smashing the big clerical estates. These laws made it illegal for civil or religious corporations to own land. Aimed at the latter, they opened the way for the hacienda's encroachment on the common lands, and for new claimants, in cahoots with the ruling groups, to become, literally, lords and masters of all they surveyed. During the Porfirio Diaz epoch, Mexico became a group of big private empires. The peasant, the farmer, was dispossessed, forced to work for wages or in serfdom on one or another of the huge estates. It was the landless peasant who swelled the ranks of the armies that overthrew Diaz in 1911, and the dictator Huerta in 1914. And for this big share in the revolutionary tasks, the peasant was promised land, plus political liberty. "Land and Liberty" was the slogan of the arch-figure of Mexican agrarianism: Emiliano Zapata.

Twenty years later the peasant still had practically no land, and hardly any more liberty than before. All he could show for his pains was a rain check for the Revolution, indefinitely postponed. There was so little of land or liberty in possession of the peasant that you could hardly notice them. Some land had been parceled out, some had been transferred to the new-rich aristocracy, the generals and politicos and industrialists, but most of it was still in the hands of the hacendados.

The prevailing system of farming was still the hacienda system. Any attempts at parceling came to a dead stop against the Chinese wall of the politicos' properties, acquired, without benefit of purchase, in the heat of revolution.

The Cardenas administration revived land distribution on a big scale. The time had come for the rain check to be turned into a meal ticket. His agrarian policies carried Cardenas to swift peasant popularity, and soon the machete was again slashing the brush and the peasant again became Mexico's man-of-the-hour. Land-hungry and just plain-hungry peasants cheered as the Cardenas administration sped up the acreage allotments, marking off new ejidos and homesteads. Land-poor Mexico, with the heat of government power, was thawing out its greatest frozen asset, the soil. Peasants in faded straw sombreros and the characteristic ankle-tied pantaloons of unbleached domestic—poor man's wool of Mexico—trooped to the nation's capital. Barefoot, or in crude, thong-fastened huaraches, they hang around the Agrarian Department's new streamlined, ultra-modern building on Calle Lopez. A few leave each day, new ones straggle in. Those who remain squat on their hams, waiting, as they have been waiting for centuries.

The government issues statistics to show that more acreage has been distributed since Cardenas took office than during the preceding twenty years; that the cost of distribution has been greatly cut. The government tells of great new enterprises, in the Laguna cotton district, in the sugar-cane plantations of Morelos, in Yucatan's henequen fields, in the lower valley of the Rio Grande. Agricultural credit banks are established; collective farm credit societies are formed; crop lien and other agricultural loans go to help buy seed, implements, pay living expenses. Irrigation projects, hydro-electric projects, highway projects, new railways are announced, to help speed the crops, to develop backward communities.

Some peasants don't ask for lands. They hang on to what little they've got as tenant farmers and sharecroppers on the big estates, rather than run the risks of the new-fangled schemes. Even there, the protection of the 1917 Constitution and its Labor and Agrarian chapters, extends to them: minimum wages, schools for their children, decent places in which to live, all these the peasant is supposed to get.

Conflicts arose between the land workers themselves, as well as between landless and landowners, between communities claiming restitution of the same land, between government land-law enforcers and men who don't want their lands cut up, between the federal men and the local kingfish. Blood flowed into the soil again. The blight of stored-up hatred— fed by intrigue, sabotage, incompetence and negligence— starved the crops. Mexico was still hungry. Another big question mark: Can Cardenas solve this fundamental problem his way, or are the obstacles too great for him to overcome? A glance at a bit of history, with emphasis on the basic land problem, will be helpful in understanding what Cardenas and Mexico's three million peasant families are up against.

2

One of the hardiest myths in Mexico's history is that the pre-Conquest Indians lived an idyllic existence, that before the Spaniards arrived and broke up the Aztec playhouse, everything had been hotsy-totsy. Nothing could be further from the truth. The aristocracy ruled among them like aristocracies in European monarchies: nobles, army, priests, to keep the people in line. In addition to working a piece of land to feed himself and his family, the plebeian Indian had to labor on the tracts set aside for the king, on the nobles' lands, on the army lands and on the land of the gods, the temple tracts. Besides these lands set aside for the special benefit of the upper castes, there were tracts known as the "common lands," forerunners of ejidos. Those were worked in common by the peasants. The returns, after tribute to the Aztec emperor had been delivered, were divided among the land-workers. Control of the privileged classes extended even to the common lands. The tribes subject to the Aztecs had to pay a number of extra tributes in the form of foods, handicraft articles and personal services. These subject peoples later provided man power for Cortez and his little band of conquistadores.

The Conquest changed the territorial divisions of the former Mexican kingdoms. It also wiped out the paternalistic concern that the decadent, but wise, Aztec rulers showed toward the people who kept them in gold ornaments and fine feathers. The land was redistricted by the Spaniards into aggregations of towns and communities, with a Spaniard as boss of each district. As for the mass of the population, it continued paying tribute to the Spanish overlords as it had paid tribute to the Indian overlords. The avid conquerors, who had lived on the coarse diets of war while they dreamed of great piles of gold that would make them fabulously rich, made their first mistake by trying to turn the new country into a big sweatshop. The level-headed counsel of their home government, eager to sink the roots of an enduring empire in the new world, went unheeded. The Spanish fighting men wanted land and slaves, women and gold. In their wake came new adventurers lusting to share in the pillage of this fantastic treasure house: traders and priests. A system of *encomiendas* was established, whereby each *comendador* was given not only a big slice of land, but a certain number of Indians who were to work for him, and for whose welfare he was to be responsible. The *comendatore* or group-leader system, implanted in fascist Italy, is a distant derivation of this ancient mode of conquest. The *comendadores* got their work out of the Indians, all right, but the Indians did not get much welfare. The savage brutality of these sixteenth-century "civilizers" is notorious and hardly needs elaboration. Some of it would be unbelievable if we didn't have the bloody examples of our own very civilized epoch to teach us that such things can actually happen.

The Indians stood it as long as they could and then took to the hills. Some of the moderating influences among the conquerors, notably a few courageous friars such as Bartolome de las Casas, "father of the Indians," intervened on behalf of the conquered natives. The devastation had reached such a stage by 1573, that Philip II was forced to heed the advice of his more far-seeing counselors. He issued his famous decree which provided, among other things, that the sites where towns and communities were established should have sufficient water for the population and for crops, enough forest land, arable soil, and a special tract—an ejido—one league square where the Indians could graze their stock. Later decrees provided foundation grants for each town and village, measured off from the atrium of the church. The purpose of these grants was to give the Indians a place to build their living quarters, as well as to provide common lands for subsistence purposes. These lands were theoretically inviolable and it was during this period that the communal exploitation of land first really became organized, only to be shattered later by encroachments of the feudal land barons, lay and clerical.

The Mexican war for independence, 1810-1821, which was at the same time a civil war between the native big shots and the mass of the population, revolved around the recurring hunger for land and liberty. The grabbing of land was like winding a watch spring, tighter, tighter, until it popped. With land, of course, went power. Since most of the land at the time of the first independence movement was in the hands of the Spaniards, the resentment of the landless was trained on them with greatest force. The *criollo* aristocracy, however, did not want the rabble to go too far. As in the case of the conservative opposition to the Diaz oligarchy later, they were willing to kick out the old rulers, and wanted to convince the masses that everything would be fine and dandy with a new set of rulers. The parish priests who joined the peasantry in the first declaration of independence—unapproved by the big shots and their faithful allies, the top-clergy—were excommunicated and later executed for their pains. And the worried Spanish government, symptomatically, began handing out bits of land to appease the people.

How closely the land-hunger was part of the independence movement can be seen from the manifestoes of Jose Maria Morelos y Pavon, a priest who became the apostle of small-tract ownership as against the estate system. He proposed, in 1812, the breaking up of all the big haciendas into small farms, maintaining that the root of all the troubles was the ownership of the bulk of the land by a few individuals. What was worse, these individuals cultivated only a small part of their holdings and the rest remained idle, while the people starved. Morelos passionately urged destruction of all irrigation works, aqueducts, dams and other appurtenances of the haciendas, in order to smash the economic power of the land lords, at that time the firmest bulwark of the Spanish King and principal supporters of the royalists. In 1813, Morelos affirmed his fervor for freedom by issuing a decree that abolished all slavery and castes, and ordered free elections. Mexico's march since that time has been toward these democratic ideals, which seemed utopian then, and which to many die-hards still seem utopian today.

By 1856 the land-grabbers had again wound the watch spring to the breaking point. Mexican independence, won in 1821, made no fundamental changes in the country's economic structure. The post-independence period found the same land system in effect as during the colonial epoch. Among the biggest land lords was the Catholic Church. Its tremendous wealth and power were barriers against which rising republicanism crashed time and again without appreciable effects. By 1833 a movement had already begun toward checking this monopolistic spread of the Church as land lord, and a mild restrictive decree was issued, forerunner of the later legislation that was to nationalize mortmain holdings. It was during this epoch that Joel Poinsett, the United States' first ambassador, appeared on the scene. Progressive liberals introduced legislation to nationalize Church properties. A bill by Lorenzo de Zavala, who later figured with Poinsett in extensive colonization plans which preceded the secession of Texas, was defeated by the clerical party. The latter supported the dictatorial ambitions of General Antonio Lopez de Santa Anna. Some of Mexico's greatest difficulties during the War with the United States were traceable to the Church's efforts toward defeating nationalization attempts.

The nationalization law of June 25, 1856, was the first clear victory in the liberals' campaign to break up feudal land monopolies. It was followed by the Wars of the Reform, during which a second and more general nationalization law was decreed. But the Constitution of 1857, the first liberal charter, failed to protect the ejidos from the effects of its Article 27, that prohibited civil or religious corporations from owning land. This gave the land-grabbers a new chance to swallow up townships and villages, producing another tremendous growth of the haciendas. Men who raised their voices in the Constitutional Convention of 1857 and in the agricultural regions, on behalf of the immense landless population, were bitterly attacked. As usual, most of the generals sided with the big land lords, but there was an occasional voice of protest from the military. For instance, General Juan Alvarez, in a manifesto issued in 1858, said:

"The majority of the hacienda owners and their employees traffic in, and become enriched with, the miserable sweat of the unfortunate peasants; the peasants are snared like slaves, and debts are imposed upon them, passing even to the eighth generation, increasing in size and augmenting the personal labor of the unhappy victims. At the same time, humaneness, reason, justice decline, and with them declines the compensation for so much anxiety, so many tears and so much weariness.

"Expropriation and abuse grow and the insatiable greed of some hacendados never diminishes. They have gradually taken possession of privately owned lands, lands of ejidos, entire communities, and with unparalleled boldness claim ownership, although there is no legal title to back them up. So it is with good reason that the communities clamor for justice, protection and support; but the courts are deaf to their clamors and petitions; scorn, persecution and imprisonment are the reward of those who claim what is justly theirs."

General Alvarez' manifesto could easily have been issued again, without even changing a comma, at any time during the period preceding 1910, the "golden age" of Porfirio Diaz. The famed dictator rose during a time of national confusion and unrest, a critical stage in the growing middle class's onslaught against monopolies in land and commerce. In a world fermenting with the yeast of free competition, Mexico was still a cloistered refuge for feudal power, fighting with its back to the wall against the revolutionary bourgeoisie. Diaz, after he was securely in power, frankly set about establishing a dictatorship, with a slogan that has a familiar ring, "law and order." All powers of the federal and State governments were concentrated in the dictator's hands. The Constitution, for all practical purposes, was suspended. With

Diaz, capitalism got into the saddle in Mexico, and in its organized, dictatorial form it seemed to foreshadow some of the later fascist patterns. Diaz opened the country to foreign colonization and to foreign capital. As in other matters, Diaz' legislation permitted the people with the right connections to run rough-shod over the rights of Pedro Citizen.

The pre-Diaz land laws that established the so-called "surveying companies" provided the machinery for swallowing up the little landholder all over again. Under these laws, on the pretext of putting public lands and unclaimed lands into productive use, the surveying companies were entitled to whatever properties they marked off, provided that no previous claims had been filed. There was a rush to the land office. The big hacienda owners were strong enough to withstand the onslaught of the surveying companies—usually foreigners in league with Diaz henchmen—and then they, too, became surveyors and joined the fun. The little farmer, the rural communities with unregistered ejidos, were engulfed by this new ground swell of monopoly. Among those served with a slice of Mexico was Mr. George Hearst, father of the illustrious publisher, who got a hunk of Chihuahua into which you can put a couple of New England states and still have room for a wall around it, a mere quarter of a million acres known today as San Juan de Babicora ranch. Other beneficiaries were Harrison Gray Otis, of the Los Angeles *Times,* who drew vast acreage in Lower California and Sonora; the Haff interests, with three million acres; the Colorado River Land Company, with eight hundred thousand acres; the Harriman interests, with endless tracts, timber lands, railway concessions; and others. When the party was over, close to two hundred million acres of land in Mexico—nearly half the total area—had been presented, with titles and all, legal-like, to a comparatively small number of men and companies, to have and to hold forever. This went on for more than fifty

years, and in 1904, Diaz, seeing the error of his and his predecessors' ways, tried to change things with a new law, but it
was too late. In addition, the Diaz gang controlled all industrial concessions and banks, the latter absorbing many
rural properties on foreclosures and through forced tax sales.
The banks issued paper money with no security and had
other privileges which really made the highly-touted Diaz
credit system and budget-balancing a house of cards ready to
tumble with the first harsh wind.

The land lords who, with the mining interests, were the
pillars of the Diaz structure, spent little time, as a rule, on
their haciendas, run mainly by straw-bosses and overseers.
Their system of operation, as a whole, was inefficient and
criminally wasteful. The key to successful farming was to
squeeze as much work as possible out of the land-workers
and give as little as possible in return. It was a form of capitalism bared of all its trimmings, exposed in its ugliest moods,
with no responsibilities toward the workmen; slavery, without the tempering mercy of the slaveowners' concern for his
beasts of burden. There were some exceptions, some benevo-
lent hacendados, but this benevolence was purely voluntary, a
gesture of charity, virtuous only by contrast with the prevailing barbarism of the overlords. All the abuses known to
company-towns existed: private police, company stores which
charged outrageous prices and where trade was compulsory,
hacienda-dances where the owner sold booze and so got what
little was left of the peons' wages, forcing him to borrow and
put himself and his family and future generations in hock.
The pitifully inadequate hacienda school and the hacienda
church were all part of the same set-up. Was it any wonder
that a people so bound would understand instinctively a manifesto which called upon them to unite, reminding them of
what they knew only too well—that they had nothing to lose
but their chains?

The system of peonage was universal, as much in the henequen plantations of Yucatan, the tobacco plantations of
Oaxaca, as in the maguey groves of the central plateau, the
big ranches and farms of the northern States. In one of the
smallest States, and one of the most fertile—Morelos—the
abuses of the hacienda system were glaringly evident, and it
is there that the agrarian revolution of the twentieth century
found its point of departure. Morelos is a semi-tropical State,
once part of the estate which the King of Spain granted to
Cortez along with some 25,000 vassals. Sugar cane was the
State's main crop. By 1908, eighty-five per cent of the acreage
was owned by twenty families. The bulk of the cane was
used, not for sugar, but for the manufacture of alcohol, which
became the principal industry. The march of the hacendados,
who spent their big fortunes abroad, left a wake of destruction as complete as that of a plague of locusts. Forests were
mowed down, towns and villages vanished within the expanding hacienda walls. And at the height of production,
only three per cent of the total area of the haciendas was
under cultivation. The rest lay idle while corn had to be
imported from other States.

The people thirsted for drinking water and the haciendas
squandered the precious fluid on their fields, just as they
squandered the human labor that worked those fields. On
the Santa Ines hacienda, for instance, approximately 75,000
quarts of water were used for each kilogram (two and two-
tenths pounds) of sugar produced; on the Temixco hacienda,
65,000 quarts. Still the land-grabbing continued, and the
slightest protest was crushed with the one efficient organization that the haciendas and the whole Diaz structure maintained: armed terrorism.

And this factor is important in understanding the background of Mexico's land troubles. Even Diaz himself, before he became incrusted as dictator, wrote a personal letter

in which he cited the injustice being done by cutting up the ejidos, stating that the "small property" was really distributed to the hacienda owners. Suppose, in order to see the picture still more clearly, that you own a home and a small piece of land, perhaps a farm, where you have worked, and your family has worked, for generations. The fellow next door has a big estate. He decides to branch out, takes your place, evicts you, and doesn't pay a nickel. If you protest, you go to jail or are put on a hacienda chain gang. And suppose you had a family and you had to support that family, what would you do—you, with your experience and superior education and the benefits of civilization? Then, think of what the peasant could do under the circumstances, without these advantages. Eventually he took the only course—revolution. He wanted the land back, but in such a way as to prevent the same situation from developing again. He wanted a system that would safeguard him against any individuals who might attempt to grab the others' land, an operation sometimes erroneously described and praised as "initiative" and "enterprise." If this fact—the need for collective protection against avaricious and disproportionately strong individuals—is borne in mind whenever a discussion of Mexico's land problem is presented, a lot of the confusing smoke-screen thrown about the question will vanish into thin air.

The land-grabbers turned the beautiful State of Morelos, a climatic and scenic paradise where Mexican rulers always built their country palaces, into a swamp of vicious greed. There, a peasant lad grew up, his heart a heavy lump of resentment against injustice, his guts burning with an unquenchable flame of vengeance, the compass of his life set on a dead course: to right the wrongs done to his people by the despoilers. That man came to be called the Attila of Mexico, firebrand, the whip of hell and destruction. But to the peasant of Mexico he is the martyred father of the Agrarian

Revolution, the apostle of Land and Liberty. Today there is hardly a section of Mexico which hasn't a town, or a school, or a street, or all three, named after Emiliano Zapata.

3

Many a peasant in the State of Morelos today will still tell you that Emiliano Zapata wasn't killed, that the body publicly exhibited on April 10, 1919, was not Zapata, but a wax dummy. Zapata still rides, they will tell you, over distant mist-hidden hills, awaiting the proper time for his return, to finish the job he started on November 28, 1911. That was the date of the Plan of Ayala, the peasant's declaration of independence, his ultimatum to the men in power that the Mexican Revolution will remain unfinished until the needs of the farm population are satisfied. These peasants, some of whom rode with the agrarian hero, have almost sanctified the man. They see him as a new savior, a Christ on horseback and with cartridge belt across his chest, immortal, the Christ who said, "I come not to bring peace, but a sword." The other Christ, the cheek-turning Christ, they save for the day when there may be peace on earth.

Emiliano Zapata was born in the village of Anenecuilco a few months after Porfirio Diaz became president. He grew up in the fields, on his father's little farm, and his earliest recollections were stories of destitute peasants dispossessed, told around a village lunch-stand or in front of the hut where the family gathered of an evening to watch the sun go down. Once he asked his father why the peasants didn't get together to protect their lands.

"Nothing can be done against the hacendados," Gabriel Zapata told him. "They are too strong. They have everything. We have nothing."

It wasn't long before the village cops made things too hot

for quick-tempered Emiliano, and the boy, then twenty, pulled out for the neighboring State of Puebla, where he got a job on a ranch. After a couple of years as a cowboy, he returned to his home, to work on the family tract. The march of the hacendados brought them, a few years later, to the limits of Anenecuilco and the neighboring village of Ayala. Young Zapata, his brother Eufemio, and several other villagers, decided to see a lawyer, carried their complaint to the courts in Mexico City. There they found that it was all part of the same run-around, a colossal shell game in which the sucker never got a break.

Zapata called the villagers together, suggested that since there was no other way, they defend their land with guns. This suggestion by Zapata was tantamount to signing his own death sentence. The hacendados didn't kill him outright then, but did what was often the same thing: they had him conscripted into the army, favorite medicine for troublemakers. During the Diaz epoch, and later, conscription was used to fill the barracks to which few would go voluntarily. More than one man, perhaps on his way home from work, perhaps stopping for a drink at a pulque saloon, disappeared, and was never heard of again. Zapata served six months in the Cuernavaca garrison, and was released through the influence of a rich rancher, a former employer who liked the way Emiliano could handle horses and take care of them. Several times he tried to return to his home village, but the hacendados managed to keep him out.

It was not until 1909, when the gubernatorial election campaign was in progress, that Zapata was allowed to come back. Since there were always election fights and this was a particularly hot one, they figured something might happen to the young troublemaker who had become so popular among the peasants. The men of Morelos still had hopes, although faint, of trying to correct the abuses of the Diaz regime by way of the ballot. All previous elections had been stolen and this was no exception. Zapata campaigned for Patricio Leyva, representing the small middle-class groups, against the Diaz candidate, Pablo Escandon. Leyva was declared defeated, and persecution of those who backed him was intensified. But the campaign revealed to the people of the State that they had found a leader. While Madero in the north was preparing his movement that would be launched with the Plan of San Luis Potosi, dated November 20, 1910, a little group of farmers, a newspaperman, a couple of lawyers, gathered in the hills. They decided to join the movement and sent a representative to San Antonio, Texas, headquarters of the Madero revolutionary junta.

A series of isolated uprisings in the State early in 1911 brought more repression. There was no other way out: Zapata and his companions rode away to join forces with Gabriel Tepepa, who had risen against the Diaz government in the little town of Tlaquiltenango. Soon the various guerrilla bands, formed by the Zapata group as they passed from village to village, moved toward unification and the thirty-four-year-old Emiliano was named commander-in-chief of the Morelos Revolutionary Army.

Diaz capitulated after a truce with Madero, that little fellow with a big heart, who thought that men, facing loss of power they had wielded for years, would act rationally. Madero had the country in the hollow of his hand for a moment. Hopes for freedom and justice rose high. But Madero, member of a rich family that looked on the Revolution as an investment, was not the man Mexico needed at the moment. This vegetarian, naturopath, pacifist, wanted to give the country a sun-bath and a change of scenery, when it clamored for an emergency operation. Madero hesitated, on the brink of social revolution, and he was lost. The hopes that the men of the soil had raised were swamped under the intrigue of the Diaz crowd that stayed in the National Palace while formalistic Madero went through the motions of an election.

These intrigues eventually split Madero and Zapata. When Madero came to Morelos, he was guest at a banquet. The governor, a Diaz man, was host. The landowners and other conservatives were there. Zapata was invited. Madero might sit at the table with those gentlemen and keep calm. But that was no place for Zapata, and he refused to attend. Later, in Mexico City, Madero, still blind to the urgent needs of the agrarians, tried to buy off Zapata with enough so he "could get himself a ranch." The men of Morelos saw which way the wind was blowing. They declared against Madero, who was blamed for the surprise attack by federal troops on Zapatistas. This occurred after Madero had given his word that no such thing would happen, and had tried to induce Zapata to lay down his arms. But Madero was already hamstrung—the counter-revolution was on the march. General Victoriano Huerta, who was to become dictator in 1913, headed the forces that moved against Zapata. When the reaction was ready to put Madero out of the way, they found their man in Huerta.

The assassination of Madero in February, 1913, then already president, was like an electric shock that made the lukewarm anti-Diaz groups realize that a mere change of men was not enough. The killing of the pacifist President was the spark that set off a bloody social war. Zapata and his army of peasants continued fighting against Huerta as they had fought against Diaz. They joined forces with Carranza. When Carranza also tried to put a brake on the agrarian demands, the Zapatistas still insisted that something be done about the land. To win agrarian support, Carranza issued his January 6th decree, in 1915, ordering parceling of lands. Zapata was forced to fight the Carrancistas who were against him, and who finally trapped him, through a subterfuge, and killed him in April, 1919, in ambush. Before that happened, Zapata had written a letter to Carranza, summing up the disillusionment of the peasants, a bitter picture of betrayal, that the underdogs would recall again and again, as the revolution was shunted up the blind alleys of personal gain by ambitious politicos and foreign pressure. Zapata's letter said in part:

". . . And in agrarian matters, the haciendas have been given or rented to the favorites, the generals; the old land lords replaced, in many cases, by new land lords with guns at their belts; the hopes of the people mocked. Ejidos are not returned to the communities which, in most cases, continue to be deprived of them; nor is the land distributed among the working people, among the poor peasants and those who are really in need.

"In labor matters, by intrigues, bribes and disrupting maneuvers and corruption of the leadership, the disorganization and death of the unions has been achieved; the unions, sole defense, main bulwark of the proletariat in its fight for betterment. The majority of the unions exist in name only. Members have lost faith in the former leaders, and the most conscientious, those of greatest worth, have scattered, discouraged. . . . Your soldiers steal seeds, cattle and work stock; in the small towns, they burn and loot homes of humble citizens and in the larger cities they speculate with the stolen grains, hold up automobiles in broad daylight, organize robbery into an industry, such as the notorious maffia known as the 'The Gray Automobile,' unpunished because the leaders of this gang and their accomplices are people close to you, or holding high positions in the army . . . and this is the government which you call the representative of law and order."

The pressure from the agrarian sector became stronger every day. Carranza sent General Pablo Gonzalez to wipe out Zapata, to raze the State of Morelos if necessary. And the forces of General Gonzalez, on behalf of law and order, swept through the State like all hell let loose. The sugar mills and farm implements which Zapata, the soldier, had left untouched, because he knew that Zapata the peasant would want to use these after the fighting was over, were burned to the ground, hacked to pieces by the punisher sent from Mexico City. Whole villages were set to the torch, villages where Zapata and his men were welcome, where they had been met with open arms. In many cases the entire population went along with the Zapata army when it left, fearful of the arrival of the federals. The destruction and pillage could not long continue one-sided. Soon some of Zapata's bands were paying off, an eye for an eye, and in some cases two for one. Bands of marauders, taking advantage of the chaotic situation, committed nameless atrocities under the protection of agrarian or anti-agrarian slogans. Zapata was finally slain, still fighting for agrarian justice two years after Article 27 of the 1917 Constitution had made land distribution a part of the basic law.

4

Zapata died, but his cause lived on in Article 27, destined to become the most revolutionary instrument in Mexican reconstruction. Article 27 definitely placed limitations on private property when such property conflicted with the public interest, qualified the former concept of absolute private property so that private property derived from society rather than the other way around. This is substantially the concept of property under a regime of social democracy, in which the main tendencies are toward centralization, toward conservation of natural resources, toward directed economy, and in general, toward greater intervention of the government in the mechanics of national economy. The emphasis of this intervention can vary, of course, on behalf of one group or another, one economic class or another, and the struggle for political control becomes a struggle for the privilege of determining that emphasis.

Curiously enough, the principle of making property a social function produced the paradox of giving the recipient of the land parcel absolute hegemony over his piece of land. Under no conditions, according to the basic principle of Article 27, can this property, birthright of the family, be alienated or attached, or be made subject to any liens or court action of any kind. These legal walls were placed around the ejido in order to prevent a recurrence of that absorptive process by which the land-grabbers had nullified every attempt at distribution of farm acreage in the past. Theoretically the man on this parcel would have absolute security of land. Here was a new kind of private property, so much a personal thing, so much a part of the man who worked it, that it could not be sold, any more than the man could sell himself into slavery. It could not be taken for taxes, nor be made subject to foreclosure. He could devote his full energies to the task of cultivating this piece of property, to making it a place of beauty, a joy forever for his family and his descendants.

All in all, a delightful picture to contemplate—on paper, like the real-estate prospectus that turns a swamp into an enchanted lake. Article 27 stated specifically that the Congress and the various State legislatures shall pass the necessary laws and shall proceed to division of the big estates. Seventeen years passed before a workable agrarian code was approved by Congress, a code tending toward standardization and co-ordination of diverse legislation that had confused the land problem and had caused interminable delay in parceling. That was in March, 1934, and that same year—the first year of the Six-Year Plan—during the administration of Abelardo L. Rodriguez, the autonomous Agrarian Department was created, replacing the former National Agrarian Commission which had been a dependency of the Ministry of Agriculture, traditional stamping ground of the big landowners.

From its inception, the agrarian reform encountered every possible kind of obstacle that a law can run up against in the process of being enforced. It found opposition within the ranks of the men of the Revolution, who differed on the precise form to be given the parceling system. Some argued on behalf of properties they themselves owned and which might be affected, others on behalf of properties they were in the process of acquiring, or hoped to acquire. Some spoke obviously as representatives of the landed interests. Outside the ranks of the men of the Revolution, the opposition took more forceful measures, stopped at nothing to check the distribution: sabotage, bribery, persecution, boycott, murder. Every attempt to turn the land reform from a paper project into reality made one fact stand out sharply: the big landowners, whose monopoly and absorption the Revolution fought to break, were still the giant power they had always been. There were new faces among the land lords, faces of former men of the Revolution. But the hacendado had landed on his feet, and was again at grips with agrarianism.

Land lordism was able to stage a come back because of the inadequacy of early agrarian legislation designed to put into effect the provisions of the 1917 Constitution. The first laws consisted of little more than an emotional attack on the huge estate system, a gesture toward the peasants who had made up about seventy per cent of the armies that overthrew the Diaz and the Huerta dictatorships. The second phase of this legislation passed from a more or less negative attitude toward provisions for land distribution on a limited scale, the evident aim being to parcel land only when absolutely necessary. It was during this second period, 1923 to 1928, that the peasants began organizing into federations, in a relatively small way, and the first attempts were made to establish a nationwide peasant confederation.

The farm legislation matured with the Agrarian Code of 1934, which definitely set forth the principle of the peasant's right to land and the duty of the State to find that land for him. It discarded the notion that the aim of the ejido was to provide subsistence farms where the land-worker could supplement the wages he drew on the hacienda or in industrial plants. This latter interpretation was the one which the conservative interests had tried to give the agrarian movement. The result was that in many cases peasants got tiny pieces of land, not even enough for subsistence, and without seed or implements to work this land, and the unconcerned politicos felt that the Revolution's debt to the peasant had thus been discharged. In other places, politicos on the make—and in some cases, the impatient and baffled peasants themselves—took over lands without the formalities of the agrarian laws. These laws had become, under biased enforcement, impediments instead of aids to the peasants' attempts to get the land they needed. Numerous armed clashes resulted. Land lords with private armies of "white guards" refused to accept the agrarian legislation. They persecuted the peasants, many of whom were hanged to roadside trees as a warning. Agrarian engineers who arrived to survey lands for parceling were assassinated. Terrorism prevailed in Mexico's farm areas. The peasants were fighting their Revolution all over again. By 1933, the little faith they had in fake leaders—many of them stooges of the hacendados—had vanished, and the peasants moved toward more extensive organization into leagues and federations. To permit the peasants to protect themselves from "white-guard" raids, previous administrations had armed the peasants. One of the first acts of the Abelardo Rodriguez administration was to force disarming of the peasants. One of the first acts of the Cardenas administration was to re-arm the peasants, and then to convert these armed farmers into reserves of the regular army, thus giving them an organized and official status as rural defense corps against marauders and "white-guard" raiders of their ejidos.

5

Lazaro Cardenas came into office with the new Agrarian Code already on the statute books, and with the autonomous Agrarian Department already established. The Rodriguez administration had begun to apply the code, emphasizing stabilization of the farm-credit structure which had been functioning haphazardly since 1926, when the first National Agricultural Credit Bank was established by Calles. The beginnings of the epochal agrarian reform which has marked the Cardenas administration actually date, then, from 1934— first year of the Six-Year Plan which was also the final year of the Abelardo Rodriguez administration. During the two years of Rodriguez' presidency, a total of 105 land-parceling decrees was issued. During Cardenas' first four years, a total of more than 2,000 similar decrees was issued. At the close of the Rodriguez term, membership in farm-credit societies totaled 100,000. By June, 1938, the membership had jumped to nearly 500,000.

In addition to direct repression of land-demanding peasants, sabotage of their demands through complications of red tape, and delays in passing on claims, a number of other means were employed by the land lords in an effort to make the Agrarian Code as dead a fish as other statutes had been. Since President Rodriguez had obligingly deprived the peasants of their arms, and since most of the military commanders and local kingfish were in league with the land lords, physical obstruction of land parceling was a more or less simple mat-

ter. The killing of several agrarian engineers finally forced
Rodriguez to provide such officials with an armed guard. The
land lords, and with them most of the Calles clique that had
acquired good-sized estates, seized on the cry of "small property" as a rallying point for invalidating the agrarian program.

Article 27, and the Agrarian Code, specifically grant protection to the "small property" as well as to the ejido, on the
principle that both these forms of farming will tend to weaken
the main enemy, the big landowners. The "small-property"
clauses grant immunity against parceling to any farm tract
with an area less than two hundred and fifty, or less than
four hundred, acres, depending on the location of the land,
type of soil, nature of the crops. That concept of "small property" helps to make clear the size of the big estates. Soon the
land lords found a solution. Relatives, friends, hired stooges,
all were drafted. They registered different parts of a big
estate as their "small property" tracts. This recognition,
granted to the right people by the government officials, left
the hacienda intact except on the records. Not only intact,
but inviolable, since the law said that small tracts could not
be parceled. A favorite way of getting around the farm law
was organization of fake "peasants' leagues" after the fashion
of company-unions. These groups would apply for an ejido
on a certain estate. The Agrarian Department would order
the "parceling" and then the peasants would go back to work
on the hacienda under the same conditions as before. Sometimes politicos and others who wanted to grab off a piece of
land formed fake peasant organizations and pitted them
against the regular peasant groups.

The "small property" was not always a stall. There are
many perfectly legitimate small property-owners, farmers and
cattle ranchers, who are not on ejidos. Even when it is legitimate, the land lords prefer the small-property deal rather than
the ejido deal, for a number of reasons. The small farmer,

with his limited resources and antiquated implements, can't possibly compete with the hacendado's extensive credit and modern agricultural implements. In the acquisition of water rights, the hacendado always has more weight than the little farmer. On the market, the hacendado determines the prices at which the little farmer must sell his crops. The "small property" is even better for the hacendado than share-cropping, another favorite form of hacendado farming. The share-cropper has legal protection: the land lord must provide him with decent living quarters, a tract for subsistence farming and grazing of domestic animals, must provide schools for his children. The "little-property" man has none of these special benefits, and in many cases actually operates on a share-crop basis—the near-by hacienda advancing the seed—but without the theoretical benefits of the landless share-cropper. In many cases, too, the little farmer becomes an employer of labor. He prefers to get it, naturally, as cheaply as possible. He thus becomes an economic, social and political ally, a shadow of the big land lord, and he becomes an enemy of the land-parceling program because it withdraws the landless proletariat from circulation by giving that proletariat tracts of land to work on ejidos. As an employer, too, the small farmer plants himself in opposition to organized labor, and it is from his ranks that some prospective fuehrers and duces of Mexico hope to conscript the man power that can be hurled against the urban proletariat.

It is not to be assumed, however, that every man who advocates "small property" is by virtue thereof a fascist. There are many peasants who prefer a fenced-in chunk of land where they can grow or not grow crops, white-wash or not white-wash the adobe shack, as the spirit moves them. There are also economists, technicians and politicos who see in a system of widely-distributed small farms the best bulwark of democracy, security, prosperity, and all the other beautiful things that organized society can provide at its best. They will cite such countries as Holland and Denmark as examples of how small individual farming can become positively Elysian. And some of the most honest economists in Mexico will concur in the laudatory approach toward the small farm. But there are small farmers and "small farmers."

There is the small farmer in whom the most ardent advocates of the collective ejido system declare they find the best ally of the ejido farmer, the one who will really fight shoulder to shoulder with them to break down the hacienda system. The "dyed-in-the-wool-and-a-yard-wide" small farmer is the fellow who doesn't hire any peon labor. On his land the work is done by the farmer himself, his sons and his family.

There is the small farmer who does some of the work himself, directs operations on his tract, but employs laborers to do most of the heavy work.

There is the small farmer who is really a rancher, whose main business is not growing food crops, but livestock, who needs big tracts of land for grazing and plenty of water for the stock.

Then there is the small farmer who is no farmer at all, but who is in the farm business. He is the fellow who lives in the city, sometimes with a mercantile business in addition to the farming, in many cases just enjoying life on the proceeds of his land. Sometimes he is a politico, maybe a senator or a congressman, a cabinet officer or a governor. Sometimes he is a general in the army. But in every one of these cases, the "small farmer" is no farmer, but a businessman, whose approach to farming is that of the owner of any business.

These men, in the farming business, were the ones who had been getting the most benefit from the agrarian program. The big dams and irrigation works constructed during the Calles regime—and pointed out as monuments to his great constructive genius—were built at public cost for the almost exclusive benefit of privately-owned lands. When the land workers tried to organize unions on these capitalist enterprises, it is said that they were sent away to the Tres Marias penal islands as "Communist agitators."

In the State of Michoacan, on November 2, 1938, some eight thousand small farm owners organized a League of Small Proprietors. The godfather of the organization is General Gildardo Magaña, governor of the State, and with eyes cast on the presidential chair. He has been among the most persistent champions of the "small farmer," advancing the argument that the small farmer—"not as an enemy of the ejido" but as an ally—can be a decisive force in breaking down the hacienda system; but, that the small farmer has to be protected from land-parceling, that he must get aid in the form of credit and implements from the government, just as the government is helping the ejido farmer.

Supporters of Cardenas' policy of greater emphasis on ejido organization charged that Magaña was seeking a formula for his presidential campaign, the formula in which he concurred with his friend, Cedillo. They charged that all the agitation about the "small farmer" was a blind to cover up the renewed campaign of the land lords against the agrarian program of land distribution. They contended that the only real ally of the ejido can be the small farmer who works his own land; and, they argue, the so-called "small farmers" on whose behalf Magaña and other State governors raise their voices, cannot really be instrumental in destroying the power of the big haciendas, because the small farm opens the way to a revival of the hacienda. They state that the idea of merely dividing estates is a mechanistic interpretation of the Constitution and the Agrarian Code. The hacienda system cannot be eliminated, they continue, merely by reducing its size, but by destroying the big land lords' economic and political power. Not the small farmer, they conclude, but the ejido, organized on a system of industrialized farming, a co-operative of peasants, with ample credit and modern machinery, will be the decisive factor in really returning the land to the men who work it. They also consider it symptomatic that most of the States in which governors have come out loudest for the "small farmer" are also the States where organized labor has had tough sledding.

6

Cardenas, armed with adequate legislation, with the lessons of many past mistakes, and with a corps of trained technicians and economists, gave the agrarian restoration movement the biggest push it has ever known. The Cardenista land program, incorporating every aspect of the Mexican Agrarian Revolution, seeks to provide an eclectic structure in which radical collectivists, radical individualists, and all intermediate degrees, can develop side by side. Maderismo, Zapatismo, Carrancismo, Obregonismo, Callismo, all can be regarded as having attained maturity by blending into Cardenismo. The eclecticism of the Cardenas farm program is regarded by many as utopian. Some critics, in the name of simon-pure Marxism, charge that such a thing is impossible, that it is based either on ignorance or bad faith, that this amounts to reconciliation of class interests and that the inevitable end of such a policy is fascism. Other critics, in the name of the sacrosanct and eternal right of absolute private property, unhesitatingly brand the Cardenas program as disguised communism, and not so disguised, either. The land program aims at avoiding the abuses of dogmatic formalism in application of the land laws, recognizing that asparagus can be grown best under one system of cultivation and hemp or cotton or bananas under another. The two-headed problem in all these forms is to give the land-worker a break, to give him a decent return for his labor, and, at the same time, not to jeopardize agricultural production and hence the national economy. Defenders of the "radical" program describe it as really a "conservative" program, and explain that by conservative they mean the fullest utilization of resources—natural and human—with the least possible deterioration in natural resources, the greatest possible development of the human.

The Cardenistas believe this can be best achieved through the development of co-operatives, necessarily government-subsidized, that the peasants' hope lies in a system of control of the land by the man who works it. Nice theory, the skeptic answers, but will it work? How is the agrarian program really turning out? Is the peasant getting the land? How about the incentive to work? How about the discipline of the hacienda? Does the farmer have any say-so, or is he just being regimented? How long can the penurious, debt-saddled government keep handing out money to the farmers?

The first answer from Mexican officials comes in the form of statistics. During Cardenas' first four years in office, more than thirty million acres of land were distributed. From 1915, when the first agrarian decree was issued, until 1934, when Cardenas took office, approximately twenty million acres were distributed, making a grand total of about fifty million acres, roughly one-tenth of Mexico's total area, distributed to about one and a half million farm families.

When the Cardenas administration began its land-parceling program in 1934, there were approximately forty million acres of arable land in Mexico. Of the thirty million acres that went into ejidos, ten million came from this arable area, and the rest from uncleared brush and forest land. So this part of the program actually made available twenty million additional acres, half of the total that had been made ready for the plow during the years of the hacienda system. Of the grand total of fifty million acres distributed since 1915, less than three million have the benefit of irrigation. About one-third of Mexico's arable area of sixty million acres was under cultivation in 1938.

Another fact to be borne in mind is that the land reform under Cardenas is not something that was initiated overnight. A big part of the applications for land, on which the Cardenas administration acted, had been on file for years, some as long as twenty years, many for ten, some relatively recent. Those files in the Agrarian Department are more eloquent than all the speeches and debates in describing the real meaning of Cardenism to agrarianism. Cardenas ordered action, definite decisions on the land applications already on file and speedy handling of the new ones that arrived, including many petitions for larger tracts than the "particles" which many had been given as parcels. He took the agrarian program off the official paper and brought it down to earth. And to the peasants, stalled for years, that was some kind of miracle.

Aside from the ejido program, the government has authorized division of some ten million acres of public lands into farm colonies with a total population of thirty thousand families. By the middle of 1938, sixty-seven colonies, comprising nearly five thousand families, had been definitely established on a million and a half acres. The rest were being delayed because the funds budgeted for surveying and engineering work had been used up.

The ejidos, which in 1938 grew approximately fifty per cent of the country's four hundred and fifty million peso agricultural production, are the keystone of the new farm regime through which the men of the Revolution hope eventually to supplant the hacienda system.

7

The word *ejido,* according to etymologists, derives from the Latin *exitus,* "the way out." The application of "the way out" to land is traced by some students to ancient days when feudal estates extended right up to the walls of independent towns. In order to permit inhabitants of the settlements to come and go without being accused of trespassing, the king established a strip of land, an *exitus,* which was made part of the town's community property.

Under the Mexican Agrarian Code, an ejido is a tract of land granted in common to a group of families, each of which is entitled to a proportionate parcel of the tract. The "ejido" is subdivided among the occupant families, and each family can farm its own plot as it pleases, choosing the crops, the form of cultivation, and financing. The family can do almost anything it pleases with the land, except sell it or mortgage it. The farmer on this parcel is entirely free to get his crop loans from private moneylenders, produce dealers or banks, as had been done for years before government farm credit banks were established. He can make these loans individually or through the ejido society, from private financiers or the government bank. The government loans are made to ejido farmers organized into co-operative societies. Ejidos of this type are known as the "controlled" ejidos, and may be worked either individually or on a collective basis, under technical direction of the government bank, which selects the crops, obtains the necessary machinery, sells the production, and distributes the profits among the farmers. This type of production has gained most headway in areas where crops can be grown on extensive acreage. The system of large-scale operation was introduced, for instance, in Yucatan's henequen plantations, after earlier agrarian programs had made the mistake of cutting up the plantations. In other places the collective system had been instituted, in the growing of truck-farm produce, such as vegetables and greens, which lend themselves better to individual farming. In such cases, the collective system is being abandoned and the individual system restored, but the marketing continues to be done collectively.

The nerve center of the "controlled" ejido system is the Banco Nacional de Credito Ejidal (National Ejido Credit Bank), established on January 1, 1936, on which date it took over the accounts of 221,680 farmers, members of 2,853 co-operative credit societies which had been organized under the old bank, the National Farm Credit Bank. By June 1, 1938, the membership of the co-operative farm societies had grown to nearly 500,000 and the total number of government-financed co-operatives had passed the 5,000 mark. "Free" ejidos, that is, not government-financed, totaled nearly 8,000. The bank was organized as a corporation capitalized at 120,000,000 pesos, of which the federal government subscribed 115,000,000, the State governments 2,500,000 and the rest was available to individual investors. The federal government agreed to pay for its shares at the rate of 20,000,-000 pesos a year. Most of the 2,500,000 shares assigned for general subscription have been purchased by the co-operative societies. Besides making crop loans, the bank finances purchases of seed, machinery, work-stock, dairy and beef cattle. The bank has, during the last two years, laid special emphasis on instituting collective farming wherever this is feasible, and only where mechanized farming is possible. The possibility of mechanized farming, industrialized farming, with its great advantages in efficiency and better returns, was a factor that led to collective organization. This is contrary to the contentions of some critics that "communistic" and "soviet" ideas were being evolved and then put into operation blindly. Another factor, equally important, was the need of credit societies which could be held responsible for loans. To guarantee the money advanced, the government intervened in operation of controlled ejidos.

The two most talked-of collective attempts are in the Yucatan henequen fields and in the Laguna cotton district, comprising acreage in the adjoining States of Coahuila and Durango. About seventy per cent of the total henequen acreage of the State is now being cultivated collectively. An integral part of the henequen-growing is the fiber-production plant for which special machinery is needed. Under the form of an Association of Henequen Producers, the State government is running the henequen industry. Machinery was made available to the ejidos, to "small farmers" and to the plantations. One criticism leveled at the Cardenas henequen reorganization was that it deprived the industry's workers of all the rights under the labor laws, that they could not protest against State dispositions, that since they were owners they could not strike. The government answered that the workers are much better off than they were under the rule of the plantation owners, that the latter had run the henequen business into the ground, that the plantations were notorious slave holes, that the plantation owners squandered their profits instead of using them to maintain the henequen fields, that for the first time in the history of Yucatan, corn was planted on a big scale, about a hundred thousand acres of it, so that grain would not have to be brought in from outside the State for the forty-four thousand ejido families.

The henequen industry is pretty specialized, after all, and the problems there did not attract as much attention as those that developed in the Laguna section, the big cotton region. There are about forty thousand families on this tract of approximately one million acres, which for years was completely controlled by five powerful families. In 1938, crops of cotton, alfalfa, wheat and corn valued at a total of thirty million pesos were produced on two hundred thousand acres under cultivation. About twenty million pesos were invested in work stock, implements and machinery, including four hundred tractors, fifteen thousand plows, and several thousand graders, cultivators, threshing machines, and other implements. During 1937 and 1938, the government built sixty-five new schools, bringing the total to nearly three hundred in the Laguna section. There are five hundred teachers for the twenty-two thousand pupils.

Collective farming is being given a bigger and more thorough try-out here than anywhere else in Mexico, and on the outcome may depend the emphasis of the future farm program. Because of its importance, the Laguna area has been a center of controversy from the time of the first big expropriation, in 1936, following a strike of peasants employed on the haciendas. In the fall of 1938 there were three hundred and twenty-five co-operative ejido societies, and many of them had begun to extend the co-operative idea to other phases of their life, establishing co-operative stores, co-operative barber shops, co-operatively owned corn-grinding mills, some of them managed by women. Development of these co-operative systems, building of more ample irrigation works, and a greater diversification of crops, previously limited practically to cotton, are among the principal aims of the government program in this section.

In September, 1938, charges of irregularities were leveled at the officials of the Ejido Credit Bank operating in the Laguna region. The manager of the bank resigned and the Ministry of Finance undertook an investigation. The general tenor of the complaints was that the peasants were very much in favor of the collective farm system, and were all for the government bank, but that their difficulties were with the bureaucracy that had been placed in charge of administering the institution. Peasants complained of haughtiness and insolence of the employees; that some of the engineers ran things as if they were operating private haciendas; that machinery and supplies were being charged to the ejido societies at prices much higher than their actual cost; that a lack of system in advances forced peasant families to go for days without food; that some of the bank employees had formed a monopoly for handling indispensable equipment; that inferior feed, containing ten per cent of soil, was being bought for the mules; that some lands had been flooded through negligence; that frequently the engineers and other government employees threatened and insulted the peasants; in short, enough charges to show that the peasants were not against the system, but against its abuses.

Right-wing congressmen, led by Emilio Acosta, an hacienda owner, asked for an investigation of the bank's Laguna operations. The Ministry of Finance and a congressional committee investigated. Peasants were assembled, and for three days the committee listened to complaints, a total of about two hundred. Each of these was gone into, and the committee returned a report declaring that the majority of complaints were not against the bank or its employees, but really consisted of petitions for drilling of new water wells, building and repair of living quarters, indicating the neglect of the hacienda owners in this respect.

Water is the big problem of the Laguna district. Whether you farm collectively or individually, capitalistically or communistically, the stuff just won't grow without water, and the people must have drinking water as well. Lack of the latter was explained by the recent establishment of many new communities, made up of peasants who had previously been scattered. Part of the water problem—at least regulation of the available supply and its conservation—will be solved by the El Palmito dam which was scheduled for completion in 1940. The congressional committee's favorable report was unanimous, signed by all, including the chief complainant, Acosta.

Some of the charges hurled at the bank officials were undoubtedly true, and can be traced to some political appointees who behaved as bureaucrats do the world over when democratic control is not strong enough. In some instances, the peasants, who were used to being bilked so much, took advantage of young, tenderfoot officials and pulled a fast one here and there, like, perhaps, a motorist who passes a red light when the cop's not looking. Sometimes the peasants bought liquor with the borrowed money instead of food for their families.

But the charges do not always originate with the peasants. Very often they come from entrepreneurs and moneylenders. These men, aroused by the bank's tendency to eliminate the middleman, will offer peasants higher prices for crops, or money at lower interest, deliberately to stir up discontent. In any case, the peasant gets the benefit. Then perhaps an implement dealer, angry because a rival firm got the contract, will say a lot of nasty things. The general sentiment among people with no axes to grind—and even some people whose lands have been expropriated—seems to be that the attacks came from two main sources. These people felt that the bank on the whole functioned well, was fulfilling its aims, that it is not perfect, but that rough spots will be ironed out. One source of attack is the politico who wants to get his hand on the controls of the banks. But the heaviest attacks—no longer against alleged abuses—but against the system itself, come from the big landowners. And the very intensity of these attacks is regarded by many as a symptom that the collective system may be working out all right after all. Typical of the criticism against the Cardenas agrarian reform is this excerpt from an article by M. H. Guerena in *Hoy*, September 10, 1938:

"The president stated that 1,570,507 peasants have received . . . 22,343,501 hectares. But the president does not state how many farm owners have been deprived of their land; nor the value of the land taken without compensation; nor the fact that the agrarian reform has destroyed agricultural credit and the few farmers still remaining on the land cannot get credit and their situation is desperate; nor did the president mention the sufferings brought upon the nation in the form of increased cost of living, due principally to insufficiency of agricultural production."

Luis Cabrera, able spokesman of the landed and corporate interests, writes in *Twenty Years After*, published in 1938:

"The Ejido Bank is the one that selects the land which seems suitable for ejidos; the bank seeks the peasants who will apply for the land; it transfers the land, it organizes the credit societies, decides which crops are to be grown, when the land is to be watered, when to harvest, advances the money for seed, buys the plows and oxen, names the foremen, pays wages and calls them 'advances' on profits, it directs the harvest, sells the crops, keeps accounts, and above all, it decides who can work and who cannot."

And if you ask almost any peasant—there are exceptions—about all this, his answer will usually be, "So what?" He'll tell you that he has more say-so about things than he had before, that he gets more good out of his labor than he did under the hacendado. And if you point out the drawbacks and ask him if he would like to return to the old system, he'll look at you with a funny expression, as much as if to say he thinks you're "teched in the haid," and that you ought to be in the booby hatch instead of running around asking a lot of fool questions.

Pick up a newspaper in Torreon, center of the Laguna district, during harvest time, and you'll find advertisements like this:

> "Mister Ejido Farmer—for good serviceable furniture, stoves, radios, remember the Blank Furniture Store—Your Credit is Good."

The peasant had never been called mister before and he never had any credit before.

Ask a merchant, and he'll tell you that the peasants are buying shoes, clothing, groceries, which they never bought before.

Ask Julian Garcia, sixty-year-old peasant, what about it. He'll answer:

"My great-grandfather did not know what it was to sleep on a bed. Nor my grandfather. And my father, like his ancestors, slept on the floor, on a straw petate. But tonight, I shall sleep on a bed, and on a mattress, thanks to General Cardenas."

Ask some of the ejido secretaries to show you their books on the 1938 crop:

La Paz Ejido—536 hectares—produced 1,033 bales, 400,373 kilograms of seed, bank repaid, other expenses met, reserve fund taken care of, net profit, 112,254 pesos to be divided among 150 ejido members.

El Hormiguero ejido produced 817 bales, 316,835 kilograms of seed, paid bank, harvest expenses, bought new machinery, put 12,800 pesos in the reserve fund, 400 pesos to the school parcel, and 51,000 pesos left for distribution to 152 peasants.

And so on, some showing bigger gains, some smaller, a majority barely breaking even, and some in the red, like farming almost anywhere that has to be done with a variety of soils, under a variety of different methods, with industrialization still in its infant stages.

Ask the National Ejido Credit Bank for figures on all the ejidos and it will tell you that in the 1937-38 season a total of 3,134,778 pesos was distributed as profits to cotton and wheat growers, compared to 1,555,370 pesos the year before, and that the yield per acre in cotton, wheat and rice has been increased, surpassing the average yield on non-ejido farms and haciendas. Figures showed that corn and bean production dropped in 1938 under the 1937 totals. The government said it was because the peasants were eating more and putting less on the market, whereas formerly the market came first and the peasant got only a measured amount of corn for his subsistence. Aside from this, it is a fact that farm production fluctuates widely, depending on the weather. Lack of funds is, of course, the big problem. In 1938, private financing supplemented the ejido bank in some sections. The Anderson, Clayton Company of Texas has been handling most of the cotton crop of Mexico in the past, and continued to do so in 1938, advancing money to some of the farmers. Other private speculators participated, and in one region near Matamoros, buyers netted a return of 297,000 pesos on advances of 150,000 pesos, which is nearly one hundred per cent. This may be one reason that entrepreneurs do all they can to fight the bank and the ejido.

The government statistics generally look good. The opposition offers other statistics and other interpretations which make things look not so good. There are bright spots in the agrarian picture, and there are plenty of dark ones. The hacendado is far from being whipped. Although peasants are armed, organized into rural defense corps as reserves of the army, killings continue. Every day reports come in of bloodshed over land. Hacienda white guards raid ejido lands. Ejido farmers move in on a "small farmer's" land. Two ejido groups claim the same tract. White guards spread terror against agrarians. Parceling engineers are assassinated.

Armed agrarians abuse the power given them, lord it over other peasants. And, almost everywhere, the local kingfish again appears as the ultimate obstacle to land reform. And the little kingfish traces back to bigger kingfish, up to the statehouse, to the national capital. The government is friendly today, but still the kingfish of the provinces are supporters of the government, and in turn they are backed by it. Will the government be friendly tomorrow? And if not, what can the peasant expect from the kingfish who today is bound by a certain amount of restraint? The peasant has been gypped over and over again by his fair-weather political friends. He is now definitely trying to protect his gains against possible political changes. About two million peasants have placed hope in their new nationwide organization, the National Peasants' Confederation, born with great solemnity at one o'clock in the morning, August 29, 1938.

8

Elaborately-mustachioed Professor Graciano Sanchez, big chief of the Mexican Peasants' Confederation, wept while he addressed the peasants' convention in the Hidalgo theater, Mexico City, on August 28, 1938. Sanchez' voice, choked with tears, broke as he pictured the gathering: realization of the dream of many years, something for which he had labored fervently since, as a rural teacher, he had ridden with the agrarians in Tamaulipas. Later that day, Sanchez almost wept again, not sentimentally, but angrily, when an insurgent movement in the convention threatened to oust him and other politicos. But Sanchez won and he became secretary-general of the newly formed National Peasants' Confederation.

The auditorium echoed with the chorus of the "Agrarian Hymn" welling from three thousand peasant throats:

"Ay . . . ay . . . ay . . .
In our struggle and our toil,
Many valiant brothers died,
In reconquering the soil!"

Around the balconies of the theater, banners proclaimed:

"Stand Ready to Defend Cardenas Against Reaction!"
"Revolutionaries: On Guard in the Class Struggle!"
"Zapata: You are Not Dead. You Live in Our Hearts Today!"
"United in Action. United in Work. United in the Revolution!"
"For the Economic and Cultural Liberation of the Peasant Woman!"

President Cardenas spoke. Sanchez, to the right of the President, held the microphone for him. Luis I. Rodriguez, president of the Party of the Mexican Revolution, stood at the President's left side.

Cardenas told the gathering that he spoke to them "as a loyal friend and as one responsible for the unification meeting." They represented every State in the union. For several years the official government party had been directing the work of unification in each State, and this meeting was the climax, uniting the various State federations. In many localities, peasants refused to join the Confederation, declaring it to be a political instrument. The day before the convention, opposing leaders had called on Cardenas to argue a serious point: should the Confederation be limited to peasants or should non-peasants who had shown themselves to be allies and fighters in the peasants' cause also be permitted to become members and officers? That question threatened not only Professor Sanchez, but also a number of congressmen and other politicos who were known in the legislative halls and government councils as the Peasant Bloc. For some time the rebel movement had been developing in the peasants' organization, aimed at ousting the politicos. It failed to carry, however, and later in the convention when Sanchez was elected, sixteen local organizations' delegates walked out of the meeting, despite Cardenas' earlier plea that they close ranks, and try to bring all other peasant groups into the one confederation.

Luis Rodriguez, president of the Party of the Mexican Revolution, the government party, said in his speech that "Cardenismo is the incarnation of the aims of the Revolution."

Concha Michel, known as a composer of revolutionary songs, and as a leader in the movement for women's rights, spoke on behalf of the Confederation's feminine sector.

Others spoke. The Confederation voted on its declaration of principles, its basic program. Summary of that program:

1. No special privileges for small property other than those privileges enjoyed by the ejido parcel farmers. Integral solution of the land problem, economic unity in which the independent property and the parcel are put on the same basis. Solution of agrarian problem with no legal restrictions or any restrictions of any kind other than the natural ones of land, water, terrain.

2. Formation of collective enterprises, State-owned and State-controlled, on land remaining after all the ejidos have been satisfied and the small property has been restricted to the same size as the parcels. On these enterprises all workers will have a right to work, either as wage labor, as share-croppers or renters. The purpose of this part of the program is to industrialize farming.

3. Collective farming of the edijos, not to create a new rural bourgeoisie, but an agrarian economy based on co-operatives. Preliminary steps should be organization of producing and consuming co-operatives and more State intervention in regulation.

4. More widespread distribution of land, establishment of more autonomous towns and settlements where civil rights can be guaranteed. Expedite land distribution.

5. Re-organization of credit. The farm banks should not be run as a profit business, nor as an abstract organization of a group of societies, but should become an organic part of the Agrarian Department and function as a credit institution.

6. The Revolution, in its agrarian aspects, must eliminate all economic subordination of man to man, so that the ejido must become the sole form of economic-technical exploitation of the soil. Share-cropping, renting, colonization, subdivision sections of the agrarian laws should be re-drafted to bring all these under the ejido system.

7. Cancellation of the agrarian debt, which is an unjust burden on future generations. The former owners got full benefit from the years of exploitation, not only exploitation of the soil, but of the men who were their servants and laborers.

Besides the above program, the Confederation presented President Cardenas with a "Three-Year Plan for Farming," to function under the Second Six-Year Plan.

There were other projects and other speakers. Two men, regarded as important behind-the-scene forces in the peasant movement, and close friends of Graciano Sanchez, did not speak: Emilio Portes Gil, former provisional president of Mexico, and Marte Gomez, governor of Portes Gil's home State, Tamaulipas, a State important in agriculture, in fishing, in oil (Tampico), and with a long stretch of its northern boundary extending along the Rio Grande.

9

In 1918, Portes Gil, then a congressman, was a witness at a duel fought in Chapultepec forest, between Cesar Lopez de Lara, ex-boss of Tamaulipas, and Luis Caballero, rival candidates for the governorship of Tamaulipas. The two fired, missed each other, but killed another witness, Lieutenant-Colonel Francisco Aguirre, and wounded Portes Gil.

In 1935, Cardenas and Calles came to a showdown, the final sequence in a political duel, and when the fireworks were nearly over, Portes Gil found himself squeezed out of the presidency of the National Revolutionary Party, in which he had figured prominently since its inception. Some said he had himself squeezed out because he didn't want to get too involved with the Cardenista program.

Portes Gil is not at all an innocent-bystander type. If he was the unwilling victim, it would just be another paradox, which would be fitting, for Portes Gil, one of Mexico's keenest politicos, is a bundle of contradictions. A passionate anti-clerical, a big-shot Mason of Mexico, he was the one who, as president, signed the truce with the Catholic clergy in 1929. Denounced, during his rise as a "radical," he has become one of the men to whom the rightist interests in Mexico look with fondest hope, a man whose name had become linked with Hoover, with the G.O.P. of the United States, and with the House of Morgan. Branded a "Communist" by Morones, Portes Gil became the instrument of persecution against the Communists when they were driven into underground activity. For years a close collaborator of Calles, he was believed to have been instrumental in engineering the Calles ouster; at least, he threw the weight of his personal political machine and his talents as a strategist on the side of Cardenas. As president of the National Revolutionary Party during those critical days, he was in a big measure responsible for holding things together.

In a country where most of the big shots in recent years have been army men, he has been among the few outstanding non-military politicos, the only civilian president among Mexico's six last chief executives. Portes Gil has been a staunch prohibitionist and an anti-gambling crusader, since he was quite young. At the age of nineteen, in 1910, he was a schoolteacher in his native city of Victoria. He attended a champagne-drenched political banquet and scandalized the nice people by delivering a fiery oration on the evils of drink. He studied law, was admitted to the bar in 1915, and soon afterward drifted to Sonora where another ex-schoolteacher-reformer, Plutarco Elias Calles, had just decreed statewide prohibition. In that State he became a judge of the Supreme Court, and a part of the Calles machine.

Portes Gil has been more influential probably than any other one man in molding contemporary Mexican legislation. Lawyers say that he was most influenced by Italian corporative jurisprudence and that this influence is reflected in current Mexican legislation. At the age of twenty-seven, Portes Gil was made legal counselor of the War Ministry by General Obregon and he redrafted the military code. In 1919, as a supporter of Obregon's presidential ambitions, he was jailed by Carranza on a charge of subversive activities. When Obregon and Calles, with their Plan of Agua Prieta, overthrew Carranza, Portes Gil was appointed provisional governor of Tamaulipas, and in 1924 was elected to that same post. It was during this period, the building of his State political machine, that Portes Gil became identified with the peasant movement, encouraged agrarian organization in the State. He met Marte Gomez, an agrarian and hydraulic engineer who had gone into politics, and Graciano Sanchez, a rural schoolteacher turned agrarian leader. Gomez, successively congressman, senator, director of the agricultural college, director of the farm-credit bank, was named Minister of Agriculture in Portes Gil's cabinet and later Minister of Finance in Abelardo Rodriguez' cabinet.

Portes Gil served four terms in Congress, introduced a labor code and a penal code which were discarded as being too radical by a very radical lot of congressmen. His penal code would have made the "unwritten law" into written law, and also would have made hunger justifiable cause for robbery. His proposed labor legislation later served as one of the bases for the Mexican labor laws now in effect and influenced many of the younger lawyers, including some of Cardenas' brain-trusters. As governor he helped promote the Tampico stevedores, dock-workers and marine-workers' guild (Gremio Unido de Alijadores), a politically controlled co-operative. This organization did some good things, and some not so good, but its significance in the rise of Portes Gil was that it became an important part of his political machine.

President Calles made Portes Gil Minister of the Interior, regarded as head of the cabinet, and from this post the Tamaulipas reformer, then thirty-seven years old, moved into the presidency, as provisional chief executive, following the assassination of President-elect Alvaro Obregon in July, 1928. Portes Gil directed the prosecution of the Catholic group charged with responsibility for the Obregon slaying. He distinguished himself as the most forcible exponent of anti-clericalism, advocating full shearing of the clergy's political power in order to bring about definite separation between Church and State. His writings on these matters have become textbooks for the younger Mexican politicos. From the presidential chair, Portes Gil moved to the presidency of the National Revolutionary Party. After that he was professor of agrarian law in the National University, Minister to France, delegate to the League of Nations. In the Rodriguez administration he became Attorney General. Cardenas appointed him Minister of Foreign Relations, a post he left to become head of the National Revolutionary Party at the time of the Calles-Cardenas split.

The division of the National Revolutionary Party into right wing and left wing, and the purge of the Party and

Congress, led finally to the resignation of Portes Gil. Since that time he has been engaged in private law practice, but his political machine has remained more or less intact. Many of his key men still hold important government positions, or are in Congress. With Marte Gomez as governor, the Tamaulipas section of his machine continued functioning. As ex-president, as ex-cabinet minister, ex-statesman, Portes Gil continued in 1938 as one of the most influential politicos in Mexican public affairs, although he repeatedly stated that he had "withdrawn from politics."

There is some doubt about whether the anti-re-election laws would prohibit a provisional president from becoming chief executive for a regular term. The most widely accepted opinion is that the law would bar an ex-provisional president as well as an ex-substitute president, like Abelardo Rodriguez, whose friends were priming him for a comeback. It is not likely that politically-shrewd Portes Gil would run personally in the face of a non-re-election argument that could be used against him. But there is no such technicality to bar Marte Gomez. The influence of both is strong in the peasant organizations.

In the 1940 elections, the agrarian sector will play an important, if not a decisive, role. As prime-mover of the "small-property" interpretation of the agrarian laws, Portes Gil, through his fronts, is expected to figure in the nominating convention in 1939, and the elections of the following year. The issue of "small property" versus "ejido collectivism" had come to the fore, in 1938, as pre-election agitation increased. A bloc of State governors, including Magaña of Michoacan and Yocupicio of Sonora, both with presidential ambitions, both generals, was formed to push the "small-property" emphasis in application of the land laws. The agrarian problem is one of several due to make the next elections the first real test of Cardenismo.

XI

RHAPSODY IN BLUE DENIM

1

THE woes of Mexico's men in blue denim have provided the principal theme for the political torch-singers of that country for more than two decades. Plaintive lyrics have been crooned for overall-wearing listeners by table-thumpers from the left wing, from the right wing, and from the wishbone. For without what the lads call a "mass base," a political career can't even get to first base. Some of these orations, shooting from the mouths of politicians in a blast of hammers-and-sickles, lay it on so thick that they seem to be histrionic caricatures, mocking the all-too-real sufferings that the Mexican people have known. But the proletariat will lend its ears, even if it doubts. For the Mexican industrial worker and the peasant are twin victims of some of the greediest, most selfish and sterile capitalists known anywhere, not excepting African and Asiatic colonies.

It is not surprising, then, to find that one of the newer and more substantial monuments of Mexico's Revolution is a modern Department of Labor building, twin structure to the Agrarian building. The two edifices stand side by side on Lopez street, in the center of Mexico City. Peasants and proletarians mingle as they go in and out of their class halls of justice. Like the Agrarian Department, the Labor Department is a product of the 1917 Constitution, specifically Article 123, Mexican labor's Magna Charta. There the worker seeks redress from underpaying, overworking employers. There he demands his three-months' severance pay to which every unjustly discharged worker is entitled. There, too, labor lawyers thrive, and corporation attorneys find goldy-green pastures on which to batten.

The overalled men have hoisted one after another politico to power and have seen many of their champions turn against them. New leaders continued to rise, appealing to the disillusioned but embattled proletariat to bear the brunt of new reform movements. Peasants and proletarian were often hostilized into hatred of one another, only to be kicked in the patches of their pants by the fellows who set them against one another. Toughened by experience, learning little by little, painfully and heroically, to sift the wheat from the chaff, the men in blue denim keep battling. Added to their other problems they now have the responsibility of two big industries on their shoulders, the railroads and the oil industry, placed in their care in a form that brings with it all the disadvantages and some of the advantages of political intervention.

Wage-hour-and-working-condition demands by the men in blue denim brought to a head the split between Cardenas, as head of the maturing anti-Calles movement, and the old dictator who wanted to continue as uncrowned king of Mexico. After a series of strikes in 1935, Calles issued a public statement condemning the Cardenas administration for not squelching the striking workers, for trying to enforce minimum-wage laws passed by the Rodriguez administration. In so doing, the old Sonora warhorse produced another Mexican paradox: the action of Calles, whose labor policy had been to keep the workers divided into various unions, now forced labor into a self-defensive united front which years of oratory and organization efforts had been unable to achieve. Out of this temporary Committee for Proletarian Defense grew the Confederation of Mexican Workers, unquestionably the most powerful labor organization in Mexican history. And with it, the star of Vicente Lombardo Toledano, brainy, cultivated, labor lawyer-philosopher-pedagogue-politico, was revealed as a planet of the first magnitude in the political heavens.

2

If Lombardo Toledano's wealthy parents hadn't lost their fortune as a result of the anti-Diaz revolution, their talented young son might have become a very successful corporation lawyer, a literary dilettante, a university professor, an old guard politician, or a distinguished member of the Mexican diplomatic service. And the organized labor movement of Mexico would have lost what is undoubtedly one of the sharpest, best-grounded political brains in the country.

Vicente Lombardo Toledano was born in Teziutlan, State of Puebla, in 1895. That same year another intellectual, who had turned his talents to the labor movement in a distant land and who was later to shape Toledano's philosophy, was writing his first strike manifesto, for the workers in the Semyanikov factory, in Russia. The man was born Vladimir Ilyitch Ulianov. His comrades called him Lenin. That same year, also, in the little town of Jiquilpan, Michoacan, there was born to the Cardenas del Rio family a son whom they named Lazaro. And the Teziutlan Copper Company, owned by Lombardo Toledano's father, was at the height of its production.

As the son and heir of a copper magnate, Lombardo Toledano got the best of care to be had. When he was about fifteen years old, he was sent to Mexico City as a boarding student in the Internado Nacional, a preparatory school which was the favorite of provincial families who could afford to pay tuition and board for their sons. Like the other young men of his class, young Toledano drifted toward the social gatherings of the "best people" of that period, most of them in one way or another connected with the Diaz regime.

The dwindling of his family's fortune brought the young law student, as in the case of other young men, to look deeper into the revolutionary convulsions which had begun to shake the nation. Lombardo had already achieved a reputation as an orator among his classmates, but the speeches of his school days were along lines quite different from those which were to make him famous as a labor leader. As a young lawyer he turned to politics as the most promising field for his talents. And politics at that time—the period of Obregon's rise—was developing a definitely laborist trend.

Toledano's philosophy was first molded in the classes of Antonio Caso, a Bergsonian, who today still heads the school of philosophy in the National University. In the thesis for his law degree, Toledano defended the idealist philosophy as opposed to materialism in a manner brilliantly becoming one whom Caso regarded as his star pupil, protégé and possible successor.

The year 1918 marked the first nationwide attempt to organize labor and that same year Lombardo Toledano was named secretary of the Popular University, a cultural center which arranged lecture courses of a popular nature. Here the future labor leader first rubbed elbows with the city proletariat. In his lectures at this time, Toledano showed decided traces of Carlyle's influence. Two years later, already a professor at the age of twenty-five, Lombardo Toledano took a combined professional and vacation trip to the Hot Lands, in the Balsas River valley, State of Guerrero. The semi-barbarous living conditions of many natives, their complete neglect in the face of devastating malaria and leprous skin diseases, the heart-breaking poverty of these people, left a permanent mark on the young professor. His brain was already churning with attempts to reconcile these things, the situation of the city workingman, the retreat of the Puebla Indians to the hills, with the idealist philosophy in which was inherent the notion that there is a Divinity that shapes our ends.

While Lombardo Toledano was in Guerrero, the Carranza government fell, and Adolfo de la Huerta went in as provisional president. Jose Vasconcelos, who later became Mexico's most famous exile and who returned to Mexico in 1938, was appointed Minister of Education following the Carranza fall. Vasconcelos, who gave many young intellectuals an opportunity to show their stuff, named Lombardo Toledano director of the National Preparatory School, a post regarded as highly important in Mexican cultural life, and formerly reserved as a mark of honor for mature men who had achieved fame and distinction.

It was during this epoch that Lombardo Toledano moved closer to trade-union circles, as did many others under the frankly laborist tendency of the Obregon administration. He was soon in the Regional Confederation of Labor (CROM), as head of the Educational Committee, a handsome, bright-eyed, long-jawed young man with wide, sensual lips, curly loose-combed hair and a faraway look, more like a poet than a labor leader. His affiliation with the CROM came through one of the veteran labor leaders with whom he had previously worked, General Celestino Gasca. In the CROM, Toledano became a collaborator of Luis Morones, whose social trajectory was the reverse of Toledano's. Morones, a plumber-electrician, rose to complete control of the organized labor movement, to a cabinet post, and wound up as a millionaire.

After the 1923 de la Huerta revolt, Toledano, not quite thirty, was appointed governor ad interim of Puebla, replacing the late Froylan C. Manjarrez, who had joined the rebels, but who later returned to the Calles fold as a loyal collaborator. At the time of his death in 1937, Manjarrez was editor of the National Revolutionary Party's official organ, *El Nacional.*

Toledano continued in the CROM at Morones' side until 1931 when the Toledano group rebelled and formed a CROM of its own, later to become the General Confederation of Workers and Peasants, which, in turn, was to be the nucleus of the Confederation of Mexican Workers.

During this period, Lombardo Toledano had maintained a strict trade-unionist point of view, holding that the labor unions should function strictly as economic organizations for defense of their rights against the employers. This was a position similar to that held by Calles—who looked on the syndicalist trade unions as the bulwark of capitalism—and Morones before the latter made the CROM an adjunct of the Obregon electoral machine in 1920. But following the break with Morones in 1931, and prior to formation of the Confederation of Mexican Workers, Toledano had been moving more toward a position in which he considered the role of the trade unions political as well as economic.

Simultaneously, Toledano's philosophy had veered from idealism and spiritualist theism toward the positivism and humanism of Auguste Comte, and then toward the dialectical, historical materialism of the Marxists. His attempts to bring into the University an alternative for the prevailing Bergsonian anti-scientific school and to open the way for the Marxist philosophy led to his expulsion from that institution. He then founded the Gabino Barreda University, named for Mexico's outstanding proponent of Comte's positivism, with the idea of finding a compromise between idealism and materialism. This school was transformed in 1935 to a "Marxist" institution and its name changed to the Workers' University of Mexico. During this period Toledano had visited the Soviet Union. What he said and did upon his return led to the accusation that he had become an agent of Moscow.

Toledano first took the philosophic socialist position in 1932 when he and his former maestro, Antonio Caso, engaged in a polemic which has become among the most famous in Mexico. Caso called his former pupil a renegade and an ingrate. Toledano replied that he had been completely taken in by the idealist philosophy and had come to realize the untenability of that point of view. The debate, waged in the newspapers for weeks, was sensational, because it represented the fundamental division between the two main currents of thought in Mexico. Lombardo's evolution was paralleled by that of many other Mexicans who had started out as Catholics and wound up as Marxists. More than once is the accusation leveled at a candidate, during an election, that he had been leader of the Catholic Youth Association and then blossomed out as a revolutionary. Occasionally there is a case of a revolutionary who later appears in the clerical ranks.

Toledano turned the tables on Caso and branded his former teacher a renegade, stating that he had passed from positivism to intellectualism to intuitionism to religious metaphysics, and that "as an inevitable consequence of this philosophical and scientific involution, from the Christian concept of life to the political doctrine of fascism." He charged that Caso had become an "enthusiastic fascist" and "leader of the conservative class" of Mexico, and cited lectures of Caso's in which the famed philosophy professor had advocated giving the University a "National-Socialist orientation."

Toledano summed up his own philosophical position:

> "... we believe that man is a product of nature; that the exterior world forms and guides his spirit; that his conscience is principally social and not individual; and that it is not man who makes history according to his will, but that history creates human ideas; that liberty

does not consist of separating man from nature, attributing divine power to him, but in proceeding rationally within the dialectical process of historic laws. . . .

"The most that spiritualism can give in the field of social doctrine is the Encyclical Rerum Novarum, and in the field of political struggle the fascist regime or the Nazi system. . . ."

In his personal life and habits, Toledano is the direct opposite of his famous predecessor, Morones. Morones was big, fat, gross, ostentatious. Lombardo is thin, rather short; he would appear almost ascetic, if it were not for his carefully dressed appearance. He is very neat, always wears well-tailored clothes of neutral shades, preferably gray, or blue, with a touch of color in his necktie and socks, and his trousers are always pressed. The years have slightly lined his poetic brow and face, but there is still something very youthful about his expression and his general demeanor.

Toledano has none of the lust for luxury that Morones showed in the notorious party-house he maintained in Tlalpam, Mexico City suburb, where the labor leader of yesterday ruled with the abandon of a latter-day Nero. Toledano is almost austere in his way of living, and his hobbies are three: his collection of cactus plants, said to be among the biggest in the world, surpassing even that of Alexander Genin, millionaire Frenchman, department store owner in Mexico City; his collection of ancient Mexican sculptures, containing some eight hundred pieces; and his library at his home in Villa Obregon, formerly known as San Angel, a suburban area where many other Mexican celebrities live.

He has three daughters, and can often be found talking with them, or reading, in the garden of his home. The light burns late at night in his study, where Toledano has turned out a prolific production of political and philosophical works. He is a hard, steady, disciplined worker, extremely nervous,

smokes cigarettes continuously. A convincing speaker, he is
not a spellbinder. Morones was the superior agitator, a rouser
of emotions. But Toledano, still the professor, drives home a
clear exposition of his argument with the steady impact of a
sledge hammer on a spike. A course of Toledano speeches will
leave a more lasting impression than a series of Morones'
speeches.

His enemies will frequently assail him as a "bourgeois" who
has been smuggled into labor's camp, a wolf in sheep's clothing. They call the workers' attention to the fact that when
Toledano travels to Europe he goes on nothing less than the
Queen Mary. But many workers don't mind that at all. They
are rather proud of having a fellow like Toledano on their
side, one who can match wits with the best of them, whether
on the rostrum, at the dinner table, in the legislative chambers, or on the strike battle-lines, one who can meet the
enemy at its own game. His admirers in labor's ranks rather
like the idea that a "bourgeois" does not have the presumption to consider himself an equal of the proletarian and yet
can be called a comrade. But don't get the idea that labor
is one hundred per cent for Toledano. The Mexican workers
have been burned too often to be anything but skeptical.
They look on many leaders as careerists, as political climbers,
and even have a word for this phenomena: "leaderism." The
political ambitions that tend to thrive among lawyers in the
Conciliation and Arbitration Boards help to keep this attitude alive. But, precisely because the political color of an
administration may have an important bearing on labor
board decisions, the labor organizations have begun to check
closely on those appointed to the arbitration boards, as well
as on the men they send to the legislatures and to Congress.

In some sectors of organized labor, there is a marked
feeling of distrust toward Toledano, a feeling that his interest in the labor movement is primarily that of a politico.

His enemies—personal, political, economic—naturally do all they can to spread this feeling in labor's ranks. And they have most of the daily and weekly press at their disposal. John L. Lewis was handled tenderly, almost caressingly, by the anti-CIO press in the United States, compared to the verbal manhandling that Toledano gets in the Mexican commercial press. Toledano fights back through the CTM daily newspaper, *El Popular*; through the CTM monthly, *Futuro*; by mass meetings, and demonstrations, and through the labor bloc in Congress. Within labor's ranks and outside, the opinions about Toledano clash. Few, however, will doubt his ability, his political awareness, his versatility, his ideological preparation, all of which are invaluable in labor's struggle against capital, and which help to make him an important influence in holding labor together. His critics frequently ask: Where is Toledano headed, and how far will labor go with him?

3

The Confederation of Mexican Workers (CTM) celebrated its second birthday in 1938 by moving into new quarters, right on Mexico City's main stem, Madero Avenue, No. 74, a building which many years ago echoed with the prayers of nuns. Into this former convent moved the general staff of the biggest trade union federation in all Mexico's history: Vicente Lombardo Toledano, Salvador Lobato, Fidel Velazquez, Juan Gutierrez, Mariano Padilla, David Vilchis, Manuel Gutierrez.

The decisions made by these men affect approximately one million men and women, according to the Confederation statistics, organized into some four thousand locals in thirteen national and industrial unions, and thirty-two State federations.

Besides the CTM, there are two other labor confederations,

and several regional federations, but the membership of all these combined pales beside the imposing mass of the CTM. The other confederations are the General Workers' Confederation (CGT) and the remnants of the CROM, which still has a dominant voice in the textile industry. Among the regional federations, the Federation of the Workers of the North, a Monterrey and Nuevo Leon State organization, which the CTM calls a "company union," and the Federation of Jalisco Workers are the most important. In both Jalisco and Nuevo Leon, clashes between the CGT and the CTM are frequent. Head of the CGT is Julio Ramirez; of the CROM, Francisco Ramirez Escamilla. The CROM recently split again over charges leveled at Morones and some of his confederates, involving the disappearance of five hundred thousand pesos of the union's funds during the time that Morones was running it.

The CTM, in line with its policy of political action, and with opposition to its organizational drives in various States, has been participating in state elections, frankly supporting one candidate or another, according to the candidate's attitude toward the CTM. Some of the sharpest conflicts have come in the States of Sonora, Nuevo Leon, Coahuila, and Durango, where the authorities were accused of forming "white unions" to fight the CTM. In the first named especially, the CTM has hard sledding, due to steady and allegedly repressive opposition from Governor Ramon Yocupicio. Toledano accused Yocupicio of attempting to have him assassinated during a visit to the northern State. Yocupicio said he had no intentions of "permitting radicals to take over the State." The Sonora governor's attitude turned eyes toward him as a possible candidate of rightist groups in the 1940 presidential election. In nearly every case where the CTM was fought strongly, the authorities made use of the CGT as a counterweight. This was the system followed by Calles, after decline of the CROM, to keep any one union from becoming too strong.

The rise of the CTM went parallel with a tremendous increase in strikes during the last five years. Statistics show plainly that while the nominal salaries of workers in Mexico have risen, the real wage, the purchasing power of the worker, has not increased appreciably, and in many cases has even declined. In order to offset this tendency, blamed on arbitrary price-raising by monopolistic speculators, the government in 1938 established a price-regulating commission. This commission undertook to stabilize basic commodity prices by offering the staples to consumers and retailers at what were considered reasonable prices. This drew a heavy protest from the dealers.

The number of strikes dropped somewhat in 1938 following the expropriation of the oil properties. The drop was traceable directly to the plea of President Cardenas that workers make a special effort to keep the wheels of national economy turning. He even went so far as practically to reprimand certain strikers who had stopped work without fulfilling the legal formalities. The President bluntly told labor that "such tactics get the workers nowhere and succeed only in embarrassing the administration during a time of national crisis when united support of all citizens is needed." The strike record shows that from seventeen strikes in 1920, the number rose to some three hundred in 1921. That was during the Obregon administration when labor organization was encouraged. In 1924, when Calles came in, the number dropped to 136, and then steadily on down until 1932 when there were fifty-six. In 1933 a total of thirteen strikes was recorded. From 1934 on, since Cardenas took office the number of strikes kept steadily mounting. The total had grown to 235 for the year 1934, the last of the Rodriguez administration, indicating that the labor movement was already trying to regain lost ground. In 1935, Cardenas' first year, a total of 642 strikes occurred, followed by 659 in 1936, and 833 in 1937. A campaign of retrenchment in the mining industry was given as one cause of the increased strikes in the last two years. A strike in Mexico, once the labor board holds it to be legal and licit, automatically permits the workers to hang their union banner at the entrance and to prevent anyone from entering or leaving. The purpose of this is to protect the workers against an employer who might want to run out on them with assets which might be legally attached if no settlement of the dispute is reached.

Among the most significant strikes of the last two years was that of the peasants employed on the haciendas in the Laguna region in the States of Durango and Coahuila. They struck on August 18, 1936, demanding that the hacienda owners grant them a collective contract and increased wages. The strike went on until August 31, 1936, when the government brought it to an end by expropriating the property in accordance with the agrarian laws. The huge cotton and grain region was divided into ejidos and the epoch of government-subsidized and controlled farming began in a big way on the Laguna lands.

In 1937, the CTM defined its attitude toward the State, in answer to charges that it had become completely collaborationist and was being made an adjunct of Cardenismo as the CROM became an adjunct of Obregonismo. The CTM stated that "as long as there is a progressive government running the country, the CTM will lend its support, maintaining its autonomy and freedom of action, because the proletariat has historic ends to fulfill which are different from the functions of government." The definition of policy continued:

"Until the state of semi-feudalism disappears from Mexico and the country loses its characteristics as a colony for outside economic forces, and as long as there is the menace of fascism or any other form which the decadent big bourgeoisie uses against the interests of the people; as long as these things constitute an obstacle to the inevitable transformation of the capitalist system, the Mexican proletariat should not only maintain the alliance which exists between it and the other exploited sectors of the population, but it should fight staunchly to keep the Government as a faithful representative of the people's interests and loyal executor of the Revolution which marches on."

At the first general Congress of the CTM, February 25, 1938, Lombardo Toledano addressed the delegates. The dispute between the oil workers and the companies had reached a critical state. Toledano asked the audience:

"Is the proletariat of Mexico ready for a sacrifice, no matter what it may be, in order to defend the autonomy of the country?"

A resounding roar in the affirmative left no doubt that at least part of the proletariat was ready. The following day Toledano issued a special plea, calling on the CGT and the CROM to join forces with the CTM and thus completely unify labor.

Six weeks earlier Lombardo Toledano, acting on orders of the CTM central committee, issued a circular to all affiliated unions, stating that the members of the unions should receive physical and military training. No guns or other weapons were to be used. Instead of guns the "workers' militia" would use gymnastic rods, suitable enough for the manual of arms, and each company would have a drum and bugle corps.

Before the year was out, the marching feet of thousands of men and women were heard daily, stomping through city streets and the roads of smaller communities. Every evening, for an hour or so after the work day had terminated, the workers marched. Their first appearance on a big scale was in the May Day parade. They wore overseas caps and coveralls, looked somewhat like the militias that were formed in Loyalist Spain.

Again the question was asked: Where is Lombardo Toledano headed? The most insistent asker of the question was the powerful Employers' Center, the general staff of industrial, commercial and financial interests of the country.

4

Employers of Mexico are organized, according to the law, into unions. In the opinion of some writers, this is evidence that Mexico is moving toward the corporate form of government. Others point out that the same tendency has always been part of social democracy. The last tabulation of employers' unions, on June 30, 1938, showed 265 such unions, with a total membership of 7,589, registered with the Ministry of National Economy. The leadership of the Employers' Center is practically the same as that of the Confederation of Chambers of Commerce.

The stronghold of the Employers' Center is the important industrial city of Monterrey, capital of the border State of Nuevo Leon, and sometimes referred to as the "Pittsburgh of Mexico." Railroads, accessibility of metal ores, and proximity to the United States, as well as the far-famed enterprise of the energetic Nuevo Leon residents—the go-getters of Mexico—all contributed to the growth of Monterrey. It is the one Mexican city whose main street looks more modern and more American than the main streets of many American cities.

It was in Monterrey that employers staged their famous "strike," to protest increasing labor organization, the increasing number of strikes, and the general policy of Cardenas on labor relations, which they described as "communism." Instead of either giving in to them, or attacking them, Cardenas blithely told them that "if they had become weary of the class struggle," they could turn their factories over to the workers, who would be more than glad to run them. Calles also had come to sharp words with Monterrey Big Business some years before. He at that time accused them of obstructing constructive work of his administration, and threw a scare into them with a now familiar five-syllable word: Expropriation.

Industrial and financial Monterrey is controlled by about ten families, big families, some of which have been in that part of the country for many generations. The Garzas, Sadas, Elizondos and others appear on the boards of the foundry, the smelter, the brewery, the glass works, the banks. The biggest potentate is Adolfo Prieto, whose interests cover many parts of the country, and extend to Spain and South America. One of the Monterrey men, Joel Rocha, wealthy furniture manufacturer, has been discussed by rightist groups as a possible candidate for the presidency. Among certain groups that quietly promote whatever ambitions Señor Rocha may have is one that calls itself the National-Socialist Party of Mexico, members of which declare themselves to be anti-Semitic.

From Monterrey on July 29, 1938, a United Press dispatch reported that the fascist and anti-Semitic Gold Shirts—who had theoretically been disbanded by an order from President Cardenas—had clashed with the CTM during a strike at the National Coal Factory. The dispatch quoted the CTM as stating that "Nationalists and Gold Shirts assaulted the strikers," and that the Monterrey police and other public authorities were supporting the strikebreakers. At this time there appeared an anti-CTM publication which headlined the prophecy that "Monterrey will be the tomb of the CTM."

Late in 1938, the fight continued unabated. Monterrey employers announced their intentions of putting a stop to further union organization. Their control of many public officials, they believed, would help them in this drive. Things got hot on September 22, 1938. The Employers' Center asked Cardenas to intervene in the Monterrey situation. A similar request was made of the State governor. The new crisis arose over the arrest of Ramon Contreras, a CTM organizer, on a charge of "frustrated homicide." His arrest led to threats of a general strike in Monterrey, which the employers laughed off, asserting that the "CTM does not represent the proletariat of Monterrey." Then the electric-light plant was shut down, busses stopped running, there was no telephone service, the roundhouse came to a standstill, the smelter and foundry furnaces cooled. This didn't last very long, but the judge who had ordered him jailed found that, after all, there really had been no legal basis for arresting Contreras, and set him free. The stoppage ended quickly.

Leaders of the CTM repeatedly charged that "reactionary" public officials in the States of Nuevo Leon, Sonora and Durango, among others, are encouraging attacks on the labor organization and financing the formation of fascist "nationalist" organizations and fascist trade unions. The CTM newspaper, *El Popular,* editorially supported candidates regarded as friendly to labor. In the fall of 1938, one of the CTM's top leaders, Juan Gutierrez, a member of the national central committee, and native of Nuevo Leon, announced his candidacy for governor of that State.

Gutierrez, representing the powerful railway workers' union, one of the strongest and one of the most conservative unions in Mexico, is regarded by some as having fully as much say-so in the CTM as Lombardo Toledano. The point made is that Toledano has no one union back of him and that the real power in the CTM, as in any labor confederation, is wielded by the direct representatives of the unions. Those who argue in this fashion forget that back of Toledano, even before the CTM came into existence, was the strong General Confederation of Workers and Peasants and its various constituent regional federations of workers and peasants, formed by Toledano's group after the split with Morones.

The charge sometimes leveled against Toledano that he was not a "revolutionary," meaning that he did not take an active part in the anti-Diaz movement nor against subsequent reactionary movements, cannot be hurled at Gutierrez, for he saw military service in 1913 and 1914. Born in Cadereyta, a small town near Monterrey, Gutierrez has been active in the labor movement since 1915, when he became a railway telegraph operator, after having served an apprenticeship as messenger boy. By 1927 he had become an official of the Railway Telegraphers' and Dispatchers' Union. For seven years after that he was the railway workers' representative in the arbitration and conciliation board. As a delegate of Mexican labor he attended the Tripartite Conference in Geneva and visited Spain, England, Belgium, France, and other European countries, studying the labor movements. In February, 1936, he was elected general secretary of the Railway Workers' Union central executive committee, and with the formation of the CTM became a member of that organization's central committee. Self-made, cautious, Gutierrez is known among the workers for his coolness, his careful consideration of any situation before acting.

In August, 1938, a palpably forged letter, purported to have been "instructions" from Toledano, then in Europe attending a convention of the Trade Union International, was widely circulated, printed in some weekly Oppositionist papers, and also distributed via chain letter. The real author of the document was said to have been a lawyer in Monterrey, but nobody could prove it, and many people were only too glad to attribute it to Toledano. The "letter of instructions" was a curious concoction which made frequent references to "our chief Stalin" and stated that "John L. Lewis, acting on Stalin's orders, plans to promote armed intervention in Mexico, so that the United States will be paralyzed and he can start a civil war."

About the same time that the "letter" appeared, the CTM and the Peasants' Confederation issued a joint manifesto calling on the workers to show their "tranquillity and patriotism" and appealing to the employing class to do likewise. This was interpreted by some as a plea for a truce in the class struggle, and the Employers' Center hastened to announce that it would be only too delighted to call a halt to the class struggle, that it had always believed in class collaboration, anyhow. But the Employers' Center had its doubts about the manifesto. Some unions outside of the CTM also expressed doubt as to the sincerity of the call, and the CROM charged that its members were being persecuted by CTM unions in several States. Some newspaper commentators argued that there could be no peace, because the slogan of the CTM, "A Classless Society," was not peaceful. The weekly, *Hoy*, in an editorial on August 6, 1938, summed up the employers' contentions for a "real unity between Mexican capital and Mexican labor." The editorial concluded:

". . . instead of running behind international organizations which go to pieces when they come up against reality, each country—and especially ours—should try to harmonize Capital and Labor, in order to be able to defend themselves from the Labor and Capital of the other countries. When, because a Mexican factory has been closed, the imports of textiles from Europe or the United States are increased, Mexico remains not only as a tributary of foreign industrialists but also of the workers who wove the fabric. What the Mexican worker fails to gain is gained by the worker of another nation.

Therefore, if tomorrow all our industry were to be declared in bankruptcy, the working classes of other countries would be pleased: with fewer competitors, they could have the right to demand better salaries and better working conditions.

"Knowing this to be true, Capital and Labor in the United States forget their differences when it comes to getting advantages from other countries. We see that Mr. Roosevelt, in spite of his anti-capitalist speeches, prepares, by means of the defense of the farm land owners, the defense of the Standard Oil and all the rest of the capitalist sharks. In this attitude he is backed up by all his citizens who, facing the foreigner, set aside their differences.

"And since Mr. Hull's note again reveals the lack of consistency of our artificial brothers abroad, we ask, with all respect, but ardently, that the Government of President Cardenas, showing a new example of patriotism, put a definitive and energetic stop to the demagogues who spread hatred, for what our country needs is that the Mexican worker become reconciled with Mexican capital, which is the only one that can feed him and sustain him."

But all these beautiful words of peace and harmony and co-operation turn to bitter mockery in the face of actual fact. One week after that editorial appeared, Mexico, used to bloody happenings, was shocked by one of the most brutal, cold-blooded massacres in all labor history: the wholesale slaughter of union workmen—twenty-six at one time—on the lumber hacienda of El Chaparro, in the State of Michoacan, on August 13.

5

The lumber workers of El Chaparro first formed a union in 1930. Members were persecuted, leaders driven out of town, hounded by the local kingfish. The workers tried to win the municipal elections. Outsiders were brought in—to vote, and some to take the jobs of the most active union men. For six years all talk of unionization was done in whispers. Not until 1936 did the sawmill workers feel strong enough again to organize openly. They formed their union under the protection of the Cardenas labor policy, and by April 15, 1938, the union had deposited, according to law, a project for renewing the collective contract with Olivares and Cuevas Hermanos, owners of the hacienda. The union said the company owed the men back pay, that funds taken by the employers on a check-off system for union dues had not been turned over to the union, that a badly-needed first-aid station had not been provided. The union wrote repeatedly asking for enforcement of the old contract, and for opening of negotiations on the new one. The workmen got no answer; so, on July 4th, they submitted a formal notice of intention to strike. On July 12th, the labor board representative met with an employers' representative and the strike committee.

On the morning of August 13th, while on their way to work, twenty-six members of the union were slain by an armed band. The slaughter had been carefully planned. As each group of workmen reached a turn in the road known as "Las Capulines," they were stopped. Union men were placed on one side of the road and non-union men on the other, separated according to a list which the leader of the band consulted. The hair-raising details of what happened after all the union men had been lined up were related later by five persons who were present: three lumber workers who survived the massacre, the wife of one, and a ten-year-old boy who was driving mules to pasture at the time. Some of the men were hanged and slowly cut to pieces with knives and machetes; some were stabbed; others' heads were mashed in with rifle butts. Most of them, tied in pairs, were shot at close range.

The brains of Eucario Suarez saved Evaristo Martinez, nineteen years old, one of the survivors. Suarez and Martinez had been tied together, arm to arm. When the volleys were fired, both dropped. The bullet that killed Suarez spattered his brains in a bloody splash across Martinez' face. The attackers left the latter for dead. He lay still, heard one of the band approach, prepare to pump more bullets into the men on the ground, heard the leader tell him not to waste his ammunition.

The workmen were not all killed at the same time. Two or three were put away, while certain lessons were driven home to the victims. For instance, Heraclio Garfias was asked why he wanted to go fooling around with such things as unions, why he was interfering with the good old patroon system. Garfias laughed. No elaborate economic theories bothered his simple brain, no ideologies:

"Why did we form a union? We formed a union so that we would get our pay on time."

"Well, you're getting your pay now, you red sonofabitch," the leader answered. A moment later Garfias got his pay: a bullet ripped through his guts.

Jose Lira, who had served a couple of years in the army, watched as three men were hoisted to a pine tree, ropes around their necks. He stood it as long as he could, he said later, but he'd rather die by a bullet than that way. So he broke loose and ran for the woods, over a low cliff. He believes a miracle saved him, but he didn't see, he didn't hear a thing while he was running. Through the woods, through a river, deep into the brush, he ran until he dropped.

A shot, fired when Lira broke and ran, hit Eucario Martinez on the arm, and he dropped. His wife, Domitila, an infant in her arms, ran toward him and covered her husband, pleading that he be spared. The leader pushed her aside, told one of his men to pound Martinez' head with a gun butt. Then, she related, the leader ordered her away, reminding her that if she said anything about what she had seen, he would come for her and her two children, tie them to his saddle-rope and drag them, feet first, till nothing was left of them.

Manuel Blancas, the ten-year-old mule driver, had a front-row seat at the massacre. He hid in the brush and saw the whole thing: the stopping of the workers; the roll call of the union members; the drinking, laughing, stabbing, hanging.

By noon the alarm had spread, the federal soldiers were in pursuit of the killers, who had completely stripped all their victims. Relatives went to the road to claim the bodies, chased away a pack of wild dogs that had been chewing at the wounds of the dead men on the ground. On the chest of one corpse was a rock, and under the rock a note:

"August 13, 1938, on this date died the Confederateds, who were reds, fallen at the hands of the Liberating Army under command of BB and his assistant CL."

All afternoon, brothers, fathers, children, friends dug holes in the ground, twenty-six graves. At night a mass funeral by torchlight, the wails and shrieks of women and children, the sullen teeth-gritting silence of the men.

The Mexico City police force was called in by the federal government to help trail the killers. Four detectives went into the hills, disguised as peasants. On September 12, the police announced that nine of the band had been captured, that three had been killed in a battle with the detectives. One of the bandits confessed that several days before he had killed a schoolteacher. He said the teacher had tried to talk him into going to work on the land. He shot the teacher, put the body in a thatch-hut and set fire to it.

Speeches were made in Congress. The CTM demanded that all "white guards" of haciendas be disarmed, that the federal government call municipal elections, supervise them.

Twenty-five widows, sixteen widowed mothers, sixty-seven children, eighteen brothers and sisters, were left destitute by the massacre.

6

Peace, harmony, reconciliation: a few weeks after Chaparro, a labor leader killed a bakery owner, a Spaniard, in the chambers of the Board of Conciliation and Arbitration. A short time later, another Spaniard, manager of a bottling works, and his son, were shot down as they drove away from a Conciliation Board session. In another session, a former leader, turned company-man, fired into a crowd of workers awaiting a strike decision.

Yet the blood spilled at El Chaparro, being spilled elsewhere, is but a drop in the gory river that keeps rolling along through the history of Mexican social struggles. Diaz bluntly told a workers' congress, through his representative, the eminent educator, Justo Sierra, that if they tried to get too strong, just to remember that there were fifty thousand bayonets ready to put them down.

The 1877 railway strike in the United States gave the Mexican labor movement its first impetus, although trade-union organization did not really get under way until the turn of the century. As early as 1855, there had been a certain amount of organization in the form of mutual-aid societies. In 1875, an obscure tailor, Jose Maria Gonzalez, disciple of Proudhon, published a little periodical called *The Son of Labor*, threw a scare into the rising Mexican middle class. Refutations of his ominous warnings filled many columns of the newspapers. Repercussions of the railway strike, the telegraphers' strike in 1883, Haymarket in 1886, the Homestead strike in 1892 and the Pullman strike in 1894, and other strikes in the United States, went rolling through the budding labor movement in Mexico. The literature of the First International, 1864, had found its way into the editorials of *The Son of Labor*.

In 1905, four years after the first Congress of the Mexican Liberal Party which for the first time included labor planks in a political platform, the tobacco workers in Veracruz struck. Soon miners, textile workers, railway workers were forming leagues of resistance, trade unions, to replace the old mutual-aid societies. The influence of the Ricardo Flores Magon group, of socialists, of exiled Spanish anarchists and syndicalists, the I.W.W., all definitely appeared in the labor movement. The armed suppression of the Rio Blanco textile workers, the crushing of the Cananea copper strike (with the aid of Texas rangers) followed. Sporadic strikes broke out elsewhere. Pablo Zierold, a German exile, formed the Mexican Socialist Party and organized the first observance of May Day—now a legal holiday—in Mexico.

In 1912 the Casa del Obrero Mundial (House of the Worker of the World) was established, under the passionate guidance of Juan Francisco Moncaleano, a Catalonian anarcho-syndicalist. Two years later, under the Huerta dictatorship, the House was raided by police and padlocked. This building later housed Sanborns' restaurant, favorite hangout of foreign tourists in Mexico City.

Against the Huerta dictatorship, the famous Red Battalions of workers were formed, to fight on behalf of Carranza and his Constitutionalist Movement. As they moved from town to town, the Red Battalions formed new Houses, established unions, so that by the time Huerta had been whipped, thousands of Mexican workers had been organized into labor unions. In 1916, Carranza, already frightened by the rise of labor, faced a general strike which demanded payment of wages in gold instead of worthless paper money. Alvaro Obregon, then a general in the Carranza army, saved the leaders from court-martial, an action which was recalled in his campaign for the presidency four years later.

The first general organization of labor, root of the contemporary movement, took place in Saltillo, State of Coahuila. That was in 1918, at the invitation of Gustavo Espinosa Mireles, who was then governor of the State, and who in 1938 became head of the government's Oil Administration Distribution Department. In the Saltillo meeting a young, plump, energetic member of the electrical workers' union appeared. His fiery orations pushed him to the front rapidly as the obvious leader of the new organization and carried him later to a position of power unparalleled in Mexican labor history. For a brief period, Morones was practically dictator of all industry. He could close factories, shops, newspapers, which opposed him. Back of him were the armies of Obregon, of Calles, then rising to political prominence as champions of the workingman, as candidates of the Mexican Laborist Party.

The Villa raid on Columbus, New Mexico, the flop of the Pershing expedition, the shelling of Veracruz by American warships, the open pro-German activities of Carranza, had brought relations between the United States and Mexico to the breaking point. Armed invasion seemed imminent. The country was in danger of imperialist aggression, the leaders proclaimed. That same nationalist spirit, which was later aroused, on a much larger scale, by Cardenas following expropriation of the oil companies, rallied around Carranza.

And it was then that a historic meeting took place, which was to be almost duplicated twenty years later. The American Federation of Labor, friendly to the Morones union, had been pressing the American government not to go into a war with Mexico, in spite of the clamor of the jingo press. In 1918, Samuel Gompers, head of the A. F. of L., and Morones, head of the CROM, met in Laredo, in an effort to unify the labor movements of the two countries, to bring workers of the Americas closer together. At this meeting the project for organization of a Pan-American Union Confederation was perfected. Twenty years later, in 1938, John L. Lewis, head of the Committee for Industrial Organization, and Vicente Lombardo Toledano, head of the Confederation of Mexican Workers, were speakers at a series of meetings in Mexico City. At one of these meetings, the Latin-American Workers' Confederation was formed, including many more countries than the Pan-American Labor Confederation, long vanished.

7

The Latin-American Labor Congress, September 5 and 8, 1938, was one of four congresses held in rapid-fire succession during that month, all in Mexico City, all with support of the Mexican government. The series was opened by the Congress of the International Institute for Industrial Relations, followed by the Labor Congress, the International Anti-War Congress, and the National Pro-Peace Congress.

A high spot of the series was the mass meeting on September 11th in the Mexico City bull ring. Speakers included prominent delegates to all four congresses: John L. Lewis; Leon Jouhaux, head of the powerful French Confederation of Labor; Edo Fimmen of the International Transport Workers; Ramon Gonzalez Peña, Asturian miner leader and Minister of Justice in the Spanish government cabinet of Juan Negrin; Ragnar Casparsson of the Swedish Confederation of Labor; S. Guruswami, of the Railway Workers' Union, Madras Province, India. These men were fraternal delegates to the Latin-American Labor Congress, did not take part in the deliberations, but spoke at open meetings.

Unlike the organization proposed in the Gompers-Morones plan, however, the Latin-American Workers' Confederation did not include the United States. Of the Latin-American countries, Brazil was the only one left out. The reason given was labor opposition to the government of Getulio Vargas. Headquarters of the new Confederation were established in Mexico City. Officers elected: President, Vicente Lombardo Toledano; secretary, northern zone, Fidel Velazquez, Mexico; first vice-president, Francisco Perez Leyros, Argentine; second vice-president, Clodomiro Clavijo, Colombia; secretary, southern zone, Jose M. Argaña, Argentine; secretary, central zone, Cristian Castilla, Colombia.

The following unions signed the first constitution of the Confederation: General Confederation of Workers of Argentina; Bolivian Confederation of Workers; Chilean Confederation of Workers; Confederation of Workers of Colombia; National Labor Congress of Ecuador; National Workers' Confederation of Paraguay; Railway Brotherhood of Cuba; National Maritime Labor Federation of Cuba; Cuban Press Association; Sugar Workers' Federation of Matanzas, Cuba; Union of Port Workers, Havana, Cuba; Cuban National Transport Federation; Cuban National Tobacco Workers' Federation; Havana Province Federation of Labor; Gas, Electrical and Water Works Federation of Cuba; Peruvian Workers' Center; Organized Labor of Nicaragua; Shoe Workers' Union of Costa Rica; Costa Rica Banana Plantation Workers; Committee for Organization and Unification of Labor, Uruguay; Venezuela Confederation of Labor; Confederation of Mexican Workers.

Motto of the Latin-American Labor Confederation: "For the Emancipation of Latin America."

8

At the open meeting of the Labor Congress:
Guruswami, Hindu labor leader, brings thousands to their

feet with an impassioned diatribe against British oppression in India.

Jouhaux, France, shoots explosive short phrases, followed by long, luxurious periods, like the pop of a cork, then the flowing gurgle of champagne bubbling into a glass.

Gonzalez Peña, Spain, tells the tragic plight of his country, his gestures the precise, sweeping, co-ordinated movements of a matador in the bull ring.

Aliaga, Spain, a tiny man, thin, short, brings down the house: no longer a man, a voice, all voice, a tremendous, resonant voice; Aliaga, man, fades away; Aliaga, magnavox, thunders: "Spain has rediscovered Mexico, and Mexico has discovered Spain!"

Melessi, Uruguay: "Peasants in my country work eighteen hours a day for eight pesos a month!"

Luces, Venezuela: "Workers in oil-company concentration camps!"

Aguayo, Paraguay: "Infamous bloody dictatorship!"

Perez Leyros, Argentina: "Masses in misery, social legislation a dead letter!"

Pacheco, Ecuador: "Land lords and clergy crushing the people!"

Rodriguez, Peru: "Thousands of workers in prisons for joining unions, homes violated, press censored, fascist tyranny rules!"

Ocampo, Chile: "Government finances Nazi gangs!"

Monterrey, Nicaragua: "Reign of perpetual terror, tortures, dungeons for workers who even breathe a word about unionization!"

Fuentes, Costa Rica: "Lands idle, thousands famish, imperialists drain resources of nation!"

Lewis, United States; Lewis, that terrible red, no flowery phrases, no violent gestures, a steady clatter of words from tight lips, like a pick-ax digging into coal: "Organize, organ-

ize, organize! There is no short cut to economic emancipation! Organize!" Alejandro Carrillo, the interpreter, em-
bellishes the rough-cut hunks of common sense, gives them
Latin flourishes, wows the audience.

At the offices of the United Press, Mexico City:

Frank Kluckhohn, New York *Times* correspondent, whose
office is just a few steps away, drops in on Bill Lander, the
able UP man. Excitedly, *Kluckhohn:* "Did you hear? They
greeted Lewis with the Communist salute!"

In the opposition press:

"The Labor Congress—a Russian salad."

"The Congress is a scheme of Moscow."

"Lombardo Toledano, Jouhaux, Gonzalez Peña, Lewis,
are all known agents of Stalin."

"Plot to make Mexico a colony of the Communist International."

"They shout Peace, but what they really want is War, so
that the Communist Party can rule Mexico!"

9

The Communist Party of Mexico first appeared as an
independent organization late in 1919, part of a growing
opposition to the "collaborationist" policy adopted by Morones in the CROM. Morones had previously been a strict
syndicalist, advocating pure unionism and no political action. In the Obregon presidential campaign he formed the
Laborist Party, which nominated Obregon as its candidate.
The dynamo of the CROM and the Laborist Party was a
small clique known as Grupo Accion, which ruled both party
and labor federation.

The Socialist Orientation Group was formed within the
labor movement to combat the Morones policies, called a
"sell-out." Simultaneously, the Latin-American Bureau, with

more or less the same membership as the Socialist Orientation Group, had been organized, affiliated to the Third International. From these two groups, the membership of the Federation of Young Communists, organized on September 16, 1919, was drawn. The following year the Communist Party was formally organized, including among its first members: Felipe Carrillo Puerto, the Yucatan leader; Manuel Diaz Ramirez, Jenaro Gomez, Jose C. Valades, Jose Allen, and R. Gomez Lorenzo.

The de la Huerta revolt in 1923 found the Communist Party, the Laborist Party and the Agrarian Party backing the Obregon-Calles government against the rebels, who had the support of the Co-operatist Party and the General Confederation of Workers (CGT) which had been formed as an independent union along anarcho-syndicalist lines. Extensive organization of labor and peasants followed the crushing of the de la Huerta rebellion and the rise of Obregon-Calles.

Until 1929 the Mexican Communist Party enjoyed a luxurious period of legality, established *El Machete* as its press organ, organized the National Peasants' League, the National Transport Workers' Union, the Unitary Trade Union Confederation, the International Red Aid, and the Anti-Imperialist League. This period also marked the rise of an obscure office employee, Hernan Laborde, who took part in an unsuccessful railway strike. Laborde later was elected to Congress, and became general secretary of the Communist Party.

Labor and peasant organization continued to grow by leaps and bounds, and with it a cultural revival that flourished in the famous Mexican mural art "renaissance." Then Secretary of State Kellogg of the United States proclaimed his alarm over the Red Menace. This was the period of Morrow influence in Mexico, the oil compromise, a truce in the Church-State war. The administration of Emilio Portes Gil brought with it the era of repression for the Communist

Party. It was ushered in early in 1929 with the assassination of Julio Antonio Mella, a young Communist who had come from Cuba. He was shot supposedly by an agent of the Cuban dictator, Machado, and with connivance of Mexico City police.. In June, the Communist Party headquarters were raided. A few months later the shop of *El Machete* was smashed and the paper suppressed. The next year—Ortiz Rubio had already succeeded Portes Gil—relations between Mexico and the Soviet Union were broken. In 1931 the Communist trade union central was raided. Added to all its other woes, the Communist Party found itself with a family feud on its hands, a split over policy which helped decimate the organization.

Jails, prisons, the Tres Marias penal islands, were full of Communists, labor leaders, leftist intellectuals. Hundreds of peasants were slain as "Communists." Suspicion of being a Communist was sufficient cause for arrest. When it recovered from the first blow, the Communist Party began its period of illegal work, became an underground force in the steadily growing anti-Calles movement, gnashing its teeth over the support which had originally been given Calles only to have him turn against his Communist backers. As the anti-Calles movement grew, the paths of the Communists and the left-wingers of the official government party moved closer together. The slackening of repression following Cardenas' nomination in 1933 permitted the Communist Party to run Laborde for president. The votes were officially tabulated, although the Communist candidate claimed that the official figures showed only a small part of the votes actually cast for him.

Cardenas began his administration by announcing that there would be freedom of the press and assembly, that there would be no suppression of political parties, nor interference with trade-union organization. To the contrary, the government said it intended to encourage union organization and unification—that was part of the Six-Year Plan. About the same time, the Communist Party announced that its revised "line" coincided with the Cardenas program, and that it would give his administration qualified support; that the Communist Party, with its new policy, would not take an oppositionist stand against a program which appeared to be pro-labor, and would back him as long as he lived up to that program and gave "progressive government" with labor and peasant rights guaranteed.

In 1938, after four years of legality, the Communist Party claimed a substantial increase in membership, was publishing a daily newspaper, tabloid size, called *The Voice of Mexico*. That name was adopted in place of the old *El Machete* of militant traditions, in accordance with the "non-sectarian People's Front" which had become the Communist Party policy. On September 16, 1938, it held a big anniversary meeting, packed the Arena Mexico to the rafters. Speakers included Margarita Nelken, Spanish Communist congresswoman, who was a delegate to the CTM's anti-war congress. Over a balcony were draped three big painted portraits of three mustached men: Lenin, Laborde, Cardenas.

The Communists have two special bones to pick with Cardenas. One is that despite his granting of legality to the Communist Party, relations have not been resumed with the Soviet Union. The other is that Mexico's President permitted Leon Trotsky to come to Mexico, and, despite loud and long protest, refused to kick him out.

10

There are two Leon Trotskys in Mexico.

One lives in the house owned by Frieda Kahlo (Mrs. Diego Rivera) in Coyoacan, Mexico City suburb.

The other is in a wax museum on Argentina Street in Mexico City. This wax Trotsky is dressed in knickers and a cap, the way Trotsky-in-the-flesh got off the boat that brought him to Mexico a couple of years ago. About twenty other wax sculptures of familiar Mexican types and of famous personalities, some of them living, most of them dead, sit, stand or recline in the little museum. Among them are Porfirio Diaz; Baby Face, the bandit; Amado Nervo, famous Mexican poet; Miguel Hidalgo y Costilla, father of Mexican independence; the late archbishop, Pascual Diaz; Roberto Soto, the music-hall comedian; an infant who, according to astrologers, is "the future king of Mexico"; the Unknown Mexican Soldier; a fish peddler; a flower girl; a nude lady being tortured on an Inquisition rack; a drunk sleeping it off; and Mickey Mouse. A placard on the jaunty figure of Trotsky explains to the public that it will have to be satisfied with this likeness, made from a photograph, "because the gent in question refuses to let anyone in to see him," and the artist couldn't get past the police guard.

Trotsky of Coyoacan repeated, in articles, in interviews, and in statements by his chief protector, Diego Rivera, that he has darn good reason for guarding himself so well. One after another of his secretaries in Europe got bumped off; his son, Leon Sedoff, was poisoned. Then, he charged, Stalin's GPU put the finger on him, sent a couple of professional liquidators over to rub him out. Therefore, the guard, and therefore the careful scrutiny of anyone who approaches the house. Only Señor Rivera can pass the guards unchallenged.

A bitter controversy developed in Mexican labor and political circles when it first became known that Trotsky was seeking asylum in Mexico. Some urged President Cardenas not to permit the Russian exile to enter Mexico, and others pressed Cardenas not to make an exception of Trotsky in Mexico's tradition of providing refuge. The Mexican government finally granted Trotsky permission to rest his weary and harassed bones in that beautiful country on condition that he keep his nose out of Mexican politics.

The Communist Party was in the forefront of opposition to Trotsky's remaining in Mexico. The issue of the Popular Front became the one about which the Trotsky controversy was intensified after he had been in Mexico for a while. When the famous "trial" took place, the CTM refused to take part in it. Since the CTM and the National Revolutionary Party had moved toward a Popular Front position, and Trotsky's writings about Spain and France expressed opposition toward the Popular Front theory in those countries, his Mexican critics declared that he was mixing into Mexican politics.

The charge heightened the feud that had developed between Trotsky and Lombardo Toledano, and by the end of 1938 articles by Trotsky appeared in Mexican periodicals, no longer dealing with European affairs, but directed at Toledano and at Hernan Laborde, Communist Party secretary. Trotsky said he was not taking part in politics, but that he had a right to defend himself from the attacks made on him. Toledano said that long before this Trotsky had attacked the CTM, its tactics, its leaders and the Popular Front, in the 1937 edition of *The Revolution Betrayed*. He added that in this book Toledano had been called a false leader and one who had been bought with Moscow gold.

In October, 1938, the Communist Party newspaper charged that certain persons in the CTM's National Study Commission were publicly espousing theories coinciding with Trotsky's, and cited an article in which one referred to "the death of the Popular Front myth." This developed a serious situation in view of the public attacks by Toledano against Trotsky, whom the CTM leader called an "enemy of Mexico, enemy of anti-fascist action, standard-bearer for the enemies of the world proletariat." Toledano, in November, 1938, again asked that Trotsky be given the boot, but President Cardenas said nothing doing.

A short while after the Four Congresses, Rivera, the CGT and several smaller unions, organized a mass meeting in which the congresses were characterized as a farce and the CTM leaders were assailed for "disorientating the masses." Among the speakers at this meeting was Mateo Fossa of Argentina, who accused the labor congress officials of having denied him permission to enter the deliberations chamber, although he carried credentials from workers' organizations in the Argentine. The meeting, held in the same Arena Mexico where the Communist Party had celebrated its anniversary some weeks back, was a contrast to the earlier gathering—many empty seats compared to a packed house. Over the same balcony where the mustached portraits had been hung in the other meeting, there now appeared a banner calling on the workers to "demand justice against the crimes of that hyena, Stalin, who lives on the blood of the workers."

Meanwhile, Trotsky, in his well-appointed study in Coyoacan, announced he was writing a biography of Stalin. People who ought to know said that it would be more sensational than the trial-of-the-Moscow-trials, which got a mighty good press. It got such a good press, in fact, that the little trickle of pilgrims to Trotsky's residence soon developed into a rushing stream of celebrity hunters. Tourists felt they couldn't go back home and confess that they hadn't seen Trotsky. It would be as devastating as not seeing the Pyramids, or Xochimilco, the Desert of Lions, or Diego Rivera Frescoes; like returning without bringing back a sarape, or a basket, or some article of native handicraft. What a life! What a world! Surely Leon Trotsky never dreamed in 1917, when the papers gave their top banners to the famous team of Lenin-and-

Trotsky, that he would show up twenty years later as a tourist attraction, a Mexican curio!

But, although the layman may look on Trotsky as a curious and colorful addition to an already fascinating and strangely mixed Mexican picture, the one-time leader of the Red Army is not regarded at all lightly by his admirers and defenders in Mexico and the United States, nor by his political enemies. Some of his defenders look upon him as a symbol of contemporary persecution, and his defense as a defense of the principle of political asylum. Others, while disagreeing with his doctrine, express respect for his talents, for his participation in the labor movement, for his prolific political and historical writings.

To the average Mexican, however, Trotsky is still hardly more than a quaint name that appears now and then in the newspapers, adding an exotic touch to the parade of Mexican political shake-ups and polemics, another momentary diversion from the hottest topic of common conversation: Bull-fighting. But for the newspapermen in Mexico, both foreign and domestic, the peripatetic Russian celebrity—former mighty army chief now under siege in Coyoacan (Aztec for "Land of the Coyotes") —continues to be a lively source of news copy.

XII

OLD BRICKS IN A NEW HOUSE

1

JUST as Cardenas has had to play ball with the generals because his position without them would not have been any too secure, so, in forming his new Party of the Mexican Revolution, he has had to make deals with civilian politicians. These compromises constitute both the strength and weakness of the Cardenas regime. Through them his "mass base" is made firm, but through them also his social program sometimes undergoes modifications. By developing soldier-allegiance to the army as an institution instead of to individual generals, by developing class-allegiance of labor and the peasants, Cardenas' new party seeks to drive toward elimination of these personalist props and pave the way for "institutional government" that Mexico has heard about for so long.

Some political critics got a big kick out of this: many months after the formation of the new Party, its building still displayed a sign that said "National Revolutionary Party." That was the name of the Calles organization. In constructing his party, Cardenas did not raze the Calles political structure. It was more of a remodeling job. And most of the key units in it are still the "old bricks" of the Mexican Revolution.

There are new ones, too; hence, one of the essential functions of Cardenismo is to serve as a mortar to keep the old and new together. As things stand today, Cardenas still needs the old bricks that have weathered some heavy political storms during the last thirty years.

2

The search for a formula that would give his government a mass base, and consolidate the Cardenas emphasis on the Revolution, had the collaboration of labor, peasant, army and political leaders. They finally arrived at an organization with a theoretical structure of "revolutionary democracy." Membership in this new party is by organization rather than on an individual basis; that is, the workman belongs through his union, the peasant through his federation, the soldier through his regiment. The only sector left open to individual membership is the Popular Sector, which is available to anybody, including politicos, but the dominant voice theoretically is that of the labor-peasant-army blocs. Leaders denied that it represented a corporate or a soviet system. Critics, nevertheless, branded it either one or the other. Some said it resembled the "Aprista" plan, the American Popular Revolutionary Alliance (APRA) system known as "functional democracy."

The Party of the Mexican Revolution was formally brought into existence on April 3, 1938, a few weeks after the expropriation of the oil companies. The call for the national convention, issued on January 18, 1938, was signed with the slogan, "Institutions and Social Reform," the National Revolutionary Party motto. The slogan of the new party, now signed to all its communications, is "For a Democracy of Workers."

The origins and aims of the new organization were summed up concisely in an address by Vicente Lombardo Toledano:

"... the unified proletariat should in the future look upon the problems of our country ... from the point of view of the entire Mexican people. The Confederation of Mexican Workers came into existence, not as just another trade-union central . . . but as an organization to fight for economic and social revindication . . . an organization of struggle on behalf of the prevailing institutions of Mexico, of the democratic institutions which make possible the normal and historical development of the proletariat. . . . The Confederation . . . attitude has been one of collaboration with President Cardenas . . . not to clash, consequently, with the rest of the forces which should organize to back the Cardenas government, and with which we have common interests. The transformed National Revolutionary Party should not be a proletarian party, a party of the Left. . . .

". . . the proletariat is not self-sufficient to fight international fascism and reaction; the proletariat is the nerve center of the people, as the class which produces human wealth. . . . And since this is to be a popular party, it is evident that this will not be an attempt to establish or organize soviets. . . . The soviets in order to realize their aims must rest necessarily on a prior revolution that would transform the property system . . . we are not going to sovietize the government, but we are going to create a popular alliance to defend the interests of the Mexican Revolution. . . .

"Being a worker is not enough to guarantee the carrying out of a program of workers as a social class . . . this will be the first opportunity for the working class, as a social class, to intervene in the orientation and direction of the country's policies."

3

The APRA, which sees in the new Cardenas party set-up an indication of the solution for Latin America, is known better in South America than in Central or North America. It had its strongest development in Peru, where it was suppressed. During the last few years a number of Aprista leaders have found, in Mexico, a haven from persecution. Head man of the Apristas is Victor Raul Haya de la Torre.

The Aprista theories trace back to those of Max Adler, Vienna Socialist, who advocated "economic democracy." Aprismo can stop fascism in Latin America, Haya de la Torre, maintains. Writing in the Mexican organ of his party, he said:

> "Under the pretext that Russian communism is making headway in our countries, Italian-German-Japanese fascism seizes upon the panic of the middle classes and brings them under its sway. This happened in Brazil, and it is an immediate menace in other countries. Only a democratic concept, democratic and revolutionary, such as Aprismo, which incorporates the middle class in a popular alliance with the working classes, and subjects them to the same party discipline, can check the fascist danger."

The possibility that this theory can serve as an instrument for fascism is noted by another Aprista writer, Guillermo Vegas Leon, who said:

> "The name of this new democratic form can be taken for the purposes of maintaining or re-establishing the bourgeoisie. Fascist corporativism represents, thus, a dangerous falsification of economic democracy."

Aprismo and the Spanish Popular Front theories seem to converge in the Party of the Mexican Revolution, which is not patterned after either but has some of both. The Spanish Civil War had significant repercussions in Mexico, revealing itself, for instance in the new party's slogan, "democracy of workers," as compared to the Spanish constitution's "republic of workers." The incorporation of the army into the PRM, while in line with Cardenas' general ideas, can also be traced to the fact that so many Spanish army officers swung toward Franco-fascism.

4

Many of the "old bricks" of the Revolution are army generals, which is in keeping with Mexican political tradition.

Since its independence from Spain in 1821, Mexico has been ruled for more years by military men than by civilians. An attempt to shake off the army rule was made during the post-Juarez term of President Sebastian Lerdo de Tejada. He and the other "civilists" got a good spanking from the generals, who threw their weight with Porfirio Diaz, and that general then inaugurated his great "era of peace" as a military dictatorship, and kept it that way. Under Porfirio Diaz, the importance of the generals increased prodigiously. It was not an accidental phenomenon, then, that in the anti-Diaz revolution so many "generals" appeared throughout the country, bearing with them the autocratic prerogatives acquired under the Diaz Augustan era.

The Diaz army was like all the other structures of his epoch: shiny, lacquered, polished on the outside; rotten and hollow within. The officers were doing nicely, thank you. But the miserable condition of the private soldiers and the petty officers was notorious. The swivel-chair generals collected big allotments for food, equipment, animals. But the men in the ranks saw only a small part of it, and there were not nearly so many men in the ranks as the books showed. When the showdown came, the army melted away. The Diaz army was mainly a conscript army. As bad as things were for the workman and the peasant in civilian life, it was hard to conceive of anybody voluntarily becoming a soldier. Conscription was not on a basis of compulsory military service as it is known in the democratic countries. It was a kidnap system. So many men were needed. The strong-arm crew went out and shanghaied them. Others were conscripted on re-

quest of employers who found this punishment very effective
for workers who protested.

The last stand of the remnants of the old federal army was
made in 1914, with the Huerta dictatorship, after the assassination of Madero. Anarchy reigned. Every leader who rode
forth with a band of thirty, forty or one hundred men, automatically became a "general." Most of these revolutionary
"generals" were not military men, but civilians, citizens in
uniform. Their military careers started with the Revolution,
and their political strength often came to be gauged by their
army power.

There was no more federal army. All the armies were
rebels against one side or the other. They were either in active
or latent uprising against the Revolution or against the
Counter-Revolution, sometimes against both. The men who
fought in these armies followed a leader more often than a
cause. Loyalties were developed strictly on a personal basis,
and this same phenomenon persisted right on through the
Carranza, the Obregon and the Calles epochs and continues
today, somewhat modified, but still there. So the weight of
the divisionary general—determined by his personal loyalties—is a considerable factor in balancing the electoral scales.

Furthermore, in the so-called reconstruction period after
1920, the army officer, more often than not, was called upon
to exercise the duties of governmental administration. Military zone commanders had more power than civilian governors in every State. The general as a rule built up a personal
political machine, with his military power as a nucleus, and
with unlimited ambitions. Every general felt himself a potential president. The general became the kingfish. In 1938,
nineteen of Mexico's thirty-three State and territorial governors were ranking army officers.

In consolidating his party structure, Citizen Cardenas and
Comrade Cardenas listened carefully to the counsels of Sol-

dier Cardenas. Soldier Cardenas knows only too well that no man has ever held power in Mexico and that no program, good or bad, has ever been carried through, without the help of the army. He knows, too, that the pressure of the generals, Cedillo among them, was responsible in a large measure for his nomination as presidential candidate. Calles had some other possible choices—Riva Palacio, Perez Treviño—but the army big shots picked Cardenas. They figured that Cardenas would be a good boy and play ball, that they could control him, and that through him in the presidency, they could break down the overwhelming control of the Callistas. The strength of the generals, and how important they are for a man who wants to hold power, is evident in the result of that pre-election conflict: Calles yielded to the generals. He figured that through Cardenas he could keep the tin hats in their place. The generals, for the most part, stuck with Cardenas when the break came. Cardenas was definitely on the upgrade, Calles on the decline.

So, a general in Mexico is always a potential candidate for governor or for president. Naturally, the top general of them all, the Minister of National Defense, is always the most possible of possibilities. In fact, the post has become a traditional testing and training ground for Mexican presidents in recent years. For instance, to consider only the most recent cases: Abelardo Rodriguez moved into the Presidency from the War Ministry, and Lazaro Cardenas was Minister of War when he was nominated. Neither Cardenas nor Rodriguez were outstanding political personalities, although both had already seen service as State governors, as active army men, as officials in the government party.

Minister of National Defense Manuel Avila Camacho, on the other hand, has been pretty much of an army man, working his way up through the cavalry. The public knows little about Avila Camacho. Occasionally his picture will appear in the papers at some official function, sitting close to the President, as in 1938, when the army officers from all over the country were called in to a banquet in honor of President Cardenas. That was part of the campaign to sell the army to the people. Special sections in the newspapers on September 16 were devoted to the army, with photographs of all the officers, Avila Camacho's biggest of all. As a cavalry man, Avila Camacho is very much interested in horses, and he is fond of polo.

With the mention of his name as a possible presidential candidate, people wondered about his political ideas, his social ideas. Would he continue Cardenas' policies? Or would he swing to the right? Nobody seemed to worry that he'd swing to the left. He is known to have told friends privately that what Mexico needs is "to get down to work, order, discipline, but most important of all, work, to construct, to build," that "business must work so others can work." Several politically-aware businessmen said they would like to see Avila Camacho president because he would be good for business, that he would not be radical, either to the right or to the left, but that he would be a good "law-and-order" man. He has army support so he could hold back any revolutions, which are bad for business. Some politicians said he would be a front for his very good friend, General Juan Andrew Almazan, intimate of Big Business in Monterrey, and that he would try to curb the Confederation of Mexican Workers. Others said he was friendly to labor but not "radical labor," that he would clash with Vicente Lombardo Toledano.

The Minister of National Defense's biggest drawback to his candidacy might be his name. Like so many other prominent men in Mexican politics, he has a brother. His brother is Maximino Avila Camacho, governor of the State of Puebla, and among the peasants of Puebla—and through their organizations, among the peasants of the whole country—the name Avila Camacho does not have such a good flavor. It is associated a little too much with armed protection given big land lords and sabotage of the agrarian program.

Governor Maximino Avila Camacho, like other members of the Avila Camacho family, owns a good bit of land himself, and he has one of the finest stables of horses in the country. The peasants are not quick to forget that while they have one hell of a time trying to get a lone twenty-buck mule to pull a plow, Governor Avila Camacho imported a magnificent horse, owned formerly by no less a horseflesh-fancier than Alfonso XIII of Spain. The governor shelled out twenty thousand pesos for this splendid animal. The Puebla peasant makes about a peso a day. If he were lucky enough to make this every day in the year, and could save it all—that is, not spend a centavo for food or anything else—he could accumulate twenty thousand pesos in a little over fifty years. And peasants are inclined to figure in this fantastic way. The Puebla governor happened to get the ex-King's horse through a deal with one of his many Spanish friends. Puebla State is the most important textile center of the country, and a big part of the textile business is in the hands of Spaniards. These friends of the governor's are very partial to a certain gent named Franco. And there's the rub.

But brother Manuel, the Defense Minister, may be able to live down this unfortunate good fortune of brother Maximino. After all, Cardenas, too, has a brother who is reputed to have become well fixed; Ortiz Rubio had a brother, too, who found happiness in road construction. Abelardo Rodriguez had some enterprising in-laws. Portes Gil had some cousins here and there. And Calles—well, he had relatives all over the place, uncles, brothers, sons, in-laws, and what not. Relatives and *compadres* (spiritual kinsmen, figuratively pals, cronies, side-kicks) of cabinet officers, generals, governors, can be found through the entire bureaucracy. There's nothing peculiarly Mexican about that, although at times ideologies seem to vanish and everything boils down to a question of who is who's *compadre*. We might stop and recall that President Taft's brother was chief counsel for the Mexican Railways while Taft helped keep Diaz in power; we might recall other cases, plenty of them in our own official families, where plump little jobs are neatly tossed in a series of lateral passes to relatives of officeholders.

Whether he becomes president or not, Minister of National Defense Manuel Avila Camacho, who is a great admirer of American efficiency and enterprise, can enjoy the satisfaction of having shared in the birth of the Mexican army. During his term as Minister, it became the biggest mass of trained men, with the best equipment and the best quarters, in the history of Mexican armed forces. For the first time Mexico has an organization that can really be called an army.

On September 16, 1938, this army paraded through the streets of Mexico City, and many a Mexican heart beat quicker upon seeing these well-drilled men, with uniforms that fit, with plenty of rifles, machine guns (made in Mexico, too), cannon, even a few whippet tanks and an anti-aircraft battery, and to cap the climax, as it were, shiny metal helmets (imported from France). It wasn't only a show, but a reminder to any general with big ideas that he'd better be good.

An old jest about the Mexican army was that there were more generals in it than privates. During the revolutionary upheavals, that sometimes came near being the truth. Today's Mexican army has 36 divisionary generals, roughly one for each State. In addition, there are 127 major generals, 226 brigadier generals, 2,708 commissioned officers and 5,822 non-commissioned officers, and 39,608 privates.

The organized army reserves—mainly peasants, who are simultaneously the Rural Defense Corps—number about 55,000 men, of which 54,000 are privates and non-coms, organized into 70 infantry and 72 cavalry units. The reserves have 56,000 rifles and 22,000 horses. The aviation reserve corps has 52 trained pilots. There are 302 landing fields in the country.

The dithyrambic eulogies of the Mexican army during the past year are regarded as symptomatic of the fascist penetration among the military. But the eulogies came from the left as well as from the right. It is of course notorious that the whole set-up of fascist organization, with its hierarchies and the authoritarian discipline, has a peculiar attraction for the army officer in any country, trained, as he is, along the lines of a caste system, blind obedience to orders, and all the rest that goes into regimentation of the individual. This approach—elaborated in some cases to intricate systems of war "esthetics"—is naturally defended on the plausible theory that an army without discipline would be inconceivable, and worthless in action. The extension of this military discipline to civilian life finds staunch advocates among the men who expect to land in the order-giving posts. Here the numerous would-be fuehrers and the brass-hats find common ground, and the converging of their aims becomes particularly clear in Mexico at the present time because of the repercussions from Spain.

The pro-Franco boys in Mexico, who are, of course, the pro-Hitler and the pro-Mussolini boys, too, the lads who think the rabble needs to be ruled with an iron hand, have been openly courting the army in Mexico recently. They have been giving banquets in honor of the army officers, and their editorial outlets have been whooping it up for the army. The life of the soldier is cited as an ideal life for the proletarian, who should be falling in line with the captains of business and industry instead of following "labor leaders who want to destroy Mexico."

And the leaders also are giving their peasant and labor battalions military training and teaching them to fraternize with the men in uniform. The men who quake in their gaiters when they see workers marching in formation issued dire warnings to the army big shots over the arming of the peasants and the "militarization" of the Confederation of Mexican Workers. But maybe the army big shots know more than others what it's all about. Is it all part of the next war build-up? One Mexican army officer said he had inside dope to the effect that compulsory military training would be established in the United States very soon and that Mexico, too, is all set for it.

But here's a concrete picture: the city workers and the peasants are learning to be soldiers, and, at the same time, the privates in the army are learning to be workers. Several "military cities" have already been built, entirely with army labor, and strictly for army use. One of the show-places of the army is the military city built under the direction of General Juan Andrew Almazan, in Monterrey. Another big "military city" was completed in 1938 on the old San Jose ranch, near Tenancingo, State of Mexico. The soldiers were the carpenters, plumbers, masons, bricklayers. They even made their own bricks, built a kiln, and did all their own electric wiring.

The Party of the Mexican Revolution explained, through its president, Luis I. Rodriguez, that the aim of the administration in "civilizing" the army is to "strengthen the unity between the workers and the soldiers." The general belief is that the new direction taken by Cardenas, giving the soldiers political life, is intended to constitute a kind of Maginot Line of the rank-and-file. It is being raised against any general whose personal ambitions might get the better of him and who might try to change things otherwise than through the regular channels.

4

Some "old bricks" of the Revolution, especially those who did not ride the Calles-Obregon bandwagon, did not hit it off so well with Cardenismo. Some go along as Opposition within the Party of the Mexican Revolution, others are part of the Opposition outside the party. The Opposition has been trying hard to find a formula that could match the program, the organization, and the high-powered publicity of Cardenas' party.

About five months after the Cedillo upset, some politicos in the PRM joined hands with politicos on the outside and formed the "Mexican Democratic Constitutional Front." The head of this organization is General Ramon F. Iturbe, congressman, ex-military, who had figured in several revolts. His co-leader is Colonel Bolivar Sierra, who is supposedly a front for General Sanchez Tapia, presidential aspirant. Both Sierra and Iturbe were booted out of the PRM. Iturbe is an old Carranza man, former governor of Sinaloa, promoter of fake oil wells, close friend of Japanese, with whom he has private dinner meetings right along.

Among the backers of the front were a number of ex-military men who had been in exile during the Calles hegemony. Most of them were members of the Revolutionary Frontier Party, a border-state political bloc identified with Monterrey industrialists, and with mining and ranching interests, but with little popular following. The best known is Pablo Gonzalez, who was a ranking presidential candidate in 1920, about the time Obregon had the same idea. Agrarians remember Gonzalez as the man who trapped Zapata and engineered his slaying.

Another sector of the Opposition placed hopes on Jose Vasconcelos, Mexico's best-known exile—Calles excepted—of recent times. Vasconcelos returned to Mexico from the United States in 1938. In Obregon's cabinet, as Minister of Education, Vasconcelos was the patron of the art upsurge that became the Mexican mural movement. He is a prolific author, idol of a group of young religious fascists in the National University.

The Oppositionists, though not numerous, are very articulate and get all the space they want in the periodicals of widest circulation. They have been generally deficient in presenting constructive programs around which a popular following might be built. Their answer usually is that there is no use, that the elections are cut and dried. One form of attack used by nearly all the Oppositionists is to charge that Cardenismo is communism. Sometimes it is Stalinism, sometimes Trotskyism. One group will say that Cardenas gets his orders from Hernan Laborde, secretary of the Mexican Communist Party. Then Cardenas issues a statement, defending his refusal to oust Trotsky. Whereupon, the Opposition discovers that Cardenas' private secretary trots out to Coyoacan every day to get his instructions on how to advance the dictatorship of the proletariat.

Another form of attack is to lambast Cardenas' collaborators. The probity, honesty, fairness of the President are lauded, with almost the same reverence as the anti-Diaz parties when they used to nominate Diaz for president and their own man for vice-president. But some of the officials of the administration—well, here's what Oppositionist Antonio Diaz Soto y Gama, an "authentic Revolutionary"—the highest praise there is in Mexican politics—had to say in an article in *El Universal*, September, 1938:

"The real danger to the Revolution is in the corruption that boils and stews within it; it is in the harmful

elements who have arisen from it or who have attached
themselves to it; the danger is in the perverse and pre-
varicating functionaries, in pharisaic leaders and simu-
lators, in false friends of the people, in proconsuls and
mandarins who treat the provinces as if they were feudal
estates and mulct them as if they were conquered lands;
it is in the legion of *farceurs* who traffic with principles,
make huge fortunes under the cloak of the Revolution
and who, thanks to dishonest and unclassifiable acts, can
and do, where all may see, live opulent and fatuous lives,
which in itself contradicts everything which they
preach. . . ."

In Cardenas, the Oppositionists were stumped by a peculiar phenomenon. They had no grounds for calling him a
thief, or a butcher, or a drunkard, or a libertine, so it became a little difficult to present him as the kind of an ogre that
your political enemy ought to be. The most serious charge
made against him is that his administration, like most administrations before his, is tending to become personalist, that
the years of talk about "institutional government" seem to
have been a cry in the wilderness. Cardenistas will answer
that the "present historical moment" is marked by involun-
tary strong-man-rule-to-end-all-strong-man-rule.

As evidence of their contentions, the Oppositionists will
call special attention to the important roles played by three
former private secretaries of Cardenas: Luis I. Rodriguez,
who is president of the Party of the Mexican Revolution;
Ignacio Garcia Tellez, Minister of the Interior and governor-
nominee of Guanajuato State; Silvano Barba Gonzalez,
governor-elect of Jalisco.

But these men, like others in the administration who are
not considered exactly ninety-nine and forty-four one-hun-
dredths per cent pure, were anti-Calles. And in the first phase
of the Cardenas consolidation that was the test: to be a "Revolutionary" but also to be an anti-Calles Revolutionary. Car-

denas' first political purges were aimed at getting rid of the incorrigible Callistas. Some Callistas became Cardenistas, and donned sackcloth and ashes. Others continued with Cardenas but did not denounce Calles nor beat their breasts.

Cardenas weeds his political garden, but at the same time he has to have men who stick to his program, who can give him personal loyalty at least on the fundamentals. The price of this loyalty sometimes amounts almost to nullification of that very program through local actions that run counter to the federal plan. What is more, the men who build Cardenismo—which in turn becomes their support and strength—inevitably tend to perpetuate Cardenismo, just as the Redeemers of Calles' day wanted to perpetuate Callismo. Mexico has not yet completely emerged from the "strong-man" tradition—"emerge" sounds strange when other countries now sink into that stage—and the local Mexican king-fish still have the last word. In a crisis, and there has been one preceding nearly every recent presidential election, Cardenas may find himself patriotically indispensable, called upon to continue as head man.

5

In 1938, during the post-expropriation months, the Opposition trained its heavy artillery on Cardenas' economics. The critics pictured him as "one so dazzled by the light of redeeming the underdog from oppression and injustice, that he fails to see the needs of the other classes." They lamented that "the Revolution, left bleeding by ambitious and avaricious leaders, now falls into the hands of a man—well intentioned—who is not an economist, a real statesman, but a dreamer, a poet . . ."

They mourned the President's "innocence" in his bold attempts to solve Mexico's complex, heart-rending, back-breaking social and economic problems the hard way, the rugged pioneering way, full of hope and promise in return for sacrifice, instead of in the impasse of "established precedent." The Opposition said: The people need bread and he gives them revolutionary lyrics; his approach to the nation's economy will bankrupt the country. They said that it was like trying to cook up a Debussy nocturne in a stew pan.

XIII

THE FORGOTTEN MEN

1

THE Green Indians have made good, returned in triumph after more than forty years of exile from the broad avenues of Mexico City. They had tasted glory before. During the early days of Porfirio Diaz' regime, they stood guard on the Paseo de la Reforma, the Champs Elysées of the Mexican capital. That was in the days when Diaz was still on the upgrade. He had already arrived as president, but was still to become dictator. He was proud of the ancient Zapotec Indian blood that flowed in his veins. Then, as he moved farther and farther away from the people, as pale and pink-faced foreigners surrounded him more and more, Porfirio Diaz began to develop a kind of self-conscious inferiority about his Indian blood. The contempt of the European, of the Teuton, the Anglo-Saxon and the upper-crust Mexican-Spaniard for the Indian, made it impossible—in this revival of the colonial caste system—for their pal, their buddy, their intimate, the great Porfirio Diaz, to continue being an Indian.

The poor old man, during his declining years, tried to turn white. He is said to have used chemicals on his face and hands, tried to hide the rich, tawny, sun-baked skin, heritage of the children of the sun. That was when he sent the Green Indians into exile. He tried to forget them, for he had come to be ashamed of them, and of the two and a half million Indians who were the work horses for the palefaces and their native overseers. Many pious orations, sermons, editorials have been written about the White Man's Burden, but they always forgot that the Little Brown Brother was the fellow who had to carry it.

But now the Green Indians are back, again on guard, their full twelve-foot-high bodies raised toward the sky on eight-foot pedestals, one on each side of the Mexico City-Laredo highway as it swings over the last hill and down toward the valley of Mexico: two mighty men of bronze, with their war clubs, turned green with the patina of the years. The working class section where they stood for so long, waiting, came to be known as the Indios Verdes, the Green Indians. If you took a bus going to the Green Indians, you were going to the people.

The comeback of the Green Indians is symptomatic of the changed attitude toward the first-men of Mexico. The Revolution needed many soldiers; the Indians needed land. The Indians were told to fight and they would have land. But it is only in recent years that they have begun getting a little. Before that, they were expected to nourish themselves on the gushing promises of the generals and the politicos. Then the pendulum swung the other way. No longer was the white man the envied one. Every politico loudly proclaimed his Indian blood, unearthed Indian ancestors. Some of them even changed their names from Spanish to Aztec.

In this orgasm of adulation, the redeemers turned their redeeming powers toward the Indian. During Calles' presidency, the Home of the Indian Student was established in Mexico City. This was to be a training school where young men of the various tribes would be taught the ways of civilization and then would go back to take light to their benighted tribesmen. A lot of them liked the ways of civilization so much that they lost all desire to return to the hovels and the misery of their fathers. The Home of the Indian

Student at first was like a veritable Tower of Babel, for the Indians of Mexico speak about forty different dialects. But it did not take the intelligent young Indians long to learn Spanish and the customs of the whites. When one group had finished their courses, and prepared to return to their native villages, General Calles called them together and made a speech, telling them that he had established the institution "to prove to the reactionaries that they were wrong about the Indians," and that the native, if given a chance, could do as well as, and in some cases, better than the white man. He wound up his speech in this way:

"I have never feared that one of you would desert me. My aim has been to convert each of you into a leader, an apostle, an agitator in the pueblos, where your brothers are, that you might bring light, remove them from vice, and defend them. I hope that you will regard with affection this mission which has been entrusted to you and that you will, with the government, make an effort to bring to those masses of Mexicans, like us and like you, a chance to enjoy the right to a bit of happiness on earth. He who deserts will be a criminal, a traitor, to his race and to Mexico. You should struggle to improve the life of your people, to elevate them spiritually, to remove them from vice, and to defend them so that they should not be exploited and that they should not continue to be exploited. That is your mission. I hope you will fulfill it and bring honor to the race to which you belong."

Some of these honest lads took this manifesto too seriously. When they tried to "bring a bit of happiness" to their people, to improve their sad lot, henchmen and hacienda white guards strung them up on trees and nailed placards on the corpses. The placards said: "Hanged as a Communist agitator." Others tried to form unions on big sugar haciendas. But they failed to take into consideration the fact that their desire not to be "criminals, traitors, to the race and to Mexico," would be ignored by those owners who had it within their power to disregard this harangue. They remembered only that their duty was "to defend" their people "so that they should not be exploited." Some were shot down. Others were sent away to the Tres Marias penal islands.

Much, much, remains to be done for these most forgotten of all forgotten men of Mexico. One of their own who has been trying to make a dent in official red tape is José Gonzalez Velasco, a full-blooded Mixteco Indian, native of Santa Maria Yolotepec, Oaxaca. He studied, became a rural teacher, later an employee in the Department of Labor. In 1938 he was a delegate to the American Scientific Congress in Mexico City, the Indian ethnological section. In his singing voice, the words rippling like a run of eighth-notes, recalling his native Zapotec language, he will tell you of the many talented Indians throughout the country who live unfulfilled lives, unhonored, unsung, mute and inglorious amid the wild, screeching parakeets, and the distant echoes of political salvation. He will show you letters he gets from his former pupils, asking what about those scholarships the government promised. Most of the pupils never get past the fourth grade because schools beyond that grade are usually found only in the larger towns. The diet of hundreds of Indian communities consists of thick corn cakes and salt, and many times no salt. They are eager to learn simple industries, to know better ways of working the soil, how to get new things from it, how to make soap, to make articles of woodwork; they want more opportunities to do sculpture, to compose music and learn about it, to write poetry. An instance of the Indian children's resourcefulness: one of the pupils invented an apparatus for making extracts from the guava. Another developed a useful small machine for juicing sugar cane. So much knowledge is stored up on the endless shelves of the libraries and universities. Why can't the Indians get at least a dribble of it?

The Cardenas administration has taken some steps in this direction. Thirty educational centers have been established in remote sections. The Indians are being taught some of the things they want: carpentry, ironwork, pottery, elements of agronomy. But there are not enough schools, and too often the adolescent students have to stay home after a short period of schooling, because there are not enough hands to feed so many mouths.

Cardenas has concentrated the Indian problems into an autonomous Department of Indian Affairs, head of which is Graciano Sanchez, who is also general secretary of the National Peasants' Confederation. Cardenas has spent many hours and days among the Indians, in their huts and at their festivals, has had many chats with the wise men of the tribes. His announced aim is to assimilate the Indians without destroying the Indian culture, to give them an even break with non-Indian Mexico. Some of his predecessors wrestled with this problem, but made little headway.

Now the voice of the Indian is being heard more than ever before in post-Conquest Mexico, and it is being raised collectively rather than in the form of individual pleas. In the University of Morelia, one hundred and eighty-four delegates representing ninety-two Tarascan pueblos, assembled in a regional congress, in September, 1938, while other Indians, in other regions, were doing likewise. Many of the pueblos asked for financial aid. Sixty pueblos needed medical services, seven wanted telephone lines. There were twenty-eight petitions for better schools; nine for any kind of schools at all, because they don't have any; nine for teachers; eight for removal of teachers because "they are not doing their duty"; four for scholarships; ten asked for corn mills; others for typewriters and sewing machines, agricultural implements, fishing accessories, pottery equipment; some wanted benches in their parks; others had benches but no parks, and still others asked (oh, "timeless" Mexico of the folklorists) for clocks! Three pueblos demanded that the government guarantee free elections and participation of the Indians in the elections. Twelve asked for protection against "two kinds of thieves—just plain thieves and the White Guards from the haciendas."

Big Chief Lazaro Cardenas, who named his little son Cuauhtemoc, after the last of the Aztec emperors, feels close to his Indian brethren, and shares none of the European disdain for the red man. He feels confident that these beautiful—but politically dumb—people can form an important part of his new, self-respecting Mexico. The Indians idolize him, but their memories are long. They are hoping Cardenas will not later try to turn white.

2

The late Manuel Garcia was one of another group of Mexicans over whom the government has special worries. Garcia went to the United States to seek his fortune, and six children and his wife waited, expecting that he would send for them. The years went by. Garcia worked in the Colorado beet fields. For a while he was an extra in a Detroit automobile plant. Then, the depression. No jobs anywhere. The immigration officers picked him up and shipped him back to the border. He got one week's work, clearing brush. Half the week's wages went to buy a machete which was an essential part of the job. Then he started walking home, back to La Barca, Jalisco. He was flat broke, dejected, miserable. Nothing left but his machete. With that national symbol he slit his throat.

During 1938, about two thousand Mexicans were deported from the United States to Juarez, just across the Rio Grande from El Paso, Texas. That was as far as they could go. Broke, they went about offering their labor very cheaply, very much under the minimum-wage scale. Daily, scores more are landing back in other border towns. Not all are being deported. Some return voluntarily, for Cardenas has invited them to come back to the homeland. He says Mexico needs them, especially those who have learned trades, who can teach the others. And he has urged them to bring their work tools along.

Many thousands of Mexicans are legal residents of the United States and have no intentions of going back to Mexico. They have become Americans, although many do not speak English. Some are members of families that have lived in this country for many generations, long before any Americans came. But a substantial number migrated during the post-Diaz upheavals. Their children were born and reared in the United States.

Yet, throughout the Southwest, the Mexican-Americans constitute a national minority, sometimes persecuted, often discriminated against, segregated. Which, Neighbor FDR, you'd hardly call being such a good neighbor. And it doesn't help personal, business, or cultural relations between the two countries. Many Mexican repatriates now doing well in Mexico—among them journalists, and others in a position to make themselves heard—took back, among other valuable acquisitions, some bitter memories of harsh treatment by Americans.

Mexican consular officials have been instructed to be more vigilant *in re* the welfare of these forgotten men. They are being formed into clubs and mutual-aid societies, and federating into a general organization known as Mexico Abroad.

3

Even Health and Hygiene are "Revolutionary" in Mexico, served to the forgotten men with the same technique as that used in political campaigns. Visit a "health mission" that happens to be in the village. Children and adults grouped around a doctor and a nurse at the schoolhouse. Placards, banners, posters, flags, all over the place. On them:

"Hygiene is an act of social fraternization."
"Cleanliness—Pride of the Working Class."
"Dirt is repugnant even on silk—cleanliness glows on percale."

Scores of missions travel the country under direction of the Federal Health Department. But there are not enough. In 1938 three hundred internes were sent to rural communities, to guide the forgotten man to health, and at the same time to encourage doctors to practice in the provinces instead of struggling in Mexico City.

Smallpox epidemics have decimated many villages. Vaccination in recent years has cut the death rate sharply. In one section of Oaxaca, onchocercosis has blinded entire communities. In the hot lands, malaria kills and kills. Malaria becomes folklore in the chicle jungles of Campeche. Malaria becomes Xtabay, siren of unearthly beauty who roams the jungles, only her long black hair covering her nakedness. Xtabay gives the Indian chills, breathes fire and ice into him. In this final delirium he becomes ecstatic, cries that he has found Xtabay, dies in her lovely, lethal arms.

4

Years of poverty, oppression, civil war, left desolation in their wake: disease, alcoholism, prostitution, insanity, crime.

So many things have needed correction that Mexico is literally a paradise for reformers. Especially when head reformer of them all is President Cardenas himself. Bone-dry and a non-smoker, he wars on booze and encourages temperance groups.

With his drive to raise the living standards of the forgotten men, Cardenas undertook a general reform campaign, apparently in earnest. Unlike his predecessors who preached reform and then turned around and opened resorts like the Foreign Club ("Mexican Monte Carlo"), Cardenas has tried putting his preaching into practice. He closed the Foreign Club, padlocked Agua Caliente, and even prohibited dice-rolling in the saloons. He promised nationwide prohibition, but in 1938 had not yet got around to it.

An important part of the war on vice and crime is the permanent athletic and sports promotion campaign, handled by a permanent Federal Department of Physical Education. In 1938, two million-peso stadiums and sports fields were completed. One was named "Six-Year Plan" and the other "March 18."

The reform program makes a special appeal to women. Cardenas wants them to take part in sports, in social work, in public affairs. His administration granted women suffrage. Women drill with the labor battalions. For the first time in history, a woman made a speech in Congress in 1938.

5

A new tempo stirs the forgotten man in Mexico City, new social ideas, new buildings—a construction boom. Listen: boom-psss, boom-psss, boom-psss. Swing it, man! Syncopated rhythm from the land of syncopation: a steam-powered pile-driver, hammering forty-foot poles down into the earth, right in the heart of Mexico City, for the new Banco de Mexico building. Sixteen hours a day, for months: boom-psss, boom-psss! Machine-age music by the Raymond Concrete Pile Company of New Jersey.

And so, all over Mexico City—from Article 123 Street to November 20 Avenue, from the Street of Bitterness to the Street of the Lost Child—this symphony of construction was being heard in 1938: steam shovels, pavement-breakers, riveting hammers, welders, melody of today, with an accompaniment of yesterday, Mexico's song of tomorrow.

Twisting narrow streets flower into boulevards. Squat flat-roofed adobe-walled structures crumble under blueprint-guided pickaxes. From the surface of the rooftops, as from the surface of a vast lake of masonry, tall buildings burst through in splendor of glass and steel and cement, stretching ever closer to the sun: apartment houses, hotels, office buildings, theaters. The most modern of "functional" architecture shoots up alongside rococo colonial edifices, just as in government buildings, many built during the colonial period, aero-dynamic "functional" social ideas push through the weight of centuries toward a ray of economic sunshine.

Most European of American cities, most American of European cities, the capital of Mexico with its population of a million and a quarter, has a personality all its own. Alexander von Humboldt, famous German scientist and traveler, called it "City of Palaces." Before him, Cortez said it was an "Indian Venice." That was before the Spaniards filled in the canals that radiated from the Zocalo. Mexicans like to have it known as the "Paris of America." Mexico City rests on a foundation that's like a huge mass of gelatine, honeycombed with subterranean streams. Many of the old, heavy buildings are sinking. Architects at the International City Planners' Congress in 1938 estimated that a hundred thousand of these buildings need reconditioning or need to be replaced by new structures. Hence the constant demand for new apartment buildings. And most of the new apartment houses are "functional," letting in the luscious sunshine which the old buildings shut out. Some architects object to the new type of buildings, call them dovecotes, charge that they ruin the harmony of the city, that solid masonry is needed.

But, harmony or no harmony, the Mexican housewife likes handy appliances when she can get them, and she likes a place that's easy to keep clean. So an exodus goes on today, from the old, damp, cold, but spacious, solid, reposeful structures of yesterday, to the new, compact, sunny apartment houses, offering a shiny welcome to those who can afford the higher rents.

But many of Mexico's forgotten men, and their wives and kids still live in unsanitary, dark, unventilated, bathless *viviendas*, tenement-type structures that stretch horizontally, rather than vertically like the United States tenements. A good example: at house number 66, Niño Perdido Street, 102 families, nearly 1,000 persons, live. There are twenty-one toilets, no baths. The *viviendas* are usually built around patios, sometimes sunny, sometimes not. You would call these places gloomy if they were deserted, but life teems in them. Multicolored garments and blankets hang out to dry. Scores of brilliantly dressed women, with beautiful hair and eyes. And hands sculpted by toil. Kids with immense eyes, pink cheeks, some very healthy-looking, although they all seem to be without a certain freshness—that glow you find in really healthy kids. Maybe it's want of air, most likely it's lack of enough vitamin foods. They can take bruises and cuts, and heal in a jiffy. But typhoid, colds, flu, pneumonia, almost any disease that tests resistance, lays them low. Yet, on the whole, you know they are in pretty good shape. A steady procession of tiny white coffins carries out those who were not. They've got to be fairly tough to survive in this environment, just as the kids in the slums and the back streets and shanty towns of the United States have to be tough, to live through the squalor that greets them when they open their eyes in this best of all possible worlds.

Mexico City is not all slums and shiny new apartment houses. There are magnificent homes, the pride and joy of many Mexican residents, the envy of many American tourists who stare goggle-eyed at the splendor of some of the residential districts, the big garden-patios, sun-splashed balconies and gorgeous tile baths. The extension of Insurgentes Avenue, Colonia Anzures, Lomas de Chapultepec will convince anybody that there are a lot of people prospering in Mexico, and that when they do prosper, they know how to apply this prosperity to magnificent ways of living, glorying in the good things of life, so often abused by those whose approach is not quite so esthetic.

In a way, Mexico City is just a big-scale enlargement of the smaller cities and towns, a synthesis of all Mexico, and yet it has a quality about it entirely different from the other cities: Guadalajara, the second biggest city, the "Pearl of the Occident"; Monterrey, industrial center, "Sultana of the North"; Puebla, "City of the Angels." The people brought up in Mexico City are as different from their mountain village compatriots as people of different countries; as different as the semi-Americanized, more individualistic farmer of the northern Mexican States in comparison with the more communal, tribal peasants of the Center and the South, where clothing is identical and so are diets and one man is usually as poor as the next.

Mexico City is to Mexico what a combination of New York and Washington might be to the United States. It is the political capital, as well as the financial and business and industrial capital, and the big central bazaar toward which all the blessings of the earth flow, emptying in cascades of fruits and vegetables and flowers, fish and flesh and fowl, on the stalls of the public market houses. And the economically dominant foreign colonies give the place a definite cosmopolitan air.

But the foreign colonies in Mexico City are not like the "colonies" that exist in the slums of large cities in the United States. In the United States, you will find the big foreign colonies constituting the majority groups: racial or national minorities to the country at large, but very definitely majorities—like separate little countries—within their municipal districts. But in Mexico, the foreign colonies are numerically small and they are not segregated. The foreigner—businessman, banker, diplomat—lives more or less as does the uppercrust Mexican. There are a few fairly defined foreign districts where small shopkeepers and small industrialists have come together, and there is a small "Chinatown." But in the main, the foreigners, residentially, are dispersed through the betterclass houses. And Mexicans populate the slums.

The biggest "foreign colonies" in Mexico City are the Mexicans from the various States who have come to live in the capital. Each State group has a club or some organization, holds its get-togethers, and often gravitates toward a provincial politico who happens to have an important job in the federal government. And so it happens that you find the characteristics of almost every part of Mexico right in the capital. You'll find the famous Guadalajara beauties and the Guadalajara candies; the Toluca dairy products; the Jalisco *tequila* and the Oaxaca *mezcal;* the March of Zacatecas, that is more stirring than the national anthem, affecting almost any Mexican like "Dixie" does a Southerner in the United States.

You will find brisk, energetic go-getters from the mountains of Sonora and Nuevo Leon, the ebullient intoxicating songs and dances of the Veracruz mulatto, and the easygoing fellow for whom time is a luxury. He comes from the tropical lands where he spends the day in a hammock, where the birds drop the seeds in the ground, the zapote tree gives fruit for three hundred years and the mango for twenty-five.

Or you may find a hacienda-owner in a swanky bar, mourning the loss of some of his land, and you may find a half dozen others delighted to get the load off their necks, for they still own the sugar mills. The agrarians sell them the cane, the mill-owner is no longer a slave of the banks, because he doesn't have to borrow money to pay wages, and he makes more money now than before the land-parceling which he fought so bitterly. So he comes to Mexico City to celebrate a very successful year indeed.

And there are plenty of places where he can celebrate. He can see the many beautiful parks, the hundreds of statues that most Mexico City residents don't see any more but which thrill the provincial; he can go to the museums, to the theaters, to the many movie houses, the bullfights, the soccer games, the bars, cabarets; to the scores of restaurants, many of them specializing in dishes of one region or another; or to the "houses of joy," among which he can also have his selection according to the region of the country he prefers. And almost anywhere he goes he can have his choice of every possible kind of liquor, foreign or domestic.

But the forgotten man drinks *pulque,* the poor man's drink, often his substitute for food. In any one of hundreds of *pulque* saloons you can find rows of forgotten men, standing, sitting, sprawled on the floor. Perhaps he is at the Kiss of the Angels, or at the Machine Gun; maybe at the Glories of Bacchus, or the Beautiful Indian, the Great Duck, the Cockroach, the Office. At one corner, the forgotten man can reach the heights and the lowest depths, taste the fruits of heaven and of hell: in front of him a *pulque* Paradise beckons, and just across the street he can find a forgotten man's forgetfulness in The Inferno.

6

Fructuoso Rodriguez is a forgotten man of the mountains. He probably never heard of Abelardo Rodriguez, the President during whose term the minimum-wage law was passed. And Abelardo probably never heard of Fructuoso, who wouldn't be found on the Country Club golf links or at the Foreign Club or any of the places you might find Abelardo and his friends. Fructuoso works ten hours a day in a little pueblo in the State of Oaxaca. He makes palm-straw hats, three a day, weaves them by hand. For these hats he gets nineteen centavos, minus the cost of materials, which leaves him fourteen centavos net.

At the 1938 rate of exchange, that was the equivalent of three cents in United States currency. This comparison with American money is made only because the hats are exported to the United States. The man who exports them gets twenty cents (United States currency) each, making a total of sixty cents, which means three pesos—three hundred centavos— for the work that Fructuoso produced for fourteen centavos. With those fourteen centavos, Fructuoso can buy about two pounds of corn, and still have one centavo left to squander, maybe for a few frijoles.

But tourism has begun to bring new hope to the forgotten handicraftsmen. Becoming one of the major industries, it brings magic dollars to Mexico, has awakened a huge demand for the endless array of hand-made articles: blankets, baskets, toys, straw mats, leather goods, hammered silver, sculptured tin.

If you ask Federico Morales, a village blanket-weaver, he'll sum up the economic and social phenomenon that pundits put into long words:

"Things have changed since I used to buy my own yarn and work in the home village and then come back to Mexico

City to peddle the blankets to haggling buyers. Now I weave on the boss's loom. And I get two pesos a day, mind you, two pesos, and every day. It's true that I have to make some awful-looking designs that the tourists seem to like, but then . . . two pesos!"

He used to make that much during a whole week before, buying and dying the yarn, then bringing the finished product to market, unable to work when money ran low and he couldn't pay for materials. His soul undoubtedly got much more satisfaction out of the blankets he used to weave on his own loom, but his stomach doesn't twitch with hunger quite so much today.

Thousands of Federico Morales all over Mexico are busy turning out products for a demand so big that it can no longer be met by the old handicraft methods. The Federicos are being put to work making curios on a fordized system, entrepreneurs are making money hand over fist, in this twentieth-century rebirth of the factory system. Much of the capital that formerly went into farming is being turned to this industry, this and to real-estate investments in the cities. So the government's agrarian program indirectly spurs on a new industrial revolution. And the men who hire the Federicos to make huaraches and all the other beautiful things, are doing quite well. In some regions they have been doing so well that the government has stepped in and organized craftsmen into co-operatives which market their wares through government supervised stores.

The Federicos themselves have become part of the curios, the sights that the visitors want to see; hence, the tourist department has been encouraging many villages to retain their old costumes and their customs. This has become part of the campaign known as "conserving national historical monuments." The tourists go into ecstasies over the quaint costumes and the primitive habits. They do not like the quaintness of impure drinking water or lack of modern plumbing comforts that have been the rule in many backward places. But the tourist is helping to change this, too. The places he frequents have acquired filtered water, baths, and all the rest of the things that make the rugged individualist's life worth living. And the craftsmen like the visitors' well-tailored clothing, their well-made shoes, the shiny machine-made things which tourists use.

So, gradually, subtly, the tourist movement, awakening new wants, conquers Mexico, helps to do away with many things it came to see. A vast new demand for machine-made goods is being born, as mass-production and its tractors, automobiles, airplanes, radios, movies, spread to the most remote, the last frontiers of the handicraft age in North America.

Some of the romanticists are horrified over what will happen to forgotten Federico's soul when he can have the insuperable, civilized thrill of flushing a shiny enamel bowl instead of squatting on the ground. And the boys and girls in the tourist racket fear that the tourists will quit coming. But it is conceivable that a well-fed, well-housed and well-clothed Mexico will still be beautiful enough, or even more so. And just think what a demand for a million toilet bowls would do for the plumbing business.

XIV

MOBILIZING THE MUSES

1

THE surrender of The Noodle was one of the greatest triumphs in the career of Agustin Arroyo, and a very definite triumph, as well, for the very modern art of journalism, advertising and publicity. For years, The Noodle had been the terror of Morelos, the very small, very fertile semi-tropical climatic paradise which also gave Mexico the famous Emiliano Zapata. Scores of army detachments had been sent out to hunt for The Noodle—his real name was Enrique Rodriguez—each time a town was raided or somebody was held up on the highway, but none ever caught up with him.

In his hillside hideaway, The Noodle received the daily papers via trusted henchmen, who also managed to get ammunition and other supplies which ran low when the bandit business was not going so well. The newspapers revealed to him that some other bandits were operating in the hills, and he was being blamed. They also told him—from March 18 on—about the critical period through which the government was passing, how Mexico was having trouble with foreign companies and foreign governments, and that one of their propaganda weapons was to advertise that travel in Mexico was unsafe. That helped to reduce tourist travel and this very directly affected business in Morelos, for Cuernavaca, State capital, is the leading tourist resort of all Mexico. And it so happened that some of The Noodle's relatives were officials in the Morelos State government.

Then, on a morning in October, 1938, from the office of Agustin Arroyo, head of the government's Department of Press and Publicity (DAPP), telephone calls were made to all the newspapers and to foreign correspondents: The Noodle has surrendered! And you can bring cameras. So next morning Mexico ate up the news and the photos, reading from left to right, Arroyo; Genaro Perdomo, uncle of The Noodle; and, in a neat business suit, collar and tie, correct haircut, freshly shaved, well-trimmed mustache, and bright, vigorous face, The Noodle himself! How different from the bandit hunts of a few years ago! Then, instead of the government's Minister of Propaganda, the man in the picture was General This or General That, and with him in the picture, if there were any pictures, was a corpse, with all the bullet-wounds retouched to show very plainly that the bandit was, as the saying goes, well dead.

The Noodle told his story and stuck to it: the major factor that influenced him toward laying down his arms and placing himself at the mercy of the government was the fact that his country was being menaced by foreign interests. Furthermore, he did not think it patriotic to go on harassing and embarrassing a man like Cardenas for whom the people in the farm villages had a great deal of affection. That was why his uncle Genaro talked to the President, and the President said he would grant the rebel amnesty on his promise to live a peaceful life.

2

Congress willingly appropriated nearly a million extra pesos for the exhausted 1938 budget of a department that could produce miracles which bullets had been unable to accomplish. Everybody saw clearly then, what Cardenas had seen when he created the department on January 1, 1937—

that it constituted a powerful new weapon for the government, giving the Cardenas administration what previous regimes had sought to obtain through armed force alone. Through paid advertising in newspapers and magazines, by subsidized radio programs over government and private stations, by motion pictures, posters, exhibitions, and other means, the DAPP is consciously molding public opinion, helping Cardenas sell himself and his program to the people, telling the story of the administration from its own point of view. The department has what amounts to a monopoly of news sources in the government offices. Reporters still cover other government offices separately, and can get a certain amount of news there, but they have come to depend more and more on the DAPP handouts, which usually give the news in addition to the puffs, and the answers to special queries.

The big shot of the DAPP, an autonomous federal goverment department with practically cabinet ministry status, is Agustin Arroyo, one of the group of Guanajuato politicos who have been prominent in the Cardenas administration. Among other Guanajuato politicos who figure in the administration picture are Luis I. Rodriguez, president of the official Party of the Mexican Revolution; Ignacio Garcia Tellez, Minister of the Interior; Federico Montes, chief of police of Mexico City. It was at a banquet given by Guanajuato politicos that Obregon was assassinated. That State, which derives its name from an Indian word meaning the "mountain of frogs," also produced Diego Rivera, the politico-painter, among other notables.

Arroyo was in the Ministry of the Interior as subsecretary to Portes Gil. His political career traces back to association with the Colunga ring in Guanajuato. As head of the Department of Press and Publicity, Arroyo is in a strategic position to control presses, for the DAPP has become the best customer of the printshops. He can patronize or refuse to patronize writers, artists, and other intellectuals. Some of the DAPP's production has been highly competent and worth while. Much of it has been very expensive tripe, obviously put through on a basis of personal or political pull.

3

The general concensus is that press freedom in Mexico today is greater than it has ever been before. Some of Cardenas' advisers have counseled him to close the lid before "the reactionaries undermine the government," as they did in the case of Madero, paving the way for an epoch of bloodletting. But Cardenas has refused to throttle papers, just as he refused to rattle the saber when some of his friends urged him to do so. Opposition papers, bitterly attacking the Cardenas program and Cardenistas, circulate freely, and what's more, even enjoy free postage, a privilege which Cardenas extended to the press soon after he took office.

There have been three or four cases of newspaper suppression by men in the Cardenas administration, during the first year or so, before Cardenas became boss. But since Cardenas made clear his stand on a free press, newspapers have enjoyed hitherto untolerated abandon in criticizing public officials, a privilege packed with much more dynamite in Mexico's highly charged political air than it is in the United States. Members of the cabinet, officials close to Cardenas, have been ripped apart by newspapers, sometimes unfairly, sometimes perhaps with justification, but the high-handed reprisal was taboo. The politicos who could dish it out learned, under Cardenas, to take it as well.

In *Hoy*, a weekly, Mexico got a new journalistic thrill, a good technical job, and a general approach like that of metropolitan papers in the United States. A news summary section in it is a direct imitation of the *Time Magazine* style—the smirk school of journalism—but with barbs much more stinging. A clash between *Hoy* and the CTM followed the magazine's publication of Cedillo's picture soon after he disappeared in the hills. With the picture was an interview, denouncing Cardenas. The photographer had found Cedillo, but the army couldn't. The CTM staged a huge demonstration against *Hoy* and the "rest of the reactionary press." *Hoy* defied Vicente Lombardo Toledano, and that didn't hurt the advertising end of the freedom of the press.

Todo, another of the *Hoy* group, has a nasty anti-United States policy, and is drippingly pro-Nazi.

In an address on July 16, Lombardo Toledano, head of the CTM, charged that *Hoy's* action in printing the Cedillo stuff was part of a reactionary campaign to discredit the institutions of Mexico and its public men. He further charged—what has been more or less generally accepted in newspaper circles—that Hitler gold is buying news stories and editorials in several of the daily newspapers as well as in the magazines of biggest circulation.

Any comment on the big Mexican papers inevitably tends to become a disclosure of further evidence of Nazi penetration. But that's the picture. You hate to harp on it, but whether you like it or not, the Franco-Mussolini-Hitler influence is the outstanding characteristic of the Mexican commercial press, which is also violently anti-government.

On the other side of the fence, definitely anti-Hitler and anti-Mussolini are three political dailies, *El Nacional, El Popular* and *La Voz de Mexico*. *El Nacional* is the organ of the Party of the Mexican Revolution; *El Popular,* of the Confederation of Mexican Workers; *La Voz de Mexico,* of the Communist Party.

Besides the daily press, there are numerous weekly and semi-weekly newspapers, most of them organs of "the Reaction." *El Hombre Libre* and *Omega,* unofficial clerical organs, give big space to attacks on Cardenas and the "communism" of his administration, and to anti-Semitic articles. Some of their writers call themselves National Socialists.

Nearly all the rightist newspapers have one thing in common: the advertisements of Dr. Raschbaum's German Clinic. The ads are identical. The heading says: "I Cure Men Only—Glandular Therapy for Sexual Debility and Sterility." The absence of these ads from the leftist papers would lead to the deduction—strictly from a technical advertising analysis—that there is a better market for this service on the right side of the barricades than on the left.

Cardenas' emphasis on press freedom brought big applause from newspaper and magazine vendors. Since he took office, the daily average sale of periodicals in Mexico City has been around four hundred thousand copies, compared to two hundred thousand before. Another Mexican paradox: the first printing press was being operated in Mexico as early as 1539, by Esteban Martin, "father of the Mexican press," but the sale of books and magazines has been almost infinitesimal in proportion to the population. The cause: schooling restricted to small groups; the masses kept as beasts of burden.

Foreign correspondents constitute a class apart in Mexico. Theoretically impartial, each one actually represents the bias of his particular country, of his particular newspaper, and his personal interests. The policies of the big papers, like the New York *Times,* for instance, become much clearer when correspondents concentrate on finding only those facts which can be fitted to print, and let the rest go by. This might be called the teleological school of journalism. The press associations tend to be more objective, but they also have axes to grind. The ANTA (Havas) gets a government subsidy. Hearst doesn't like the Mexican government policies, so the International News Service digs for the kind of news that

Hearst editors want. The Associated Press tends to be influenced by the New York *Times* needs. The United Press, by and large, gives the fairest and best-balanced report on Mexico.*

The work of the Department of Press and Publicity is not confined to newspaper activities. One of its jobs has been to mobilize the "cultural workers"—painters, photographers, technicians, theater workers, musicians, writers—into more direct collaboration with the government program. In this task, the DAPP found a wealth of cultivated talent, particularly in the plastic arts and music, which have had the active support of the federal government for many years, through the Ministry of Education's Department of Fine Arts.

4

Little men, big on a wall. Humble Indians, proud and dignified in paint. General Cardenas, then President-nominee, was delighted to see the fishermen of Patzcuaro find a place of honor in 1933 on the walls of Morelia University. He was pleased that the artist, Marion Greenwood, had pictured the Indian as he had known him for so long, with the weight of centuries on his shoulders. Even more inspiring was another wall, in the Morelia Museum, on which Grace Greenwood had painted twelve-foot men, heroic, monumental figures, Today-Men of Mexico, struggling through machinelike geometrical forms, searching for the road that would lead them to a better World of Tomorrow.

-----

* On January 16, 1939, Frank L. Kluckhohn, New York *Times* correspondent, was deported from Mexico. The DAPP charged that Kluckhohn had "maliciously misinterpreted" Mexican policies over a long period of time. Kluckhohn cabled from Brownsville, Texas, that he had "tried to be strictly impartial." The general feeling among Mexican officials with whom this writer talked was that the correspondent's "impartiality" was hypothetical because the *Times* was prejudiced against the Mexican government and that the *Times* man's dispatches reflected these prejudices. The expulsion was a marked departure from the usual Cardenas policy on the press.

Soon to feel the weight of Mexico's burdens on his shoulders and the anguish of a people's struggle against potentially helpful forces turned adverse, the President-to-be studied these paintings for a long time. He was glad they had been painted in Morelia, capital of his home State, Michoacan. And he was particularly pleased that they had been painted by foreigners, two American girls, who knew little about the country's history, but who had succeeded, as only artists can, in penetrating to the very core of the Mexican tragedy. If only more Americans would try to understand before they passed judgment. . . .

The period during which the Greenwood sisters were painting in Mexico marked the second phase of the Mexican art renaissance, about which so much has been written, particularly about its leading figures: highly-publicized Diego Rivera, defiant Jose Clemente Orozco, dramatic David Alfaro Siqueiros, the iconoclastic trinity of the mighty art movement that rose with the surge of labor and the first full breath of the Mexican Revolution. In its second stage, the movement spread to the younger Mexican artists, and attracted American painters who had rejected the modern French influence, who were rebelling against Europeanism, seeking something American—American in the big sense of the New World, which the Mexican mural school seemed to have found.

The Mexican government has for a number of years been one of the principal art patrons of the country. The Department of Fine Arts, in the federal Ministry of Education, has been able to incorporate the work of painters, musicians, sculptors, and artists in other fields, into the general educational program. The walls in the Ministry of Education, in the preparatory school, in other government buildings, were made available, during Obregon's presidency, funds were provided for materials and living expenses. On these vast stretches of blank space, the artists were to perpetuate the unfolding of Mexico's Revolution, not the Revolution of 1910 alone, but the bigger Revolution, the steady building of resistance against oppression.

With the first big growth of the labor movement after 1920, the arts in Mexico definitely discarded their seven veils and jumped into working clothes. The peasant and the proletarian were to have their day, not only in the political councils, but also in the world of culture. Then came the backwash, the "sell out" of the redeemers, the suppression of the labor movement, and with these developments the soft-pedaling of the worker-artists. But the torch of art of-by-and-for the masses was kept burning by a small, enthusiastic, financeless and rather sectarian group known as the League of Revolutionary Writers and Artists (LEAR), many of whom were members of the Communist Party. The rise of Cardenas, following several years of restraint on the labor and land phases of the Mexican Revolution, brought a new, intensified appeal to the masses. The walls of public buildings were again placed at the disposal of the painters. Simultaneously, however, the Cardenistas sought a more immediate, more widespread form of reaching the people. This need became even more urgent with the Calles-Cardenas break in 1935, which made it necessary to build up Cardenas and to use every possible means to fight off a counter-revolutionary coup which the Cardenistas thought was imminent as a result of the renewed Calles agitation in 1936. The press, the radio, the poster became the favored mediums. Funds were withdrawn from mural work and shunted toward the more direct publicity. But before this happened, one of the most interesting, although unfinished, developments had taken place— the collective decoration of the Abelardo Rodriguez Market by a group of young painters: Antonio Pujol, Miguel Tzab, Ramon Alva Guardarrama, Angel Bracho, Raul Gamboa,

Pedro Rendon, Grace Greenwood, Marion Greenwood and Paul O'Higgins. Diego Rivera was the technical supervisor of the group's work.

Alongside the Rodriguez Market, Colombia Street runs from Brazil Avenue clear out to the Federal Penitentiary. On Colombia Street, in a two-story house, Number 86, the Greenwoods, Marion and Grace, lived. And there, every day the group met to discuss the progress of their work. They straggled in toward sundown: Bracho, short and roly-poly, always thirsting for coffee, and with immense tomes on biology under his arms, for a mural on vitamins; Paul, who started as a child-prodigy pianist, and whose paintings have the rhythm of a Chopin polonaise; Tzab, part-Mayan Indian; Pujol, with a pocketful of sketches from the back streets of the metropolis where he spent most of his boyhood; Rendon, who tried to put his verses into painting.

Other frequent visitors were: Leopoldo Mendez, unquestionably Mexico's master wood-block engraver and outstanding lithographer; Alfredo Salce, who brought surrealist technique into political-revolutionary drawings; Manuel Alvarez Bravo, mural photographer; Fermin Revueltas, brilliant young painter, who died in 1936. That same year the federal district building budget lopped off the mural allotment. Earlier, Isaumu Noguchi had come from the United States to contribute a colored cement bas-relief to the collective endeavor. In 1936, too, the group scattered. The Greenwoods returned to the United States. Some of the painters became art teachers in the public schools. Pujol went to Spain to join the Loyalist army.

In 1938 the Mexican mural movement had entered a new phase. Of the three outstanding muralists, the "originals," only Orozco was painting walls with the same fervor that marked the movement's beginning. Siqueiros was in Spain, a colonel in the Loyalist army. Rivera was turning out a steady stream of easel paintings and doing such incidental work as designing rugs for American millionaires. Orozco, painting furiously in Guadalajara—he had been at it steadily for nearly two years—was bringing to the Mexican mural school his matured experience and his highly developed technical preparation. In the State capitals younger Mexican artists were decorating public buildings, chiefly in the Rivera-Orozco-Siqueiros tradition. A new emphasis had also been placed on painting of murals in the schools. In many cases the painting was done by the pupils themselves. Many of the painters had become art teachers, in line with the stress on popular culture. The Ministry of Education was subsidizing easel painters. Some artists were doing posters, others were making colored diagrams for DAPP expositions. Leopoldo Mendez had founded a Popular Art Workshop, on a self-sustaining basis, specializing on work for labor organizations and the Workers' University.

The LEAR, under a new united-front policy attracted artists and writers who had fought shy of "sectarian Marxism." Many Mexican artists have not become identified with the mural school. The majority of these look with disdain on "social art" and the "art with a purpose" schools, sticking more or less to an "art-for-art's-sake" approach of "eternal values."

5

The mural painting of Mexico has received wide acclaim, but Mexico's contribution to music, fully as significant, has been relatively slighted. On June 21, 1937, President Cardenas decreed compulsory music-teaching in all Mexican schools. This edict was a long-delayed recognition of the richest of Mexican arts, development of which had been in a state of animated suspension for many years. The Europeanism of the ruling classes disdained the treasure-store of native music, and went limping along in imitation of the Italian, German and French composers. Many believe that the contemporary music movement in Mexico, when it has attained maturity, will be recognized as marking a renaissance of the Mexican creative spirit greater in scope, and with greater depth, than the art revival. For the Mexican composer and the Mexican performer have a vast musical background from which to draw, the heritage of all the races that formed the Spaniards, and in addition, the Indian and the Negro rhythms: a veritable melodic melting pot.

The name of Carlos Chavez has been fairly well publicized, but how many persons outside of Mexico have heard of, say, Augusto Novaro? Novaro is the inventor of a new piano, a new theory of music, and a new method of tuning pianos that has been adopted by some progressive schools in the United States, Mexico and abroad. All this during his spare time, when he is not putting in a full day at operating a linotype machine.

Thirty-eight-year-old Carlos Chavez is the best known of Mexican composers and directors, has been guest conductor of the famous symphonic orchestras in the United States, and has written a book on the relationship of music and electricity. The "father" of the contemporary Mexican movement, Manuel M. Ponce, is best known for his pioneering work in the use of Mexican folklore. One of the most fascinating personalities in Mexico's world of culture, considered by many as the Mexican composer in whose works the musical revival reached fullest expression, is Silvestre Revueltas, master violinist, composer, orchestra conductor.

Silvestre Revueltas used to fiddle for a living in American movie houses. He'd rather direct a symphony orchestra for a crowd of workmen and their families than for the most select diamond-horseshoe audience in the world. One reason is that he can dress comfortably, in a shirt with open collar, when providing music for the masses. When he directs a formal concert, he has to wear the conventional full-dress, and nobody can look more miserable than Revueltas in full dress.

There is something of that same quality—of liberation from throttling bonds that choke a man's soul—in Revueltas' composition. His music could never have the flavor of conservatory hothouses, because he himself is no hothouse product. If occasionally a passage in one of his pieces seems stuffy, it quickly is revealed as a foil for a surging counter-movement: the plant confined in a hothouse straining to violent growth and breaking through the imprisoning glass, into the open air, willing to perish if necessary for this one big deep breath of freedom.

Revueltas has the qualities which have been described as essential for the man whose work is nationalist, in the sense that it is based on folklore. Simple, generous, modest, rooted in the people, bearing the people's struggle in his blood, Revueltas, in his music, sums up his Spanish heritage, the blending of Gothic and Mediterranean peoples, the Indian and Negro rhythms of Mexico's songs and dances, the tempo of the modern mechanical world, all with a cosmic sense of tragedy, of humor, of irony. You can feel all these things in his work, but you cannot single out any one, you cannot recognize snatches of popular folk music as in Chavez. The latter's music is a mosaic, well-designed and fairly harmonious. But Revueltas has poured the raw materials into the crucible of his tormented creative genius, fused and molded them into something new, something genuinely Mexican, neither a surrender to folklorism, Indianism, nor an aping of European and United States music, revealing clearly the first positive feelers toward articulate musical self-assertion of his people. If you ask Revueltas where his music comes from, he may answer:

The hard-metal hills of my native Durango.
The unreal beauty of Janitzio Island.
Weary years of exile, doing three-a-day on a Publix theater circuit.
A San Antonio, Texas, boardinghouse.
Discrimination against Mexicans in southwestern United States.
The whir of a trans-continental plane.
Co-ordinated clang of a steel mill.
Shrill, barbaric radio sounds.
Tom-tom thump of a *teponaztle* drum.

6

As in painting and in music, the same two general diverging trends are found in the other arts, literature, drama, dance, cinema—one stemming from European cultural traditions and the other trying to find its way with the Indian tradition as compass. The first leads to formalism, stylization, snobbery, technical *tours de force*. The second as dangerously leads to a negation of all cultural values other than the Indian, a kind of artistic "going native" which is the delight of tourists, folklore faddists and collectors of Mexican curios.

Music and painting are the arts which have come nearest finding a direction that is Mexican, *mestizo*, mixed-blood, American, of the new world. The cinema is rather young in Mexico. The bulk of its production has consisted of bad imitations of worse Hollywood products, "adaptations" of stories from other lands to a Mexican setting, as false as the painted maguey plants on a musical-comedy stage; or of film versions of legitimate drama off the Mexican stage, and the usual play there is to contemporary Mexico what King Arthur and his Knights would be to any Main Street in the United States. The third type of Mexican film is a patchwork of popular songs, guitar playing and dancing, with a thin thread of a story running through it. This has been the most popular, and at the same time the most interesting, but its interest and its value depend entirely on the music and have very little to do with cinema.

But there is hope in the Mexican movie world. For one thing, composers like Revueltas are producing original compositions for the pictures. Also, the producers are drawing on the best theater and literary talent of the country for film originals and directors. This may not help the famishing Mexican theater, recently given government stimulus by the creation of a "People's Theater," nor the diffused literature, but the film may be the answer to Mexico's dramatic and literary yearnings; it may be the art-form in which writing Mexico will find its best expression, just as political Mexico tries to find new forms for its democratic strivings. The photography is already superb, the sound perfected, but creative film writers and directors are scarce. The same can undoubtedly be said of Hollywood, and as in Hollywood, productions must be, first of all, box-office. The Ministry of Education and the Confederation of Mexican Workers in 1938 were trying to work out a plan for producing motion pictures that "would be closer to the Mexican reality" than the Charro horse-operas. Mexico's background in the plastic arts, in music, provides a firm, rich soil in which the new art can flourish, but it needs the fertilization of literary talent, of twentieth-century literary talent that sees things cinematically, that can mold character and situation with pictures-that-move, as the novelist and dramatist do with words.

Mexico's problem in encouraging the drama has been similar to that of music—to disseminate classical works which would create new audiences, to raise the level of popular appreciation, and to provide stimulus for Mexican dramatists. But outside of the limited encouragement given by the federal government, there has been little assistance for the Mexican drama. The commercial theater has stuck pretty close to the old Spanish comedy of incident and the gushing sentimentality of the gay-ninety "drammer." Spaniards' control of the theaters has blocked Mexican playwrights, the latter complain.

Some plays which attempted social satire—like works of Bustillo Oro and Rodolfo Usigli—were squeezed out by politicos. Julio Bracho produced O'Neill's *Lazarus Laughed*, and made Mexican theater history. The Ministry of Education has made several attempts to build up the Mexican theater. When Narciso Bassols was Minister, he tried to establish a Children's Theater for which Leopoldo Mendez and Abel Plenn prepared extensive projects. Other efforts were directed toward finding a drama basis in native dances. But political favoritisms, doctrinaire (esthetic and political) cliques, and the inevitable shortage of funds, make the going difficult for the muse of the mimes. The best theater talent— very scarce—turns to the movies.

The ferment of the post-1910 epoch has begun to find shape in Mexican literature of the last decade. Most Mexicans lived their Revolution too intensely to be writing about it. In fact, that may be one explanation for a dearth of maturity in literature and the arts, for in nearly every period, as a new generation was preparing to revaluate and draw lessons and inspiration from preceding unrest, it was swept by new upheavals onto the battlefield and the studio was left deserted. But when a relatively stable stretch is attained, the very persistence of these struggles, this hammer-and-chisel sculpting of the Mexican soul over the years, will have provided an unequaled background for new artistic creation.

The two general literary tendencies are more sharply divergent than ever before, due in a large measure to the more defined social and political alignments, and yet they seem to be drawing together into Mexico's nationalism, as if they had reached the point of widest separation and had begun to con-

verge. There are the Marxists and the non-Marxists, the revolutionaries in form but not in content, the revolutionaries
in content but not in form, the revolutionaries who hold that
revolutionary content must have revolutionary form. The
Europeanized tendency persists principally in the groups that
hold themselves aloof from the Mexican Revolution, or who
attack it. The other tendency boasts of political and social
essays, works of social satire, dynamic, explosive poetry, crude
in form, sometimes crude in language, battle cries against injustice. The welding of the best in the two tendencies—
already approached in the plastic arts through the use of surrealist technique in revolutionary drawings—is bound to produce the alloy of which Mexico's new literature will be
formed.

The spread of education, the dissemination of literature
through low-price books—hitherto made impossible by a
bookstore trust—and the rousing of Mexico's confidence in
herself, through social and economic betterment, will create
the environment which literature and the other arts must
have in order to function. A reversal of these processes must,
logically, inevitably, lead to sterility, anemia and decay of
the arts and sciences.

7

In a country which had a "scientific" party at the head of
the Diaz government, and which later turned to "directed
economy" on socio-scientific lines, science has not enjoyed
official support in the measure given the arts. The Cardenas
regime's stress on technical education may eventually bring
about a revival of science to march along with the arts. The
trend toward applied science and technology, already visible
in 1915, was responsible for crowding out the cultural aspects of science but may, strangely enough, now help to

bring about a revival of scientific philosophy. The contemporary emphasis on the arts had its philosophical roots in the anti-scientific and anti-rational doctrines preached by Antonio Caso and Jose Vasconcelos from 1911 to 1925, when the Bergsonian teachings were used as a weapon against the "cientificos" who had been identified with the Diaz regime. Hence there arose a political anti-scientific movement which found its theoretical bases in idealism.

Mexico's most developed science is biology, related, of course, to the applied science of medicine and surgery. The origin of this development may perhaps be traced to the widespread disease that thrived on mass poverty, and so the evil tended to give birth to its remedy. Funds for research in biology have been provided by the Rockefeller and Guggenheim foundations.

Many critics agree that the influence of Caso and Vasconcelos has been responsible, in a measure, for retarding the development of science in Mexico, where scientific tradition is rich. Mathematics is cultivated only in applications to engineering and architecture. There is a dearth of research facilities in a country which is one great scientific laboratory; a dearth of scientific libraries, physics laboratories, professors and students. Hence talented Mexican men of science seek their perfection elsewhere.

There are several organizations in Mexico dedicated to promotion of scientific, rationalist and positivist philosophies and studies. These groups are not Marxists, but like the Marxists they are, in the main, opposed to the school of idealist philosophy represented by Caso and Vasconcelos. One of the prolific writers on the scientific method is young Agustin Aragon Leiva, author of *Science as Drama*.

Some educators believe that one of the main functions of the Socialist School, not only in the primary grades, but in the field of higher education, will be that of destroying the prejudices against science, and that this aspect of the government school system will be more significant than the political doctrine involved.

The advocates of these measures contend that the Socialist School will lay the groundwork for a renaissance of science in Mexico. They believe that such a rebirth will recapture the Mexican scientific traditions and permit Mexico to play a more prominent role in the cultural world of tomorrow, which they foresee as an eminently scientific world.

XV

IN THE RED

1

A HANDSOME tiled monument in the Dolores Cemetery of Mexico City commemorates the life and deeds of the great Don Carlos Balmori. Don Carlos came into this world an adult—a mad multi-millionaire, with a fantastic history of world-traveling, service in the foreign legion, big-game hunting, already completed the day he was born. On the monument is a full-length portrait of Don Carlos. Nobody quite like him ever lived before. He himself lived only about twice a week. But on those nights the world was his, and all that was in it. No human being could resist this ridiculous, hot-tempered, willful, eccentric omnipotent multi-multi-millionaire, who delighted in offending people and believed that money could cure all ills. On the slightest pretext he would write out a check for a hundred thousand pesos. Human vanity, greed, avarice, treachery, cynicism, every frailty known to men and women, were bared cruelly at Don Carlos' parties.

Important people attended these parties: governors, cabinet ministers, bankers, senators, businessmen, intellectuals. Fantastically-mustachioed Don Carlos, wearing a vest of screeching hue, and an immense gold chain across his middle, always appeared with a gigantic, a monumental, diamond stuck in his necktie. He might rush up to a very respectable young matron and offer her five thousand pesos for just one night of bliss. No offense, his friends would explain; you see, he's like that, funny, you've got to humor him. But he uses his money to help people. Ah, here's the banker's wife. I've heard you can tango beautifully. Let's see you perform. Marvelous, exquisite. I will make you a famous dancer. I shall hire the best talent to prepare a ballet for you. Here's an advance of twenty thousand pesos. But you must divorce that scoundrel of a husband at once. Ah, there, Senator, I have heard much about your ability, and of your ambitions, too. My checkbook is at your disposal. Don Carlos will make you president. One hundred thousand pesos for preliminary expenses. Shine my shoes now, will you, like a good fellow. I want to say a president shined my shoes. Well, well, well, what a beautiful girl, so young, so fresh, so beautiful! And Don Carlos is a bachelor and getting old. Will you marry me? You are already engaged? To that young man, and you love him very much? Nonsense! You can marry him when I die, and you will be rich. Here's a check for fifty thousand as a pre-nuptial gift. Now go break the news to him.

And so on. About three thousand "protégés" of one kind or another filed before Don Carlos during the seven years of his mad existence. Somehow, Don Carlos always managed to hit right on the protégé's weakness. And the protégé always had to do something humiliating in return for Don Carlos' favor. Then, before the evening was over, when the girl and her fiance had almost come to blows; and the senator was dreaming of himself as president and the others were courting him for appointments; and the author envisioned his works in vellum bindings—the stickpin with the huge diamond disappeared. And it always turned up in possession of the protégé, the ingrate, the traitor, the lower-than-the-low, so impatient for wealth.

Just as the victim was about to break down or go into hysterics, Don Carlos took off his mustache, removed his hat and let down his long hair. And the folks met Conchita Jurado, a very mild-mannered, calm, sweet-faced middle-

aged schoolteacher, the prima donna of the most fantastic
theater that ever existed anywhere. The Balmori coterie
was started by a group of idle rich folk, as a "psychological
experiment," to explore the depths of human weakness, to
see humanity grovel before insulting wealth. It was a supreme
creation of the extravagant Mexican imagination. So, on the
tomb, which the surviving "Balmorians" visit yearly, is the
portrait of Conchita Jurado, who died in 1931, and that of
her other self, Don Carlos Balmori, who made so many people
ecstatically happy for a moment, only to plunge them into a
stinking swamp of remorse. And each victim got his vengeance—by bringing another victim to this master humorist, this
stripper of souls, this arch-fiend who fed on vanity, vanity, all
is vanity.

2

Under the Diaz system, foreign capital pulled a Don Carlos
Balmori on Mexico. It promised big things, and got a lot of
humiliating concessions from Mexico in return for loans that
pledged the country's future income. In the early days of the
Diaz regime, the country's financial situation was a mess.
Practically all the customs duties were being collected by
creditors. Then Diaz put into effect his program. The capitalist mode of development was given full sway, full freedom: no labor restrictions, cheap labor, government aid, low
taxes, free land. But the social side of capitalist development
was slighted; the mass of the population was kept down. Diaz
performed fiscal miracles, balanced the budget, at times even
showed a surplus in the treasury; but the fundamental economy of the country was unsound.

The 1907 depression blew the Diaz house of cards to bits.
Don Carlos demanded his diamond stickpin, and all the official sycophants saw their dream-houses tumble. The Diaz

set-up collapsed, in spite of balanced budgets, collapsed just when everything looked its loveliest. Crops failed. More small landowners were forced off the land, to look for jobs as day laborers. Strikes, political and social unrest followed. Diaz' fiscal paradise, built on an inferno of mass repression, was lost in the cataclysm of Revolution.

3

Some bill collector is always knocking at Mexico's door. In the family of nations, Mexico is one of the poor relations, a debtor nation, perpetually in the red. She has given billions in wealth, and the more she gives the more she owes, like the farm laborer under the peonage system. This important fact—the predominant position of foreign capital—is sometimes forgotten by folks with rule-of-thumb solutions and analyses.

Basically, foreign capital is neither better nor worse than Mexican capital. Capitalism's positive features and its negative features are just as plain in Mexican capitalism as in foreign capitalism, regardless of the flag under which it flies. As far as Mexico is concerned there is as little difference as, say, between New York capitalism and California capitalism and Texas capitalism.

Furthermore, if the Mexican capitalist spends all his profits abroad—as has often been the case—the difference between Mexican and foreign capitalism becomes infinitesimal. In this case, the difference is as artificial as the crackpot cries of "Gentile silver" and "Jewish gold," as false as the Nazi economics fakery that finds uncircumcised capitalism preferable to circumcised. The question is not how much money you make, but what do you do with it? That's one of the things the oil companies refused to understand. Not until 1938 did the great Royal Dutch Shell deign to construct a building in

Mexico City, and then only what amounted to a façade. The Standard Oil interests continued in ancient edifices, as if they had just pitched camp for the night and were ready to pull stakes any minute. They still had the colonial complex. They failed to differentiate between exploitation and development. The excuse given for not making permanent investments is that "conditions were unsettled." But they were not too unsettled to keep up oil and mining operations.

Mining interests have acted likewise, all take and no give, as if just passing through, like a dose of salts. The companies will retort that they paid taxes, that they gave money to public officials, supposedly for schools and other improvements, and it is not their fault that the money went into the officials' pockets instead. But they forget to add that they paid the officials to throttle labor, to keep wages down, to keep the people subdued by armed force, and in that way bolstered political tyranny, kingfishism, under which the companies could work, protected, and the people could not call their officials to account. Oh, it's a beautiful system for the absentee capitalist in the case of colonies. Isn't that what colonies are for? You send over soldiers, or you set up your private armies, and you've got the natives by the ying-yang.

Mexico is not a political colony, but absentee capitalism is the pivot on which her economy has been turning—absentee control of natural resources: farmland, mines, water power, oil.

For instance, more than fifty per cent of the national wealth is owned by foreigners, yet the foreign population is about two per cent of the total population. Ninety-five per cent of the extractive industries are foreign-owned. Sixty per cent of the manufacturing and processing industries are foreign-owned.

Foreign loans add to Mexico's financial burdens. The foreign debt which stood at 265,000,000 in 1914 had swelled, through interest, to 543,000,000 in 1938. The railroad debt, 242,000,000 in 1914, had shot up to 465,000,000 in 1938, with practically no new material purchased. All loans date from the Diaz period.

4

In the main, the Mexican Revolution was led by the radical lower middle classes, the little fellows who were trying to expand, to become full-fledged capitalists, and were thwarted and checked by the Diaz monopolists and their foreign allies. But the Revolution also stirred the poorest strata of the population, the landless and propertyless peasants and proletarians, who made up the mass of the armies. The task of the middle-class revolutionaries became that of keeping the underdogs in check. This was done in two ways: by extermination, and by granting concessions in the form of land reform and labor legislation.

In return for this thwarting and checking, the new-rich radical middle class, the Mexican neo-capitalists, got the support of foreign extractive capital (banking, mining, oil, hacienda). That, then, became the economic set-up. Foreign extractive capital allied itself with the Mexican industrial and commercial capital. But the push of Mexican capitalism continued toward economic autonomy, and as the Mexican industrialists grew stronger, organized labor also grew. The drive toward economic autonomy inevitably took the form of nationalism; and its essential aim was—and is— nationalization of basic resources, which would give Mexican capitalists a whack at industries formerly foreign-owned.

All Mexican industrial legislation tended in this direction. Labor organization was encouraged, strengthened by law, but with the politicos close at the controls, with the idea that labor could become an effective weapon against the foreign capitalists. So, ultimately, Mexican capital, at first the chief ally of foreign capital, became a competitor. Labor played the game, after its first disillusionments, but no longer blindly. It got this idea: If there was to be a restoration of resources to Mexico, why restore them only to the Mexican capitalists? Why should not the workman and the peasant be entitled to their share? In 1938, the most-repeated appeal of Mexican capital to labor was that it bury the hatchet as far as Mexican capitalists are concerned—that the Mexican capitalist is a good guy, a compatriot, and only the foreign capitalist, the imperialist, is the devil.

Other economic conflicts have arisen to complicate the Mexican scene, typically semi-colonial:

Foreign capital—mainly American and British—with commodities to sell, in need of consumers, fights foreign finance-extractive capital from the same country, interested in leaving as little as possible behind, hence retarding development, hence curtailing purchasing power.

Extractive-finance capital of one foreign country fights extractive-finance capital of another, competing for raw material sources and for placing advantageous loans.

Industrial-manufacturing capital of one foreign country fights industrial-manufacturing capital of another, and the various sectors of this type of capital in the same country fight one another, competing for markets.

Mexican industrial capital fights foreign capital of all kinds, competing for markets and raw materials sources.

Mexican importing interests fight Mexican exporting interests.

Mexican manufacturing industrialists fight Mexican manufacturing industrialists.

5

The cleavage between extractive and industrial-manufacturing capital became clear during the oil crisis. Standard

Oil set itself up as "American interests," and Royal Dutch Shell the same for British. But was Standard Oil acting on behalf of American interests? Mexico had been going through a tourist boom. New commodity markets were opening, incomes going up, living standards rising. Then Standard and Shell decided to bring Mexico to her knees on the oil question. In the absence of bayonets, which they would have preferred, they used economic pressure. It did not concern them that a depression in Mexico would mean lower purchasing power, less American goods bought, that a devalued peso would mean drastically reduced American business, which in turn would affect American jobs.

The Standard Oil and Dutch Shell game was of direct benefit to the totalitarian governments. The devalued peso made trade with the United States difficult, practically impossible. The oil companies—Shell also sells in the United States—set up new artificial antagonisms between Mexicans and Americans to check tourist travel. This curtailment cut both ways. Mexicans made less money, spent less for American goods, traveled less, American border merchants suffered, American travel bureaus suffered, American motorists didn't make the trip, American filling stations sold less gas and oil—and finally, Mexico made deals to trade oil to Hitler and Mussolini. Standard Oil, Royal Dutch Shell—"American interests" indeed! Until then, the Good Neighbor policy had been working fine. When Washington permitted itself to become chestnut-puller for the oil boys, by sending big-stick notes on land expropriation, Mexicans remarked that the Good Neighbor gag was O.K. while it lasted, but Grandma, what big teeth you have.

6

Money is like muck; not good, except it be spread. That's what the Old Bolshevik, Francis Bacon, sometimes regarded as Will Shakespeare's ghost-writer, said in his essay on "Seditions and Troubles." Since 1917, a big job of Mexican governments has been to find ways and means of giving more people a chance to enjoy some of the benefits of the mucky stuff, and at the same time to keep the incentives for business alive. This, too, has been the job of the Cardenas administration.

The men of the Revolution believe they have found the answer in "regulated economy." The Mexican form of regulated economy, like other forms of capitalism, is based on private property. It does not question the right of an individual or group of individuals to own means of production, to hire other men to work for wages, and to make a profit on this process. Nor does it question the right of the man hired for wages to seek as great a return as possible for the labor he performs, and to try to improve his position through organization. But it insists on the right of the State—the government—to intervene in the process, and to adopt measures for guarding the interests of the nation against encroachment by the most powerful economic groups.

Since the amount of capital that would take a chance under this system was relatively small, and a large part of the population was without land or jobs, Mexican regulated economy took two very decided measures. One was the nationalization of land to provide farm tracts. The other was to subsidize industries to be run as co-operatives; to help men who possessed skill and labor energy, but who had neither capital nor means of production.

Some Mexican economists regard it as axiomatic that a nation with a low supply of capital and credit—a debtor nation, in the red—must inevitably turn to directed economy, not imitatively, but in accordance with its own conditions and possibilities. Mexico is trying hard to solve her economy without the be-shirted political regimentation of Hitlerism or Mussolinism.

7

Mexico's regulated economy has turned to the co-operative—the workman's corporation—as a way out of the red. The co-operative idea is the keystone of ejido farming, and of much of the new industry rising in Mexico, spurned by capital that looked for juicier pickings. Facing this dilemma—to permit recurrence of factors which gave rise to the 1910 blow-up, that is, surrender to foreign and Mexican capital, or to pull herself up by the bootstraps—Mexico, via the Six-Year Plan, chose the latter.

The co-operative movement arose early in the anti-Diaz revolution, along with laborism and agrarianism. For a decade or more, the Laborist, the Agrarian and the Co-operativist parties figured in Mexican politics. But the early development of the co-operatives was marked by their conversion into buffers against labor organizations. Ardent co-operativists soon realized that this movement, just as the labor movement, could be steered toward the left or toward the right. A project to revise the co-op laws in 1938 raised a storm. The Co-operative Association charged that the government was trying to destroy this movement, to convert it into an accessory of the Chamber of Commerce, to establish "class collaborationism."

The revised law was prepared by the Presidential Study Commission (the Cardenas brain trust). It stated that the government aimed, through the co-operatives, merely to improve the workers' economic conditions, and "not to attempt transformation of the bourgeois economic system."

In Congress, spokesmen for some co-ops sought to change the law into what they termed "revolutionary co-operativism," which would "provide a transition from the regime of private property to socialization of the instruments of production and exchange."

It is significant that Vicente Lombardo Toledano, general secretary of the Confederation of Mexican Workers, was among the outstanding critics of the theory that the co-operative system could be the key to social and economic emancipation. Toledano's commentary is of especial interest because it helps to make clear certain aspects of Mexico's "socialism." He said, in part:

"Socialization is reached only when private property disappears as the base and aim of social institutions, so that the collectivity, composed exclusively of workers, can impose on production and distribution the modalities necessary for society, without encountering any legal obstacles. So, as long as there is private property, there can be no socialized property. The two forms cannot exist side by side. . . .

"Within the capitalistic regime, the turning over of some centers of production to the workers does not necessarily lead to socialism. It is solely an act which may temporarily help the workers, to a greater or lesser degree, but the beneficiaries do not thereby free themselves of the consequences of the capitalist regime."

In 1938, the National Confederation of Co-operatives was formed, with about 300,000 members in 2,600 co-operatives. A total of 2,867 co-ops was registered at the Ministry of National Economy in September, 1938. A total of thirty mining properties, some of them abandoned voluntarily by foreign companies, was then being worked by co-ops. More than 200 properties were being worked by private capital.

8

Cardenism is not communism, nor Nazism, nor fascism, nor "pure" democracy. Yet it has certain aspects of all four, with the modifications of its own traditions and environment. The

Indian provides Mexico with a common background, and in that sense Mexico is more of a melting pot than the United States. In our country, people of various races, creeds, nationalities settled. But we killed off the Indians, enslaved and then segregated the Negro, banned the Chinese and the Japanese. In Mexico, the conquest was biological as well as political, economic, and cultural. And the conquerors themselves bore in their veins the blood mixtures of many peoples, to be further fused with that of the Indian and the Negro. Spanish feudalism mixed with Aztec feudalism. The Virgin Mary and Tonantzin were joined in a mystic blend that became the Virgin of Guadalupe.

Fully sixty-five per cent of Mexican industry and business is conducted on the same private-property capitalist basis as in the United States. It is true that there is a tendency toward the collectivism of an under-developed economy, with a strong feudal background, and of a people only now beginning to learn the ways of political democracy. Mexico's approach toward "Marxist" teaching takes the form of "Socialist Education." In practice, despite the abundant use of very radical slogans and symbols, the Mexican Socialist school is closer to Humanism and Rationalism; stresses the idea of cause and effect, science against mysticism and fatalism; faith in the human power to achieve; something resembling Poor Richard's maxim that God helps those who help themselves.

Politically, Mexico holds to representative government, to Republicanism modeled after the United States form, and strives toward democracy. But there is democracy and false "democracy," just as there is nationalism and jingo "nationalism." In the Mexican picture, it becomes ever clearer that there is no stencil, no cut-out pattern for democracy. It is something which each nation must find for itself. It is not something that can be transplanted from one country to another, any more than you can import communism ready-made like so much caviar, in jars of red. Nor can fascism be imported. It also must have a proper soil in which to grow. Mexico's quest for democracy follows paths which cannot be identical with those of the United States. We had no feudalism to overthrow, except its approximation in the plantation system of the South. And there it was regional, rather than the dominant economic form. We have never suffered the crushing domination of a Church oligarchy. Our capitalism had virgin territory, the unhampered freedom that the revolutionary new system required. Mexican capitalism was hamstrung from the start by the power of secular and clerical land lords. The Puritan fathers fled from their oppression to a new land. But whither would they flee today? A claim has been staked to every bit of the earth. Oppressed Mexico could not flee. She had to stand and deliver. Poorly armed, unschooled, impoverished, she suffered many defeats. That she still exists at all is a tribute to a vitality of which any people might well be proud.

Mexico today is one vast laboratory of democracy. In the school, in the trade union, the peasant federation, through a free press, Mexico's men and women and children are learning the value of democratic control—sometimes learning it precisely through undemocratic procedures. It must be remembered, however, that a democracy being born today is not a democracy being born in virgin forests. Mexico has already suffered her tragedy of vast power and wealth gathered into a few hands and the helplessness of the isolated individual against that power. Mexico—working Mexico—organizes, to strengthen the individual in his challenge of the new threats against freedom—threats of economic or spiritual monopolies in a new kind of holy alliance against representative government. Some people like to call the extensive organization of workers communism, others socialism. Some say it is fascism. Cardenas likes to call it co-operativism.

Whatever you name it, Cardenism is giving the peasant more equal opportunity than he ever had. Certainly labor has more equality before the law than it had previously. The possibilities for education in Mexico today have never been matched in its history. There is no restriction on organization of political parties, within the limits of the national Constitution. Freedom of the press and assembly are unquestioned. There are no racial, religious, or economic tests for citizenship. Mexico's economic legislation is nationalist, but it is a defensive nationalism as distinguished from aggressive, imperialist nationalism. For instance, the law which makes it compulsory that ninety per cent of employees be Mexican, and that foreign-owned business must operate in the form of Mexican firms. The laws on the clergy are also defensive. They are an extension of the nationalist principle that persons with foreign allegiance must not take part in Mexican politics. The laws are not directed at individuals but at the clergy as a political institution. Clergymen—of any denomination—must be Mexican. They must confine their activities to Church work. The Church cannot own property, an extension of the nationalist principle that no part of the national territory should be alienated to a foreign power. Spellbinders who clamor for suppression of minority groups might well ponder how the pendulum of restriction has swung from the days of the Inquisition. Intolerance is a sharp-edged boomerang.

Finally, Mexico's democracy-in-the-making has the possibility of becoming a more complete democracy than others of the past or present. Greek democracy was based on slavery. Our big democracies today are tied up with political or economic domination of other nations. Mexico tries to find the way without benefit of imperial conquest.

So Mexico marches—in a rebirth of her perennial Revolution against privilege. The men who march, however, are not some new race of utopian beings, immaculate and infallible. They are the human stuff produced by centuries of oppression, hunger, prejudice, misery, tyranny, superstition, hatred, betrayed hopes. They are human beings whose generation has been one of constant civil war at home, and international wars abroad, a generation of revolution and violent change. And they have been conditioned by all this, and by the standards of contemporary society, with all its good features and all its bad. Mexico's march is not over a broad, paved highway, at the end of which the final destination is clear. The march is over a winding road, which sometimes seems to be turning back on itself. It is over a road piled high with obstacles placed there by the powerful forces that would like to disrupt that march.

Personalism—the kingfish and redeemer tradition—is one of the big obstacles. Cardenism seeks to combat it by way of institutionalism, which Calles also preached but could not make effective. Cardenas has deprived himself of executive-decree powers that predecessors had enjoyed. His administration has seen the passage of a revolutionary civil-service law that gives public employees full protection of the labor laws, including the right to strike. There is a definite swing toward giving civilians a greater share in public administration. Some of the generals are not any too happy about it, either.

What happens in Spain, what happens in the international fight for Latin-American trade, what happens in the United States elections, will have immediate repercussions in Mexico. Victory for Franco might easily result in a Mexican attempt to follow the Franco route. That's another reason Mexico marches. And there's always the steady pressure of Washington, of London, of Berlin, the men who need raw materials and the men with things to sell.

9

Great Britain and Germany are the United States' two big business competitors in Latin America. United States export capital (finance and extractive) runs up against the same type of British capital more than any other in the fight for raw materials. United States industrial-manufacturing capital must compete not only with British but with German, Italian, Japanese and native capitalists in the fight for markets. The outstanding characteristic of Latin-American development today is its industrialization. That means an increasing purchase of machinery and decreasing purchases of consumers goods. It is Utopian to think that the United States can have all the trade. That would be possible only if the United States could buy all of Latin America's products. Until that happens, Latin America has to sell to Europe and Asia, anywhere she can, and the way things are now, she has to buy where she sells. The old mercantile maxim, "the customer is always right," again asserts itself. When two countries are buying and selling to each other in more or less equal amounts we have the closest approximation to peace possible in our present stage of development.

A lot of poppycock has been written about Germany's "unfair" methods of competition, its barter methods and so on. Nazi "totalitarian" business methods have the same relation to commerce that "totalitarian" bombing of civilian populations has to war. It is a matter of degree. There is never anything "fair" about war, never anything "humane" about it. You fight to win. The only rule for military tactics is, "Will they achieve their objective?" The only rule for commercial tactics is the same, translated into business language, "Will they pay?" How "fair" is competition, even within a democratic country like ours, where certain "fair-trade practices" can be enforced? What chance has the little independent against the powerful mass-production corporation?

In Mexico, and in all of Latin America, the mercantile basis of international politics is revealed with ever greater clarity. The United States proposal for an anti-fascist pact runs smack against the refusal of "democratic" South-American countries to offend their Nazi and fascist customers. Mexico denounces fascism, but the fascist countries are the only ones she can do business with. We denounce, deplore and abhor everything that Hitler and his gang stand for. But have the Nazis had any trouble buying cotton from American firms? Or oil? Or scrap iron? Or anything else that we have an abundance of and want to sell and the Nazis can pay for? Foreign policy is inseparable from business policy. The only foreign policy of the United States of enduring value in Latin America will be one which helps create conditions whereby Latin America finds it most beneficial to do business with us.

The Good Neighbor policy—streamlined version of the Monroe Doctrine—is one of the best things that has happened in the United States-Latin-American relations, but its lovely sentiments must be implemented by deeds. Pretty speeches are not enough. Latin Americans get plenty of those, and much more flowery and polished than we can produce. We are not being Good Neighbors when we give active support to tyrannical governors. We are not being Good Neighbors when we give aid—through loans or otherwise—to a government which drives down its country's living standards, which sets up despotic rule that thwarts the development of representative government. It was not Good Neighborly to bolster a regime like that of Porfirio Diaz, whose repression of the big masses of people brought inevitable chaos from which Mexico is just beginning to emerge. And Diaz was the prototype of all Latin-American despots. It looked like good business to support him. Maybe it was for a while. But we saw the ultimate results of it. And Americans were among the biggest losers. The reason given for supporting him was "law and order," stability. Business, progress, prosperity, need stability, undoubtedly. But there is "stability"—the mechanical—of tyranny, and there is stability—the organic—of democratic control, the only real stability. How much better would it have been for business if Mexico had been able to achieve fuller development, high literacy, with millions demanding new products, higher standards of living.

But, whether we like to believe it or not, the essence of colonial policy has been to keep living standards as low as possible. Maybe business will come around to seeing the benefits of higher living standards, although it seems improbable in view of precedent. It is possible to conceive of such a thing as "enlightened" capitalism that is willing to take a cut in immediate profits in return for stability of production assured by generally higher purchasing power. It is a little difficult to see the imperialist in the role of social reformer, especially when raising of living standards in one place may mean raising them elsewhere. But then trade, twin brother of politics, makes strange bed-fellows. Sometimes there is only a flat choice left—reform or revolution, a mild laxative now instead of a blasting cathartic later.

10

The Latin-American countries liked the Good Neighbor policy so well that they actually tried to make sure, at the Lima Conference, that it would work. Several suggestions were made, among them that of Dr. Francisco Castillo Najera, the Mexican ambassador to Washington, who proposed that export capital surrender its recourse to diplomatic appeal. The theory was that genuine friendship and better relations could be developed among the nations by eliminating international conflicts over the mishaps of adventuring capital. The United States government agreed with this theory, and accepted, in the Good Neighbor doctrine, the thesis that capital invested abroad "should be subordinate to the authority of the people of the country where it is located." In other words, if a Mexican happened to invest in United States industry, we would expect him to obey our laws and not to claim exemptions. And we would not tolerate his going beyond the Supreme Court to appeal for foreign pressure.

Undersecretary of State Sumner Welles said in an address on January 18, 1935:

"American capital usually is invested abroad because of the possibility of a return greater than if it were invested domestically. Greater risks are involved and therefore a greater return is expected. One of those risks is the possibility of domestic violence which may cause damage to the capital invested."

But the other side of the Good Neighbor policy, which the United States was not willing to surrender, can also be found in a speech by Welles, on December 6, 1937. He said:

". . . should the legitimately acquired properties of aliens residing in a foreign country be expropriated for the purpose of advancing the public welfare of that country, such aliens are entitled to equitable compensation therefor."

Further, in the same address, Welles said:

"The day has passed when a citizen of the United States, acquiring property in another American republic, can undertake to maintain that, because of his citizenship, his person and his property are free from the jurisdiction of the laws and of the courts of the other American republic where he lives, and that he is supported in such a contention by his own government. On the other hand, should his property be subject to condemnation by due process of law, he is, of course, entitled to demand fair compensation therefor, and in that contention he will be supported by this government, just as this government would recognize such right on the part of citizens of other American republics residing within the United States. As I have said on other occasions, the Good Neighbor policy is essentially a reciprocal policy."

The Latin-American countries contend that appeal to a foreign country actually gives the foreign citizen the same status as if he had full extra-territoriality. They argue that the foreigner should be on the same basis as the citizen who has no appeal beyond the highest tribunals of his own country. At the bottom of the nationalist legislation in most of the "backward" countries is the attempt to build a defense against the extra-territorial status which foreign companies have enjoyed in many cases.

11

When Mr. Hull's notes to Mexico on land expropriation developed a harsh tone, the Good Neighbor policy was pooh-poohed by many Latin Americans. The situation created by the oil company and land expropriation brought into clear relief the dilemma of the average American, "the American people," with regard to Latin America generally and to Mexico in particular, because she is our next-door neighbor. The people of the United States on the whole undoubtedly would like to be friendly, and would certainly like to see this country get the benefits of such trade as can be developed between the two nations.

But, the dilemma:

On the one hand, the theory of the oil companies that the interests of Standard Oil, and Shell, and Electric Bond and

Share, and the American Smelting and Refining Company, *et al,* are identical with the interests of the American people at large. In this case we would follow their propaganda advice and boycott Mexico every time one of these firms has difficulties. Thus, we throw open that great storehouse of natural resources and that great potential market to the Nazis and Italian fascists, who have already made big inroads, and give Great Britain more advantages than she already has. A logical development of this abandoning of Mexico would be a tremendous growth of the influence of fascism and Nazism, economically and politically, and if permitted to continue, it would probably end by our going to war against Germany or Italy or Japan or all three.

On the other hand, we can reject the Standard Oil thesis, and we can intensify our friendship and our trade and cultural relations with Mexico. We can ignore the oil company propaganda and continue that great stream of tourism which in a few years has done more to break down the international barriers of prejudice than any other one force in decades. The columns of tourists plus law-abiding capital form an army of peace and good-will, whose achievements are more lasting and more satisfying than the conquests with warships, warplanes and totalitarian bombings. Any forces—Mexican, American, or European—that obstruct such a true rapprochement of these two neighbor nations cannot be regarded as friendly to the best interests of the American people or the Mexican people.

This rapprochement, mutual respect, real neighborliness can be built only on a foundation of complete autonomy, the same self-determination, the same sovereignty for Mexico that we demand for ourselves. We must be careful to distinguish between genuine nationalism—the yearning of a people for education and for a better life generally—and the jingo whose fake "nationalism" is strictly anti-United States, a ruse to retain or regain special privileges and to sell out his people to some other imperialist interests. To this type of Mexican chauvinist—desperately trying to smuggle Hitler and Mussolini into his business boudoir—any kind of imperialism is better than the American kind. Hitler imperialism is a godsend to imperialists of all countries, because it puts the world on the defensive. It spreads fear, which becomes a smoke screen for confusing two sets of divergent interests—those of the monopolies, the trusts, the imperialists, on the one hand, and those of Mr. Average American, Mr. John Citizen of any country, on the other.

Enlightened opinion cannot look upon American imperialism as more virtuous than any other brand. But neither can it sit back and smugly permit the Unholy Alliance—Duce, Fuehrer, Mikado—to assault representative government on this continent. Do our cultural, political and trade relations with Mexico, with Latin America, have to be imperialistic? They certainly tend more in that direction under the onslaught of the European imperialisms—not forgetting the British. The trend of imperialism is to become totalitarian. Then it can best fight other imperialisms, other totalitarian powers. In discussions of Latin-American trade, we can already find sly references to "limitations inherent in our political system," which place us at a disadvantage in competition against totalitarian traders. There are two schools of thought among Americans doing business with Latin America. One holds that the best way to meet totalitarian competition is to become totalitarian ourselves. To the others, such a contention sounds like cutting off your nose to spite your face, like jumping from the frying pan into the fire. The non-totalitarian groups hold that wide-awake business methods, intelligent survey of markets, carefully-planned and steady advertising, establishing of relations on a basis of mutual respect, will achieve more than totalitarianism.

There is much more than just our Latin-American trade involved in the clash of these points of view. There is the danger of totalitarianism gaining a political foothold in this country under the pretext of fighting foreign totalitarianism. If there is a lesson for us in the Mexican people's sufferings from the *cacique*—kingfish—system, it is that authoritarianism, totalitarianism, every kind of bossism, arises automatically when democratic control is relaxed. In times of stress, people fall back on forgotten wisdom that has been discarded as trite. It is then they appreciate such platitudes as the one that eternal vigilance is the price of liberty. And that the best defense is to take the offensive. At home, our best weapon against totalitarianism is to hold rigorously to democratic control, to scotch any abuse of political or economic power, to fight for equal opportunity. This will serve, too, as an inspiring example for the Latin-American believers in democratic control. That is the common ground on which permanent friendship with our Latin-American neighbors can be built: democratic control—control by the people, no matter what the outward political form. When the power of the Colossus of the North is applied in this direction, the word "American" will begin to recover its continental significance. An impregnable barrier against totalitarian invasion or usurpation will have been erected. The achievement of this goal is a challenge to our best statesmanship.

12

On the night of September 15, 1938, eve of Mexico's Independence Day, the huge crowd that gathers annually in front of the National Palace actually heard—for the first time—the customary ringing of Mexico's liberty bell, and the President's shout of *"Viva Mexico,"* commemorating the anniversary of the declaration of separation from Spain. The

Department of Press and Publicity had installed a microphone and loud-speaker system.

On that same night a diplomatic reception is also customary. Ambassadors and ministers gather to greet the President and to convey best wishes to the Mexican people. Usually a champagne supper is served. For some unexplained reason the champagne was missing this time. Nevertheless, etiquette called for a toast. While the foreign envoys looked down their noses at empty champagne goblets, President Lazaro Cardenas del Rio raised a cup of rich, stick-to-your-ribs chicken broth: to a peaceful out-of-the-red future for Mexico, to a healthy, hopeful *Mañana*.

THE END

MEXICAN STATISTICS

MEXICAN statistics are of three kinds—official, anti-official, and non-official. The first are tabulated in such a form as to prove that everything is hotsy-totsy. The second just as eagerly are lined up to demonstrate that the country is going to the dogs. The third emanate from private sources, and are often doctored for various reasons, including taxes.

Figures that come nearest being accurate are those at least a year old; then they are no longer controversial. Even census figures are not totally valid. One reason for this is the lack of communications to many sections and the illiteracy prevailing in many places. In the 1930 census, for instance, figures on land covered only two-thirds of the country's area. Then again, peasants are skeptical as to the purpose of the census. Their experience has been that every time somebody came around asking questions they lost a pig or a burro or a bushel of corn, or one of the family was carried off to the army.

In arriving at the statistics used in *Mexico Marches,* the writer has consulted official figures, wherever available, as well as the "anti-government" statistics, and where possible, private sources which he regarded as authoritative. Estimates were then made, based on the various sets of figures, and these estimates are the ones used throughout the book. These approximations will not fit one statistical table or another, but the writer believes that they will prove nearer correct.

Statistics will vary, for instance, on the corn crop. One group will attempt to show that there is less corn on the market and hence the agricultural program is a failure. Another will demonstrate that actually more corn has been harvested, but that less was put on the market and the peasants are actually eating more corn although selling less.

Certain basic estimates will run through nearly all sets of statistics. Such as, for instance, that approximately sixty-five per cent of the Mexican population are directly dependent on agriculture.

The figures on foreigners vary even more than the crop estimates. Official tabulations will show fewer resident foreigners than are actually to be found in Mexico, because many persons listed as tourists or temporary residents have settled in Mexico, but have not legalized their status. From the official sources, chambers of commerce representing various nationalities, from offices of lawyers specializing in immigration matters, from newspaper estimates, the following approximations were reached with regard to the composition of Mexico's foreign population:

Thirty per cent of Mexico's 400,000 foreigners are Spaniards. Of the rest, about 30,000 come from China; 30,000 from Guatemala; 22,000, Syria and Arabia; 13,000, United States; 10,000, Germany; 8,000, Canada; 7,000, Italy; 6,000, France; 5,000, United Kingdom; 4,000, Russia; 4,000, Poland; 3,500, Japan. The rest are of various nationalities, including a substantial number from other Latin-American countries.

About half of the land under cultivation is planted in corn, the national staple, yet not enough is grown to satisfy the country's needs. Mexico has been importing corn nearly every year, some more and some less, depending on crops, which in turn depend directly on weather conditions as the principal factor. Some Mexican economists have suggested that Mexico stop growing corn altogether, that the land be used for some profitable export crop and that corn be imported. Corn, cotton, and wheat are the three principal agricultural products. Other important crops are rice, sugar cane, bananas, henequen, beans, chickpeas, chile peppers, tomatoes, coffee. Total agricultural production ranges around five hundred million pesos annually.

Mexico's billion-peso industrial production divides up approximately as follows on the basis of output value: food industries, 30 per cent; textiles, 20 per cent; electric light and power, 10; metal products, 10; graphic arts, photography and motion pictures, 5; furniture, 4; chemicals, 3; tobacco, 3; paper, 3; clothing and hides, 2; construction materials, 3; petroleum products, 2; glass and ceramics, 1; miscellaneous, 4.

During the last three years, oil production has averaged around 175,000,000 pesos annually. About one-half of Mexico's total production of oil is consumed on the domestic market.

Raw materials predominate in Mexico's exports; machinery and manufactured goods in the imports. Seventy-five per cent of the exports are mineral products, 24 per cent agricultural and 1 per cent manufactured goods. Practically all the mines are foreign-owned; hence most of the proceeds from these as well as from foreign-owned or foreign-financed farms do not return to Mexico. The value of the total annual mine production is about 500,-000,000 pesos.

Silver, zinc, lead and copper are the principal mineral exports. Most of the silver and copper goes to the United States. Germany is a big importer of Mexican zinc, lead and oil. Italy's main purchases are lead, oil and cotton. Japan buys zinc, oil, lead and cotton. Next to silver, lead, oil and copper, the United States' main import from Mexico in 1937 was henequen. The British imported silver, lead and oil principally.

United States' sales to Mexico have consisted mainly of automobiles, trucks, tractors and parts for these. Recently General Motors (Opel) cars, made in Germany, and Italian cars (Fiat) have been cutting in on sales of American-made cars. Next in order of total value, sales by United States to Mexico consisted of petroleum derivatives, copra, iron and steel pipe, radios, tools, machinery, plows. Great Britain's principal sales are cotton thread and textiles. Germany sells Mexico nearly as much iron and steel pipe as the United States, and, next in order, paints and varnishes, and hand tools.

INDEX

Abelardo Rodriguez Market, the, 339
Acosta, Emilio, 247, 248
Acosta, Miguel M., 164
Adler, Max, 300
Agrarian Code, 234, 235, 236, 239, 243
Agrarian Department, 215, 232, 242, 260
"Agrarian Hymn," 252-253
Agrarianism, problems of, 212-213; obstacles to reform in, 233
Agrarian Party, 290, 359
Agriculture, 245, 246, 247
Agua Caliente, 25, 121, 322
Aguayo, quoted, 288
Alaman, Lucas, 197
Alcoholism, war on, 101-102
Aldasaro, Felix, 200-201
Alexander I, of Russia, 56
Alfonso XIII, of Spain, 305
Alfaro, Jose Luis, 171
Aliago, quoted, 288
Allen, Jose, 290
Almazan, Gen. Juan Andrew, 82, 304, 308
Altamirano, Manlio Fabio, 165
Alvarez, Gen. Juan, quoted, 221
Alvear, Luis, 125
American Federation of Labor, 285
American Popular Revolutionary Alliance (APRA), 298, 299, 300
Americans, antagonisms set up, 357
American Smelting and Refining Company, 15, 167, 370
Anderson, Clayton Company, 251
Anderson, Sherwood, 16
Andino, Carias, 65
Anti-Calles movement, 124, 261, 291
Anti-Clericalism, 200
Anti-Imperialist League, 290
Anti-Nazi League for German Culture, 72
Anti-Re-electionist Party, 113, 138
Aranha, Oswaldo, 63
Argaña, Jose M., 287
Argentine, the, 61, 62
"Army of Liberation," 30
Arriaga, Camilo, 152
Arroyo, Agustin, 331-334
Arroyo, Luna Antonio, quoted, 77
Article 3 (Const. of 1917), 88, 154, 155, 168, 177, 179

Article 27 (Const. of 1857), 220
Article 27 (Const. of 1917), 24, 36, 143, 155, 231, 232, 236
Article 123 (Const. of 1917), 156, 161-162, 260
Article 130 (Const. of 1917), 154, 155
Associated Press, 337
Association of Henequen Producers, 245
Association of Petroleum Producers, 39
Avila Camacho, Manuel, 303-304, 305, 306
Avila Camacho, Maximino, 304-305
Aztec Indians, 217

Bacon, Francis, 357-358
"Ballad of Petroleum," quoted, 50
Balmori, Don Carlos, 350-351, 352
Banco de Mexico, 14
Basilica of Guadalupe, 209
Bassols, Narciso, 69, 164, 165, 177, 178, 346
Belem dungeon, 147, 151
Benavides, Oscar, 63
Benitez y Cabañas, Luis, 201
Berlin-Rome-Tokyo axis, 52
Blancas, Manuel, 282
Blanco, Lucia, 160
Bloc of Intellectual Workers, 18
Bojorquez, Juan de Dios, 164
Bolivia, 62
Bolivian Confederation of Workers, 287
Bonillas, Ignacio, 109
Bracho, Angel, 339, 340
Bracho, Julio, 346
Bravo, Manuel Alvarez, 340
Brazil, 61, 62, 63, 287
British government, 30, 37
Brownsville, Texas, 125, 160
Bucareli treaties, 59, 111
Buenrostro, 25
Bustamante, Rosalio, 152

Caballero, Luis, duel of, 255-256
Cabezas, Father Dionisio, 201
Cabo, Dr. Matilde Rodriguez, 72
Cabrera, Daniel, 152
Cabrera, Luis, 156-158; quoted, 249
Cacique (chieftain) system, 83

Calles, Plutarco Elias, 21, 27, 35, 37, 59, 82, 90, 108, 109, 111, 114, 115-120, 122, 125, 126, 136, 165, 192, 235, 257, 261, 302, 303, 305-306, 315, 364; and Cardenas, 89, 124, 127, 131, 256, 261; and Cedillo, 84; and Mugica, 85; and Obregon, 110, 112; and Rodriguez, 122, 123; quoted, 104, 110, 116-117, 118, 145, 316
Calles, Plutarco, Jr., 126
Calles, Rodolfo, 126
Callismo, 240
Callistas, 119, 160, 303, 312
Campeche, the "Green Siberia," 151
Campo, Francisco, 63
Canabal, Lenin, 97
Canabal, Pio Garrido Lacroix, 97
Canabal, Tomas Garrido, 21, 64, 79, 88, 96, 97-103, 160, 205
Canabal, Zoyla Libertad, 97
Cananea, 20, 284
Capitalism, 352-357, 358, 367, 371
Cardenas, Alberto, 138
Cardenas, Cuauhtemoc, 137, 319
Cardenas, Damaso, 138
Cardenas, Francisco, 138
Cardenas, Jose Raimundo, 138
Cardenas, Lazaro, 17, 22, 27, 28, 30, 31, 65, 67, 88, 92, 93, 94, 121, 124, 126, 127-146, 159, 163, 164, 166, 168, 179, 205, 212, 216, 235, 253, 262, 271, 275, 276, 279, 280, 285, 292, 297, 302-303, 305, 311, 312, 318, 319, 320, 322, 333, 339, 362, 364, 373; and the Army, 82, 128-130, 308-309; and Cabreras, 157; and Calles, 89, 119, 124, 125, 256, 261; and Canabal, 103; and Cedillo, 80, 93; and the Church, 206, 207, 209-210; and education, 185, 186, 187, 188, 341, 347; and land, 94, 213, 215, 239, 240, 248; and Mugica, 161; and oil, 11, 13, 20, 21, 22, 25, 34, 46; and the press, 291-292, 334, 336; and Trotsky, 293, 310; quoted, 19, 21-22, 23, 24, 139-142, 145
Cardenismo, 240, 242, 272, 297, 309, 310, 312, 360, 363, 364
Cardenistas, 81, 240, 241, 311, 312, 339
Carrancismo, 240
Carrancistas, 110, 229-230
Carranza, 35, 36, 108, 109, 110, 111, 127, 147, 154, 156, 160, 229, 284, 302
Carrillo, Alejandro, 72, 189, 289
Casa del Obrero Mundial, 284
Casauranc, Dr. Jose Manuel Puig, 123

Caser, Franc, 75
Caso, Antonio, 263, 266, 348
Casparsson, Ragnar, 286
Castañeda, Eduardo Perez, 46
Castilla, Cristian, 287
Catholic Action, 63, 207, 210-211
Catholic Church, of Mexico, 154, 174, 177n., 191, 192, 202, 205-206, 209; and Canabal, 97, 99-100; and Diaz, 155, 200; and socialist education, 179, 203; conflict with State, 37, 59, 88, 114, 173, 177, 258, 290; monopoly of, 82, 148; undermining of, 55, 56; unrestricted, 88-89; wealth of, 196, 197, 200, 214, 220, 363
Catholic clergy, of Mexico, 37, 176, 178, 187, 194, 197; and Constitution of 1917, 161, 201-202; and Mugica, 160; Calles fight with, 117, 118; drive against, 204; power of, 111, 155; intrigues of, 197; resolution of, 177; supported Cardenas, 28; truce with Portes Gil, 256
Catholic Party, 202
Catholics, of Mexico, 194, 199, 200, 203, 204, 206, 207, 210
Catholics, of Spain, 206
Catholic Youth Association, 209, 266
Ceballos, Ciro B., 147
Cedillo, Cleofas, 85
Cedillo, Elena, 89
Cedillo, Higinia, 87
Cedillo, Magdaleno, 85
Cedillo, Saturnino, 21, 30, 79, 80, 82, 85, 86-96, 96-97, 239, 303, 335
Central America, 64, 65
Central American Unionist Party, 64
Central League Resistance, 98
Chamizal question, 58
Chapultepec, 20, 23, 107, 108, 134
Charles I, of Spain, 195
Charles IV, of Spain, 51
Chavez, Carlos, 342, 343
Chiapas, State of, 208
Chicago Tribune, the, 49
Chihuahua, State of, 17
Chile, 61, 62
Chilean Confederation of Workers, 287
Cinema, in Mexico, 344-345
Clavijo, Clodomiro, 287
Coahuila, State of, 17, 108, 270, 272, 285
Colombia, 61, 62
Colorado River Land Company, 222
Columbus, New Mexico, 285

Committee for Industrial Organization, 14, 286
Committee for Organization and Unification of Labor, Uruguay, 287
Committee for Proletarian Defense, 261
Communist Party, 90, 91, 138, 183, 289-292, 294, 310, 339
Comte, Auguste, 265
Conciliation and Arbitration Board, 268, 283
Confederation of Central America, 64
Confederation of Mexican Workers (CTM), 69, 185, 261, 265, 269, 270-273, 275, 278, 282, 286, 287, 292, 294, 335, 345
Confederation of Workers of Colombia, 287
Congress of the International Institute for Industrial Relations, 286
Conquest, the, 175, 217
Conquistadores, the, 194, 195, 214
Constitutional Convention of 1857, 220
Constitutionalism, 109
Constitutionalist Army, the, 108
Constitutionalist Movement, 284
Constitution of 1824, 55, 148
Constitution of 1857, 143, 148, 149, 154, 159, 220
Constitution of 1917, 11, 35, 38, 59, 62, 109, 112, 143, 146, 147-148, 151, 154, 161, 168, 201-202, 216, 233
Contreras, Ramon, 276
Control de Petrolo, 46
Coolidge, Calvin, 59, 117
Co-operative Association, 359
Co-operativist Party, the, 290, 359
Corona, Gustavo, 188-189
Cortez, Hernando, 11, 224
Costa Rica, 62, 64, 96
Costa Rica Banana Plantation Workers, 287
Coughlin, Rev. Charles Edward, 76n.
Coyoacan, City of, 292
Cristeros, 113, 173, 202, 204
Cuadra, Manolo, 65
Cuba, 61
Cuban National Tobacco Workers' Federation, 287
Cuban National Transport Federation, 287
Cuban Press Association, 287
Cultural Mission, 186-187

Dance, development of the, 346

Daniels, Josephus, 19, 76, 123, 124
Davila, Jose Eduardo, see Eduardo I
Dearborn Independent, the, 75n.
De la Huerta, Adolfo, 84, 108-112, 264
De la Huerta rebellion, 135, 264, 290
De la Luz Avalos, Maria, 171
Department of Fine Arts, 338
Department of Indian Affairs, 185, 318
Department of Labor, 260, 317
Department of Press and Publicity (DAPP), 14, 28, 332, 333-334, 337, 373
Diaz, Pascual, 293
Diaz, Porfirio, 13, 20, 34-35, 83, 101, 127, 142, 149, 150-151, 152, 153, 155-156, 159, 175, 176, 200, 214, 221, 222, 223, 224-225, 283, 293, 301, 306, 310, 352, 367-368
Diaz army, the, 301, 302
Diazism, 153
Doheny, Edward L., 35, 45
Dominican Republic, 64
Drama, in Mexico, 345-346
Dr. Raschbaum's German clinic, 336
Durango, State of, 17, 270, 272, 276

Economic sanctions, 29
Ecuador, 62
Eduardo I, 192, 193
Education, government plans opposed, 177; State control opposed, 182
Ejido, derivation of word, 243; factor in land parceling, 240; keystone of farm regime, 242; system of, 95, 213, 243-244; statistics on, 251
El Chaparro, 279-282, 283
Electric Bond and Share Company, 62, 369-370
El Hormiguero Ejido, 250
Elizondos family, 275
Ellis, Havelock, 179
El Machete, 290, 291, 292
El Monitor Republicano, quoted, 199
El Nacional, 25, 66, 123, 265, 335
El Palmito dam, 247
El Popular, 269, 276, 335
El Presidente Rodriguez, 123n.
El Universal, 15, 16, 163, 310-311
Employers' Center, 274, 276, 278
Employers' Union of the Petroleum Industry, 18, 41
Employers' unions, tabulation of, 274
Escamilla, Francisco Ramirez, 270
Escandon, Pablo, 228

Escobar, Martinez de, 168-171
Escobar revolution, 82, 87, 119
Estrada, Gen. Enrique, 136
Excelsior, 15, 70-71, 74
Expropriation, 11; aroused national spirit, 285; decree of, 24, 41; growth of, 38; Hull's messages on, 59; law of, 24, 44; newspapers in drive against, 29; popular reaction to, 27-28; strikes dropped after, 271

Falange Español Tradicionalista, 69
Fascism, 80, 362; and Aprismo, 300; in Mexico, 366, 370
Fascists, and Mexican trade, 57, 66; penetrate Brazil, 63; Central America, 65; Latin America, 66; Peru, 63
Federal Department of Physical Education, 322
Federal Health Department, 321
Federal Labor Law, 156, 162
Federation of the Workers of the North, 270
Federation of Young Communists, 290
Federation of Jalisco Workers, 270
Fimmen, Edo, 286
First International, 284
Flores-Hale concession, 58
Ford, Henry, 75n., 76n.
Foreign Club, 122, 322
Foreign menace, in Mexican history, 34, 35; Mexico's ball-and-chain, 51-52
Fossa, Mateo, 295
Franco, Gen. Francisco, 67, 80, 210, 305, 335, 364
French Confederation of Labor, 286
Freud, 179
Fuentes, Jose, 288
Futuro, 269

Gabino Barreda University, the, 265
Galindo, Dr. Jose Refugio, 203
Gamboa, Raul, 339
Garcia, Julian, 250
Garcia, Manuel, 319
Garfias, Heraclio, 281
Garzas family, 275
Gas, Electrical and Water Works Federation of Cuba, 287
Gasca, Gen. Celestino, 264
Gaxiola, Francisco Javier, Jr., 123n., 165
General Administration of National Petroleum, 46
General Confederation of Workers (CGT), 270, 290

General Confederation of Workers and Peasants, 265, 277
General Confederation of Workers of Argentina, 287
Genin, Alexander, 267-268
"German Information Service in Mexico," 73
German Pro-Culture League, 78
German school, the, 174
Germany, 29, 49, 57, 60, 65, 71
Glyka, Alexander, 15
Gold Shirts, 78, 79, 91, 92, 193, 194, 275
Gomez, Arnulfo, 113, 114
Gomez, Jenaro, 290
Gomez, Marte, 255, 257, 259
Gompers, Samuel, 285, 286
Gonzalez, Jose Maria, 283
Gonzalez, Gen. Pablo, 230-231, 309
Gonzalez, Silvano Barba, 311
Good Neighbor policy, 53, 59, 61, 366, 367, 368
GPU, the, 293
Gray, Juan, 25
Great Britain, 148, 155, 365, 370
Green Indians, 314, 315
Greenwood, Grace, 337, 338, 340
Greenwood, Marion, 337, 338, 340
Gremio Unido de Alijadores, 258
Grupo Accion, 289
Guadalajara, 17, 184, 325
Guadalupe Hidalgo, treaty of, 53
Guanajuanato, 17
Guardarrama, Ramon Alva, 339
Guatemala, 65
Guerena, M. H., 248-249
Guerrero, State of, 17, 111
Guggenheim Foundation, the, 348
Guruswami, S., 286, 287
Gutierrez, Juan, 269, 276-277
Gutierrez, Manuel, 269

Hacendado, 214, 233, 237
Hacienda system, the, 215, 223-224
Haff interests, the, 222
Haiti, opposed to labor legislation, 62
Handicrafts, the, 328-329
Harriman interests, the, 222
Havana Province Federation of Labor, 287
Haven, Gilbert, 197-198
Haya de la Torre, Victor Raul, 299, 300
Haymarket, 283
Hearst, George, 222
Hearst, William Randolph, 336

Heller, Dr. Krum, 78
Hermanos, Cuevas, 280
Hermanos, Olivares, 280
Herzog, Jesus Silva, 41
Hidalgo y Costilla, Miguel, 35, 51, 55, 196, 293
Hitler, Adolf, 31, 54, 92, 125, 174, 357, 366
Hoffman, Dr. Walter, 70, 71
Holy Inquisition, 195, 196
Home of the Indian Student, 315
Homestead strike, 283
Honduras, 62
Hoover, Herbert, 256
Hoy, 94-95, 157f., 248-249, 278-279, 334, 335
Huasteca Petroleum Co. (Standard Oil), 18
Huerta, Victoriano, 35, 56, 86, 108, 127, 154, 160, 202, 229, 286, 302
Hull, Cordell, 59, 212, 279, 369

Icaza, Xavier, 72
Independence Day of Mexico, 372
Indians, of Mexico, 153, 185, 195, 316, 317-318; and the arts, 344; background of, 361; exploited, 192; labor of, 197; myth of pre-conquest, 216-217; problems of, 159; under the conquerors, 217-218
Industrial workers, 260
Industrial Workers of the World, 284
Instituto Socialista de Mexico, 68
Integralistas, 63
Internado Nacional, 262
International Anti-War Congress, 286
International City Planners' Congress, 323
International Jew, The, 75, 75n., 76
International News Service, 336
International Red Aid, 290
International Transport Workers, 286
Italian Bank of Lima, 63
Italy, 29, 49, 57
Iturbide, Agustin de, 51, 55, 56, 136, 309
Iturbidists, 56-57
Iturrigaray, Jose de, 195

Jacobins, 161, 162
Japan, 29, 49, 57, 60, 72
Jara, General Heriberto, 72, 159
Jesuits, 192, 200
Jewish Menace, The, 75
Jewish problem, the, 75-77
Jimenez, Pedro M., letter cited, 201

Jouhaux, Leon, 286, 288
Juarez, Benito, 52, 149, 150
Juarez, City of, 320
Juarez Constitution of 1859, 149
Juarez Reform Movement, 197
Julio, General, 106, 107
Jung, 179
Jurado, Conchita, 351-352
Jurado, Field, 60
Juventud Obrera National Sindicalista, 69

Kahlo, Frieda (Mrs. Diego Rivera), 292
Kellogg, Frank B., 290
Kernan, Rev. William C., 76n.
Kingfish system, the, 82-84
Kluckhohn, Frank, 289, 337n.
"Knights of Guadalupe," 193

Labor, and Toledano, 268; attempt organize, 263; board of, 39, 40, 272, 280; forced into united front, 261; movement, 271-272; unions, 116
Labor Congress, 286
Laborde, Hernan, 138, 290, 291, 292, 294, 310
Labor Department, 260
Laborist Party, 285, 289, 290, 359
Laguna district, 17, 215, 246, 247, 249-250, 272
Lander, Bill, 289
Land laws, 222
Land lords, 117, 118, 234
Land lordism, 233
Land parceling, 213; Cardenas' program of, 93; Carranza's decree of, 229; in San Luis Potosi, 94; statistics on, 235, 241-242
La Paz Ejido, 250
Las Casas, Fr. Bartolome de, 194-195, 218
Latin America, 369; and the Good Neighbor policy, 367; competition in 365; economic nationalism in, 62; fascist penetration of, 66-67; heritage of, 61; legislation of, 62, 64; optimism in, 61; rejection of Monroe Doctrine, 52; United States and, 52, 61
Latin-American Bureau, 289
Latin-American Labor Confederation, 287
Latin-American Labor Congress, 286
Latin-American Workers' Confederation, 286
La Valentina, 126

La Voz de Mexico, 335
Lazarus Laughed, 346
"Leaderism," 268
Leagues of Resistance, 101
League of Revolutionary Writers and Artists (LEAR), 339, 341
League of Small Proprietors, 239
Leftist Socialist Party, 138
Leiva, Agustin Aragon, 348
Lenin, 265, 292
Leon, Guillermo Vegas, 300
Leon Toral, Jose de, 114, 204
Lewis, John L., 14, 269, 278, 286, 288, 289
Leyros, Francisco Perez, 287, 288
Leyva, Patricio, 228
Liberal Congress, 151, 152
Liberal Party, 151, 284
Liberals, 76
Lima Conference, 61, 367
Lira, Jose, 281
Literature, of Mexico, 346-347
Lobato, Salvador, 269
Lombardia hacienda, 138
London, 51, 364
Lopez de Lara, Cesar, 255-256
Lopez de Santa Anna, 220
Lorenzo, R. Gomez, 290
Los Angeles, 125
Los Ecos, 158
Lower California, 58
Luces, 288

Machado, 291
Maderismo, 240
Madero, Francisco I., 35, 36, 56, 108, 116, 127, 153, 154, 203, 228, 229, 302
Madrid, 51
Magaña, Gen. Gildardo, 95, 239, 259
Magon, Ricardo Flores, 152, 153, 284
Magon, Enrique Flores, 152
Manjarrez, Froylan C., 264
Manrique y Zarate, Bishop Jose de, 205
Martin, Esteban, 336
Martinez, Domitila, 281
Martinez, Eucario, 281
Martinez, Evaristo, 281
Martinez, Hernandez, of Salvador, 65
Martinez, Archbishop Luis M., 208, 209
Marxists, 265
Mata, Filomena, 152
Maximilian, of Mexico, 52
Mein Kampf, 125
Melessi, 288
Mella, Julio Antonio, 291

Mendez, Leopoldo, 340, 341, 346
Merck, Ernest von, 79, 91
Mexican Agrarian Revolution, 240
Mexican-Americans, 320
Mexican army, 306-309
Mexican Constitutional Democratic Front, 136
Mexican Eagle Oil Company, the (Royal Dutch Shell), 18, 30, 35
Mexican Labor News, the, 157
Mexican National Orthodox Apostolic Church, the, 192, 202
Mexican Railways, the, 306
Mexicans, 58, 320, 357
Mexican Workers' Confederation, 14
Mexico, absentee capitalism in, 353-355; and oil fight, 41-44, 46; and Trotsky, 293, 294; competition for, 191; deals with Latin America, 49; description of, 11, 12, 60, 214, 361; economy of, 358, 359; education in, 175, 181, 183, 184; farmers and peasants in, 16; fascists and fascism in, 66, 366; foreign domination in, 51-62; freedom of the press in, 334; grievances of, 57-60; guardian of Spanish children, 69; haven for Aprista leaders, 299; independence of, 71, 148, 195, 196, 218-220; industrial centers of, 17; labor movement in, 283; laboratory of democracy, 362-364; political camps of, 54-55; reform in, 153, 197; relations with the Soviet Union, 291; relations with the United States, 53-54, 61; representative government, 361; ruled by military men, 301, 308; stand with Loyalists, 67; statistics of, 374-376
Mexico City, 17, 28, 51, 103, 107, 184, 194, 287, 322-327
Mexico: Our Next-Door Neighbor, 197
Michel, Concha, 254
Michel, Primo Villa, 143, 164
Michoacan, State of, 127, 279
Minimum Wage legislation, 166
Military cities, 308
Mining Code of 1884, 36
Ministry of Agriculture, 91, 186
Ministry of Education, 50, 172, **173**, 178, 180-181, 338, 341, 345, 346
Ministry of Finance, 246, 247
Ministry of Foreign Relations, 23
Ministry of National Defense, 172, 173, 303
Ministry of National Economy, 274, 360

Mireles, Gustavo Espinosa, 285
Missionary Herald, the, 198-199
Molina, Rafael Leonidas Trujillo, 64
Moncaleano, Juan Francisco, 284
Monroe Doctrine, 50, 60, 73, 148
Montes, Federico, 333
Monterrey, City of, 17, 184, 274-276, 304, 309, 325
Monterrey, State of, 270
Monterrey, of Nicaragua, quoted, 288
"Monument to the Revolution," 142
Morales, Federico, 328-329
Mora y del Rio, Archbishop, 203
Morelia, State of, 69, 184
Morelia Museum, 337
Morelia University, 337
Morelos, State of, razed, 215, 231
Morelos Revolutionary Army, 228
Morelos y Pavon, Jose Maria, 55, 219
Morones, Luis N., 108, 124, 264, 267, 285, 289
Morrow, Dwight W., 37, 38, 76, 104, 118, 290
Morrow, Mrs. Dwight W., 15, 16
Mother Conchita, 114
Mugica, Francisco, 89, 90, 158n., 158-161
Mural painting, of Mexico, 337, 341
Murillo, Gerardo, 73-74
Murillo, Maria, 171
Music, of Mexico, 341, 344
Mussolini, Benito, 38, 63, 357

Najera, Francisco Castillo, 183, 367
Nascimento, Manuel de, 63
Nation, the, 76n.
National Agrarian Commission, 233
National Agricultural Credit Bank, 235
National Catholic Confederation of Labor, 203
National Confederation of Co-operatives, 360
National Confederation of Catholic Workmen's Circles, 203
National Council of Higher Education and Scientific Investigation, 188
National Ejido Credit Bank, 244, 246, 248, 251
National Farm Credit Bank, 244
National Labor Congress of Ecuador, 287
National League for Defense of Religious Liberty, 202
National Lines of Mexico, 25
National Maritime Labor Federation of Cuba, 287

National Military Academy, 73
National Museum of Mexico, 147
National Oil Workers' Union, 17, 18, 39, 41, 44-46, 48-49
National Palace, 13, 17, 18, 78, 84, 91, 132, 194, 372
National Peasants' Confederation, 185, 252, 254-255, 318
National Peasants' League, 290
National Preparatory School, 264
National Pro-Peace Congress, 286
"National Redemption Loan," 29
National Revolutionary Party (PNR), 23, 25, 27, 84, 91, 119, 124, 143, 163, 164, 177, 204, 258, 265, 294
National Study Commission, 294
National Transport Workers' Union, 290
National University, 187, 263, 310
National Workers' Confederation of Paraguay, 287
Nazis, drive in Latin America, 52, 65, 70-80, 335, 365, 366, 370; religion, 174
Negrin, Juan, 286
Nelken, Margarita, 292
Nervo, Amado, 292
New York *Times,* the, 49, 289, 336, 337
Nicaragua, 60
Noguchi, Isaumu, 340
Noodle, The, 331, 332
Northe, Dr. Heinrich, 72
Novaro, Augusto, 342
Nueva Italia hacienda, 138
Nuevo Leon, State of, 82, 270, 274, 276

Oaxaca, State of, 16, 317
Obregon, Alvaro, 35, 38, 60, 84, 108, 109, 110, 111-115, 118, 135, 156, 175, 204, 271, 284, 290, 302
Obregonismo, 240, 272
Ocampo, 288
Official Gazette, the, 209
O'Higgins, Paul, 340
Oil, 27-50; administration, 46-48; companies, 29, 35, 37, 40, 41-44, 45, 117, 157; industry, 36, 39, 261; lands, 11, 33, 34, 62; rush, 32; worker, 39
Oil Administration Distribution Department, the, 285
Omega, 336
Ordaz, Dr. Felix Gordon, 72
Ordinance of Aranjuez, 1783, 36
Organized Labor of Nicaragua, 287
Oro, Bustillo, 346

Orozco, Jose Clemente, 338, 340, 341
Orozco, Pascual, 86
Osuna, Antonio R., 65
Otis, Harrison Gray, 222

Pacheco, 288
Pachuca, State of, 17
Padilla, Mariano, 269
Painting, of Mexico, 344
Palacio, Riva, 121, 303
Palavicini, Felix F., 158, 158n., 162-163
Pan-American conference, 1938, 61
Pan-American Labor Confederation, 286
Pan-American Union Confederation, 286
Pani, Alberto J., 164, 165
Panuco, 33
Papal Encyclical, 204
Paris, 51
Party of the Mexican Rebellion (PRM), 136, 297, 298, 300, 308, 309
Pastoral letter, 205-207
Paul III, 51
Payne, John Barton, 59
Pearson, Weetman (Lord Cowdray), 35
Peasants, the, hostile to labor, 261; victim of capitalists, 260
Peasants' Confederation, 278
Pelaez, General Manuel, 33
Peña, Ramon Gonzalez, 286, 288
Peonage, system of, 223-224
Perez, Joaquin, 202
Pershing expedition, 109, 285
Peru, 61, 62, 63, 299
Peruvian Workers' Center, 287
Peso, the, rate of exchange crashed, 29
Petromex, 46
Petroleum, laws of 1925, 37, 60
Philip II, of Spain, 218
Pius IX, 198
Pius XI, 193, 210
Plan de La Noria (1871), 150
"Plan of Action," 180-181
Plan of Agua Priete, 111, 115, 257
Plan of Ayala, 86, 226
Platt, Juan, 121
Platt Amendment, 61
Plenn, Abel, 346
Poinsett, Joel, 55-56, 220
Ponce, Manuel M., 342
Popular Front, 294
Popular University, 263
Portes Gil, Emilio, 38, 90, 204, 205, 255, 256-259, 290-291, 305

Presidential Study Commission, 359
Prieto, Adolfo, 275
Pro, Padre Miguel, 114, 204, 209
Pro, Humberto, 114
Proletariat, hostile to peasants, 261
Protestantism, 56
Protestants, of Mexico, 76, 197, 199
Protocols of Zion, the, 75, 76, 90
Puebla, State of, 17, 264, 304, 305, 325
Puerto, Felipe Carrillo, 98, 110, 290
Pujol, Antonio, 339, 340
Pullman strike, 283

Queen Mary, the, 268
Queretaro, State of, 36, 52, 147, 162
Quetzalcoatl, the Plumed Serpent god, 191

Radical Socialist Party, 98
Railroads, 261
Railway Brotherhood of Cuba, 287
Railway strike (1877), 283
Railway Telegraphers' and Dispatchers' Union, 277
Railway Workers' Union, 276, 277
Railway Workers' Union, Madras, India, 286
Ramirez, Julio, 270
Ramirez, Manuel Diaz, 290
Ramirez, Col. Roberto Calvo, 171
Raymond Concrete Pile Company (N. J.), 323
Red Army, 296
Red Battalions, 109, 284
Redeemers, 21, 109, 111
"Redeemers' Row," 108
Red Menace, 290
Red Shirts, 88, 205
Reform Laws, 149, 197, 200, 214
Regeneracion, 153
Regional Confederation of Labor, 264
Reichswart, 73
Rendon, Pedro, 340
Reventlow, Count Ernst Zu, 73
Revolution, the, 11, 21, 103, 143, 154, 160, 187, 188, 202, 213, 355; advance guard of, 153; and the cacique system, 83-84; and Calles, 119, 126; and Cedillo, 86; and the oil rush, 32, 33; depicted, 339; land parceling of, 160; men of, 176, 200, 233, 358; needed men, 315; start of military careers, 302; strategist of, 109; unfinished, 226, 142-143
Revolutionary Frontier Party, 309
Revolution Betrayed, The, 294
Revueltas, Fermin, 340

Revueltas, Silvestre, 342-344, 345
Reynolds, Robert R., 74
Rio Blanco, 20, 159, 284
Rio Grande, valley of, 215
Rivas, Antonio Sanchez, 171
Rivera, Diego, 293, 295, 333, 338, 340-341
Rivera, Librado, 152
Rocha, Joel, 275
Rockefeller Foundation, 348
Rodriguez, Abelardo, 58, 90, 120-124, 126, 164-167, 177, 204, 232, 234-236, 259, 271, 303, 305, 328
Rodriguez, Enrique, see The Noodle
Rodriguez, Fructuoso, 328
Rodriguez, Luis I., 72, 253, 254, 308, 311, 333
Rodriguez, Nicolas, 78, 80, 91
Rodriguez, 288
Rojas, Jose F., Jr., 15
Roosevelt, Franklin D., 52, 76, 122, 123, 279
Roosevelt, Theodore, 53
Roosevelt letter, 122-123, 123n.
Royal Dutch Shell Oil Company, 18, 30, 167, 353-354, 357, 369
Rubio, Manuel Romero, 33
Rubio, Pascual Ortiz, 90, 119, 120, 164, 291, 305
Ruiz y Flores, Archbishop Leopoldo, 204
Rural Defense Corps, 172, 307

Sadas, family, 275
Saenz, Aaron, 89
Saenz de Sicilia, Gustavo, 92
St. Louis, Missouri, 152
Salce, Alfredo, 340
Saltillo, 285
Salochi, Gino, 63
San Antonio, Texas, 228
Sanborn's restaurant, 284
Sanchez, Professor Graciano, 184, 185, 252, 255, 257, 318
Sanchez, Gen. Guadalupe, 33
San Juan de Ulua fortress, 151, 204
San Luis Potosi, City of, 17, 151
San Luis Potosi, State of, 30, 88-89, 94
San Nicolas University, 188
Santa Rosa de Lima church, 209
Santillan, 25
Sarabia, Juan, 152
Sarabia, Manuel, 152
Schools, development of rural, 184-185; government control of, 176; spread of, 183-184

Schoolteachers, 168-172, 173, 183, 185, 186
Science, of Mexico, 347-349
Science as Drama, 348
Scottish Rite Masonic lodge, 55
"Seditions and Troubles," 358
Sedoff, Leon, 293
Serrano, Gen. Francis, 113, 114
"Sexual Education," 178, 179
Shoe Workers' Union of Costa Rica, 287
Sierra, Col. Bolivar, 136, 309
Sierra, Justo, 283
Sinaloa, 309
Siqueiros, David Alfaro, 338, 340
Six-Year Plan, 28, 90, 143, 146, 161, 163-167, 213, 232, 292
"Small Property," 236-239
Social Democratic forces, 57
Social Justice, 76n.
Socialist education, 165, 166, 168, 177, 179, 182-183, 187, 204, 361
Socialist Orientation Group, 289
Socialist Party of Mexico, 71, 284
Solana, Rafael, 16
Somoza, Antonio, 65
Son of Labor, The, 283, 284
Sonora, State of, 17, 109, 110, 116, 127, 270, 276
Soto, Roberto, 293
Soto y Gama, Antonio Diaz, 152, 310
Soviet Union, 126, 291, 292
Spain, 66, 72
Spaniards, 68-69, 219
Spanish Loyalists, 67
Spanish Popular Front, 300
Stalin, Joseph, 90, 278, 293, 295
Standard Oil Company, 18, 62, 167, 354, 356-357, 369, 370
Steinmann, Walter, 78
Stephens, John Luther, 198
Stilwell, H. G., Jr., 125
Strikes, statistics on, 271-272
Suarez, Eucario, 25, 281
Sugar Workers' Confederation of Matanzas, Cuba, 287
Swedish Confederation of Labor, 286

Tabasco, 21
Taft, William Howard, 37, 306
Tamaulipas, 17
Tapia, Gen. Sanchez, 309
Tejada, Sebastian Lerdo de, 150, 301
Tejeda, Adalberto, 69, 138
Telegraphers' strike (1883), 283
Tellez, Ignacio Garcia, 21, 311, 333
Tenancingo, 308

Tepepa, Gabriel, 228
Tezuitlan Copper Company, 262
Third International, 290
"Three-Year Plan for Farming," 255
Tijuana, 121
Todo, 335
Toledano, Vicente Lombardo, 14, 25, 72, 92, 97, 157, 185, 189, 262-269, 270, 273, 277, 286, 287, 294, 298, 304, 335, 360
Tourists, affecting Mexico, 329-330
Trade Union International, 277
Transocean, Nazi news agency, 73
Tres Marias penal islands, 90, 291, 317
Treviño, Perez, 303
Trotsky, Leon, 90, 292, 293-296
Twenty Years After, 249
Tzab, Miguel, 339, 340

Ubico, Jorge, of Guatemala, 65
Ultimas Noticias, 74
Uncle Sam Bared, 73
Union of Educational Workers, 172, 185
Union of Port Workers, Havana, Cuba, 287
Unions, 273-274
Unitary Trade Union Confederation, 290
United Fruit Company, 62
United Press, the, 337
United States, the, 287; a melting pot, 361; and military training, 308; basic charter of, 148; business relations with Mexico, 367; Calles up against, 117; identified with Semitic enemy, 76; investments abroad 368; investments in Latin America, 61; Mexicans deported from, 320; oil interests of, 155; policy of, 366; recognition from sought, 111; recognized Texan independence, 51; relations with Mexico, 53-54; role in Latin America, 52, 365; strikes in, 283; State Department of, 58-59, 63, 64
University of Morelia, 188, 318
University of Puebla, 209
Uruguay, 62
Usigli, Rodolfo, 346

Valades, Humberto Macias, 152
Valades, Jose C., 290
Valle Nacional, 20
Vampire of the Continent, The, 73
Vargas, Getulio, 64, 287

Variety, 105
Vasconcelos, Jose, 264, 310, 348
Vatican City, 51
Vatican International, 191
Vela, Gonzalo Vazquez, 181, 185
Velasco, Jose Gonzalez, 317
Velazquez, Fidel, 269, 287
Venezuela, 61, 62, 287
Veracruz, City of, 20, 51-52, 109, 285
Veracruz, State of, 16, 17, 284
Vilchis, David, 269
Villa, Gen. Francisco, 35, 58, 108, 150, 285
Villa Cuauhtemoc, 34
Villalobos, cabinet member, 25
Villa Obregon, 267-268
Villarreal, Antonio I., 138, 152
Vincent, Stenio, 62
Voice of Mexico, The, 292

War Department, 93
Wars of the Reform, 148, 149, 220
Warren, Charles Beecher, 59
Washington, D. C., 51, 364
Welles, Sumner, 368, 369
Wenzel, Bruno, 75
West, DuVal, 58
White guards, 20, 33, 173, 234, 251-252
White, Owen P., 149
William II, of Germany, 109
Wilson, Woodrow, 76, 204
Wilson, Henry Lane, 56
Wilson Unmasked, 73
Women's suffrage, 322
Workers' University of Mexico, 157, 189-190, 265
World Service, 76n.

XEFO, 23
Xtabay, mythical character, 321

Yocupicio, Ramon, 259, 270
York Rite Masonic lodge, 55, 56
Yucatan, 215, 245

Zacatecas, 17
Zapata, Emiliano, 86, 108, 109, 126, 150, 214, 226-231
Zapatismo, 240
Zapatistas, 229
Zavala, Lorenzo de, 220
Zierold, Pablo, 284
Zimmerman, 60
Zocalo, the, 121, 323
Zolorzano, Amalia (Señora Cardenas), 137